Mormon Women
at the Crossroads

Mormon Women at the Crossroads

Global Narratives and the Power of Connectedness

CAROLINE KLINE

UNIVERSITY OF ILLINOIS PRESS
Urbana, Chicago, and Springfield

Library of Congress Cataloging-in-Publication Data
Names: Kline, Caroline (Caroline Esther), author.
Title: Mormon women at the crossroads : global
    narratives and the power of connectedness / Caroline
    Kline.
Description: Urbana : University of Illinois Press, [2022]
    | Includes bibliographical references and index.
Identifiers: LCCN 2021057722 (print) | LCCN
    2021057723 (ebook) | ISBN 9780252044366
    (cloth) | ISBN 9780252086434 (paperback) | ISBN
    9780252053351 (ebook)
Subjects: LCSH: Mormon women—Religious
    life—Mexico. | Mormon women—Religious life—
    Botswana. | Mormon women—Religious life—United
    States. | Race—Religious aspects—Church of Jesus
    Christ of Latter-day Saints.
Classification: LCC BX8643.W66 K55 2022 (print) |
    LCC BX8643.W66 (ebook) | DDC 289.3/32082—
    dc23/eng/20220119
LC record available at https://lccn.loc.gov/2021057722
LC ebook record available at https://lccn.loc.gov/2021057723

Contents

Acknowledgments   vii

Introduction   1

CHAPTER 1: Mexican Women, Agency, and Liberation   25

CHAPTER 2: African-Born Women Navigating an American-Born Church   53

CHAPTER 3: Privilege, Complexity, and Women of Color in the United States   99

CHAPTER 4: Toward a Mormon Womanist Theology of Abundance   131

Conclusion   161

APPENDIX A: Oral Life History Interview Questions for Women in Mexico   171

APPENDIX B: Oral Life History Interview Questions for Women in Botswana   175

APPENDIX C: Oral Life History Interview Questions for Women in the United States   179

APPENDIX D: Demographic Information   183

Notes   185

Bibliography   223

Index   241

Acknowledgments

I am indebted to many individuals who have supported and assisted in the production of this book. First, I extend my deepest thanks to the many anonymous narrators who trusted me with their stories and generously shared their insights and experiences. The hours I spent with these women were a privilege and a pleasure.

I will always be grateful for the outstanding support offered by Silvia Carlson, April Carlson, and Juanita Ceballos Fernandez, without whom I could never have conducted the research project in Mexico. Silvia and Juanita connected me with a network of Latter-day Saint women in Veracruz, arranged interviews, and were in all ways generous in their support of this project. I will never forget the many hours of hospitality and help Juanita and her family offered me, as well as Juanita's work transcribing dozens of interviews. Silvia was an excellent interpreter, and April a skilled interviewer and translator, as well as an insightful colleague. I look back and find it miraculous that I found such an amazing group of women to help carry out this project in Mexico.

I also thank the many people who helped facilitate and carry out the research trip in Botswana, in particular, Karen Torjesen, Deidre Green, and the Mokgares. My time in Botswana—and most especially the many hours I spent talking to women there—are experiences I will never forget.

Advisors and colleagues have been instrumental in the formation and development of this project. I particularly thank Patrick Mason for his helpful comments and support throughout the years. He generously guided me throughout the process and toward the University of Illinois Press for publication. I'll always be grateful. Claudia Bushman, who began the Mormon Women's Oral History Project at Claremont Graduate University, has a special place in my heart. She first introduced me to the method of oral history, and taking her classes on Mormon women was a highlight of my graduate school career. I'm grateful for her vision and belief that the words of everyday women have infinite worth and meaning. I extend my heartfelt thanks to Joanna Brooks for helping me shape the project and for offering helpful feedback on the chapters.

As I've readied this manuscript for publication, others have stepped in and offered their insight and encouragement. Heather Sundahl has been a wonderful reader, commenter, and cheerleader. Whenever I felt stuck, knowing that I could turn to Heather made all the difference. Emily Clyde Curtis has similarly offered both moral support and skilled close reading. Liz Johnson, a former director of the Mormon Women's Oral History Project, spent many hours formatting the oral histories I conducted and entering them into the archive. My deepest thanks to these wonderful friends, and the many more who are unnamed, who believe wholeheartedly in the importance of telling women's stories. I'm also grateful to Dawn Durante and my anonymous reviewers, who offered incisive and helpful suggestions for sharpening up the manuscript.

I owe a debt of gratitude to the many women in the Latter-day Saint community whose insights have been particularly helpful to me as I've grappled with issues of gender, race, and culture within Mormonism. Kalani Tonga, Mica McGriggs, Bryndis Roberts, Amy Hoyt, and Kay in Botswana have offered me their wisdom and their feedback.

Finally, I thank my family. My husband Mike is always the first reader of my drafts and consistently offers good advice as to where I can cut the fat from my chapters. Moreover, he is the best of partners and has supported me and this project without hesitation from the beginning. I end with my gratitude to my mother Helen, who has helped me in a thousand ways throughout this project and throughout my life. She has been an unfailingly wise, generous, and exceptional parent and friend.

Introduction

I asked Luciana, "Do you think that men and women are equal in the Mormon church?" It was my second week in Veracruz, Mexico, and I had just spent an hour asking this older woman about her childhood, the challenges she has overcome in her life, and the best and hardest parts of being a Latter-day Saint woman. Through my colleague, who was interpreting for us, I had learned about her difficult marriage, which ultimately ended in divorce, and the way her adopted faith had sustained her in the challenging years of navigating single motherhood.

Her brow furrowed a bit at my question. She looked perplexed. It was the same look several other Mexican women had given me when I asked about their perspectives on and experiences with gender equality in the Church of Jesus Christ of Latter-day Saints. She said, "*Pienso que sí* [I think so]?" her voice lilting up, as if she were asking a question.

I noted from the beginning the discomfort that questions about gender equality provoked in many of the women I interviewed. I felt bad that this topic was unsettling, but I continued to ask about it because women's status and perspectives on gender were central concerns of mine. It would take dozens more oral life history interviews with Latter-day Saint women in Mexico, Botswana, and the United States before I came to realize why this question was unsettling: it led them to suspect that I was evaluating their lives and stories through a lens—that of gender equality—that did not fully reflect their dominant moral concerns or paradigms.

They were right.

I had embarked on this project to explore the worldviews and navigations of Latter-day Saint women of color in the United States and the global South with a commitment to honor these women's stories and to let their concerns and emphases expand my inquiry. As a tradition born in the United States in the nineteenth century and still predominantly directed at the highest levels by white male leaders in the United States, the Church of Jesus Christ of Latter-day Saints experienced significant membership growth in the global South in the latter half of the twentieth century. Filled with paradoxes and tensions, not the least of which revolve around race and gender, Mormonism has proved itself to be a vibrant new religious movement, requiring much of converts but also delivering high levels of satisfaction to many of its practicing adherents. How and why women of color in Mexico, Botswana, and the United States adopt and adapt this American-born faith into their particular contexts and how issues of gender register to them in their diverse positionalities were central questions of mine.

As a graduate student I participated in the Mormon Women's Oral History Project at Claremont Graduate University, interviewing (mostly white) American Latter-day Saint women about their lives and experiences and seeing in these interviews the depth and complexity of their stories. Whether they were Mormon feminists like me or traditional religious women, their oral histories revealed thoughtful navigations of their gendered lives.[1] Unlike some early feminist scholars who had ignored traditional religious women or depicted them as oppressed or suffering from false consciousness, I focused in my analysis on women's agency—their resistance, their support, their creative propagation—as they consciously embedded themselves in a patriarchal system. Oral life histories, I had discovered, were useful vehicles for this kind of analysis, because they revealed the arc of a woman's life and the various ways she was actively working to create, change, support, or push against various structures or systems in her life. Traditional religious women, I knew, might affirm complementarian gender roles, but they were not disempowered victims. I myself was a member of this unabashedly patriarchal church, and my lived experience told me that this kind of reduction was unfair.

Despite my sincere commitment to respecting the worldviews of the women I interviewed, there was an inevitable tension between that commitment and the Western liberal feminist lens through which I view the world. As a feminist, I saw the ways in which certain structures, systems, and teachings subordinate women. I spent my graduate student career employing feminist theoretical, theological, and ethical approaches to various Mormon texts and practices. Balancing out my commitment to recognize the complexity and depth of the diverse worldviews, cultures, and social locations of Latter-day Saint women, alongside my commitment to critically analyze the systems that marginalize women, proved difficult. I eventually understood that my white middle-class American feminist positionality, so often grounded in questions of gender equality, revealed itself in a handful of questions that I asked my narrators.

This orientation toward questions of gender equality and emancipation has long framed the field of women's studies in religion, which emerged in the academy in the late 1960s and early 1970s. Over the course of three years spent analyzing the scores of oral histories gathered for this project, however, I found that the paradigm of women's equality or emancipation—the paradigm that has dominated scholarly work on women and religion for decades—was not in itself a sufficient paradigm through which to evaluate these Latter-day Saint women's actions and choices. As Amy Hoyt and Saba Mahmood have argued, too often scholars have evaluated traditional religious women's agency in light of Western liberative norms, which do not necessarily reflect these women's dominant priorities and values.[2] Mahmood and Hoyt helpfully expand notions of female agency beyond resistance to norms, describing frameworks of agency that include upholding norms, resisting norms, and complicated mixtures of both.

In this book I build on Hoyt's and Mahmood's work by analyzing the complex, agentive navigations of gender norms of global and American Latter-day Saint women of color in three separate, geographically situated case studies. I argue that although the paradigm of gender equality is important and useful in pinpointing structural inequities, it is insufficient for analyzing the worldviews, actions, and moral priorities of nonfeminist Latter-day Saint women of color. I argue that these traditional religious women should be analyzed using a different paradigm: that of non-oppressive connectedness, human and divine.

Although this worldview of non-oppressive connectedness encompasses elements of female empowerment and liberation, it is characterized by a broader moral focus on fostering positive, productive, and vitalizing relationality in a variety of realms. In this paradigm, gender inequality and gender complementarity are not primary moral evils or concerns. Indeed, the nonfeminist women I interviewed often found what could be described as liberation in their membership in this patriarchal church. Oppression and alienation from both God and other humans were the states against which these women were actively working. This ethical imperative of non-oppressive connectedness emerged as a theme in the stories of dozens of practicing Latter-day Saint women of color around the world as they discussed how Mormonism satisfied this moral and relational orientation in their various cultural contexts with varying degrees of success.

In listening deeply to these diverse women's joys, challenges, hopes, and disappointments—and in expanding my analytical vision beyond questions of gender equality—I came to see the ways in which multiple markers of identity and experience such as race, class, gender, and culture intersected with one another in these women's lives. In these diverse intersections of identity, various insights, survival strategies, and ideals emerged that often centered on creating positive relationality. Intersectional feminist theoretical frameworks, therefore, underpin much of my analysis.

The term *intersectionality* was coined in the 1980s by the law professor Kimberlé Crenshaw as she explained the necessity of accounting for multiple grounds of identity (sex and race in this case) when analyzing issues of discrimination.[3] Failure to attend to these overlapping identities elides the vulnerabilities of women of color, she argued.[4] Intersectionality, a concept that continued to be developed in the 1990s by Black women, is now used by a variety of scholars to analyze how "gender, race, social class, sexual identity, and other forms of difference work concurrently to shape people and social institutions within multiple relationships of power."[5] Attention to the intersections of multiple identities and contexts in my interviewees' lives revealed perspectives I was not anticipating. Indeed, in examining gender at the crossroads of religion, nation, race, and class, a new moral paradigm emerged. Rich insights and wisdom born of bearing the complexity of these positionalities materialized. And ultimately, the narrowness of a dominant focus on gender equality was elucidated under the lens of an intersectional analysis.

Related to the intersectional nature of this project is the illuminating framework of womanist thought, which culminates in Chapter 4's explication of a Mormon womanist theology of abundance. Black feminists developed womanism as they recognized that white feminist thought does not always match Black women's experiences and priorities. Alice Walker first defined the term *womanist* in 1983, finding inspiration in the Black folk expression "womanish," which describes a strong, responsible, courageous, spiritual Black woman who loves expansively and desires the uplift of her entire community.[6]

Like intersectional approaches, womanism considers the unique matrix of oppressions faced by women of color. It also has a rich tradition of laying out a normative vision of ethics and theology, one that emphasizes commitment to "survival and wholeness of entire people, male *and* female."[7] Thus, priorities of womanist ethicists and theologians are survival, community building, and establishing a "positive quality of life."[8] There is, therefore, some confluence between womanist thought and the paradigm of non-oppressive connectedness, which prioritizes positive, uplifting relationality. The nonfeminist

Latter-day Saint women with whom I spoke might not point to structural gender equality as a priority, as many womanists would, but they are committed to developing uplifting, non-oppressive connections and relationships grounded in a determination to craft a better quality of life and to strengthen their communities.

Womanist and intersectional approaches are foundational to this project, which examines the intersections of gender, race, class, and culture in a global Latter-day Saint context. As I increasingly came to understand, these women's diverse positionalities and contexts complicate the frameworks and focuses of white Western feminists. Ultimately, these voices from the peripheries of the Mormon movement bring forth new possibilities and paradigms for understanding the lives and choices of many religious women around the world.

In order to give appropriate context to this project, I begin by discussing various fields and critical frameworks that converge in this study, and I lay out a brief overview of Mormonism. Then, I describe the methods and methodologies I utilized. My concluding remarks offer an outline of chapters and my vision for how this project presents important interventions in the fields of women's studies in religion and Mormon studies.

Women's Liberation, Gender Equality, and Women's Studies in Religion

Women's studies in religion emerged in the late 1960s alongside the women's liberation movement when feminists began to analyze the ways in which patriarchal systems marginalize women and deny them equal rights and opportunities. Scholars such as Mary Daly, Rosemary Radford Ruether, Judith Plaskow, Rita Gross, Carol Christ, and Elizabeth Schüssler Fiorenza turned their gazes to religion and critiqued the incessant androcentrism and patriarchy that undergird most of the world's major faith traditions.[9] This scholarship became so influential that the category of gender has become an important focus of scholarly analysis in the realm of religious studies, with many scholars not only incorporating women's experiences into their work but also challenging the production of knowledge itself as biased and distorted.[10]

The Jewish feminist Judith Plaskow describes the link between the field of women's studies in religion and feminist critique in her overview of the inception of the field: "Connections between feminist critique and social change have been evident in all areas of women's studies in religion from its beginnings."[11] Thus, the field of women's studies in religion has been largely grounded in a feminist critique, advocating social change with the aim of equal opportunities and visibility for women. In her analysis of the field, Plaskow saw three overlapping and consecutive stages of scholarship:

> Initially, the preponderance of works in the field focused on the analysis and critiques of male texts, institutions, and traditions. Then, without critical work being abandoned, there was a gradual shift toward recovering women's history within and outside patriarchal traditions. Most recently, there has been a burgeoning of constructive writing focused on the reform or transformation of existing traditions and the creation of new ones.[12]

Although the first stage Plaskow mentions is the one to most explicitly tie women's studies in religion to critiquing patriarchy and thus gender inequity, the following stages she cites likewise are linked to visions of women's increased voice, opportunities, and leadership in religious communities. Even the stage of recovering women's history was conceptually linked to women's liberation since, as Fiorenza argues, accepting male texts as accurate representations of women's reality consents to the erasure of women's actual experiences and thus is a collusion with patriarchy.[13]

More recently Black, Hispanic, African, and Asian scholars have emerged as prominent contributors in the field of women's studies in religion. Delores Williams, Mercy Oduyoye, Ada Maria Isasi-Díaz, and Kwok Pui-lan are only a few of the scholars who have added their voices, visions, and nuances to the field.[14] These women, while still critiquing gender inequity and patriarchy, also point out other oppressions that women of color, global and American, face in their lives. For them, gender inequity is only one oppression among many with which women in their communities contend. Therefore, recognizing the ways in which gender oppression interacts with other oppressions of race, class, colonialism, and more is paramount.

For scholars in the field of women's studies in religion, who employ a variety of methodologies ranging from theology to history, textual studies, and anthropology, transformation of current patriarchal systems is an explicit or implicit project. The work of the above-mentioned feminist scholars has changed the very face of religious studies, effecting an important shift by uncovering the ways in which religions and the field of religious studies itself have been premised on gender-biased assumptions. These contributions have been monumental. Yet as Hoyt and Mahmood argue, it is crucial to recognize that feminist theory itself, which undergirds many of these scholars' analyses of religion, was premised on liberal Western assumptions that prize equality, independence, and autonomy. Thus, the thoughts, experiences, and actions of religious women who embrace patriarchal systems and who do not fight for structural equality and autonomy have been largely unexamined by the most prominent authors in the field of women's studies in religion.

Religious Women and Agency

In the 1990s and the 2000s, scholars using ethnographic methodologies began to write careful and nuanced analyses of the lived religion of women who embrace and support their patriarchal traditions. Scholars such as Robert Orsi, R. Marie Griffith, and Saba Mahmood took traditional religious women's viewpoints and experiences seriously, and the question of agency—how these women's beliefs and religious communities did or did not engender liberation, voice, piety, connection, transformation, and various forms of resistance—was often of central interest to the authors. Orsi, for example, in his study of Catholic women's devotion to the cult of St. Jude, uncovers the ways in which their patriarchal faith could lead to healing, action, self-expression, and even at times emancipation.[15] Griffith, likewise, finds that evangelical women who embrace notions of women's fragility and dependence can find transformation and power in their submission to male authority, as this behavior leads to better treatment in the home.[16] Griffith critiques feminists who discount or show contempt for traditional women, asking whether liberation must be defined in secular terms and urging scholars to view conservative women not as oppressed but instead as creative thinkers and self-transformers amidst a world of grief and disappointment.[17]

In the first decade of the twenty-first century, the anthropologist and religion scholar Saba Mahmood systematically dismantled the dominant concept of women's agency, arguing that scholars who follow liberal Western notions of individualism and autonomy have often conceptualized agency as resistance to social norms and structures. Thus, ordinary women who uphold their traditions' injunctions and gender roles have received scant attention or been dismissed as oppressed and unworthy of scholarly attention. Mahmood argues that Western conceptions of agency must move beyond the notion of agency as subversion of authority.[18] Agency discourse, she writes, should encompass actions that support patriarchal norms and structures.

Following Mahmood's lead, Amy Hoyt and Catherine Brekus have further worked to add nuance to and reconceptualize agency in a way that honors and acknowledges the complexity, creativity, and choices of religious women who support patriarchal systems. In her work on Latter-day Saint women's agency, Hoyt finds women enacting a complex agency in which they simultaneously resist and uphold religious boundaries.[19] Brekus, likewise, advocates a reconceptualization of agency, one which recognizes that agency is on a continuum and which reconsiders the association between agency and intentionality.[20] Developing a model of agency that moves beyond associations with freedom, liberation, and intentionality, Brekus argues, could lead to the development of better understandings of how religious change takes place and how Latter-day Saint women contribute to Mormon history.[21]

These broader concepts of agency are useful as analytical lenses for scholars examining traditional religious women. These newer understandings of agency can encompass a vast array of decisions and actions, but their power lies in their insistence on examining people as rational, thoughtful subjects who creatively navigate their lives and produce new meanings, understandings, and ways of being in the world. This lens of complex agency stands in stark contrast to other analytical lenses—for instance, the lens of false consciousness—that have been deployed to depict traditional religious women not as subjects navigating their lives but as objects of oppression, not as producers of meaning but as blind consumers of beliefs.[22] Examining women through a nuanced lens of agency illuminates the lives, worldviews, and decision making of multitudes of women whose complicated lives resist the simplistic reductionism of oppression-liberation analyses.

In my project this more expansive concept of agency—how women creatively propagate, change, resist, critique, and justify gender norms, often simultaneously—is central. My analysis contributes to the conversation by showing *how* women employ their agency in their positionalities as women of color of various nationalities and *to what end* they employ it. I argue that although themes and concerns emerge in women's oral histories that are specific to their particular contexts, a major moral imperative for many of these women—a moral orientation that drives many of their agentive actions—is that of non-oppressive connectedness. Latter-day Saint women's choices to support, question, or propel this patriarchal, community-minded tradition reveal the central values that ground their lives.

This project expands on Hoyt's fine ethnographic work concerning a group of American Latter-day Saint women. Her argument—that feminist theory's emphasis on equality and emancipation shuts out the experiences of traditional religious women who have different understandings of women's distinct roles and notions of male-female interdependence—is an important intervention in feminist theory. My project adds to and complicates the discussion of Latter-day Saint women's gendered navigations by incorporating issues of race, class, and culture. I find that while an exclusive paradigm of gender equality illuminates issues of structural inequity and androcentrism—a crucial and important intervention—it falls short as an analytical lens when examining these women of color. That said, discussions of the extent to which Mormonism empowers and liberates women are fruitful, so long as they are combined with analyses that also recognize other dominant values centering their lives. The paradigm of non-oppressive connectedness, human and divine, acknowledges an orientation toward and awareness of issues of oppression, and it also acknowledges a moral focus on relationality and connection with God and other humans. Gender equality may not be a central paradigm in the lives of nonfeminist Latter-day Saint women of color, but rejecting injustice on a broader level, decrying mistreatment on a personal level, and embracing productive and sustaining relationships are central. Focusing on these values is, therefore, central in my analysis.

Connectedness, Relationality, and an Ethic of Care

When Latter-day Saint women of color enact their agency, it is often with the goal of creating or sustaining positive, ennobling relationships. That relationality, as opposed to justice or equality, can be a valid area of ethical or moral concern is an argument that the psychologist Carol Gilligan made in 1982. Gilligan's *In a Different Voice: Psychological Theory and Women's Development* changed the face of Western ethics and psychology by advancing a revolutionary concept: that the ethical orientation that tends to focus on care and relationships, more often associated with females, is just as moral as the ethical orientation toward justice and rights, more often associated with males.[23]

Gilligan's work is particularly important for Latter-day Saint women because it elucidates and validates a relational orientation that is often central for them. Hoyt touches on the relational orientation of Latter-day Saint women when she describes the gendered cosmology that anchors Mormonism, a cosmology in which "men and women are radically different from one another and . . . become perfected only through their ongoing interdependence."[24] Male-female interdependence, Hoyt suggests, is a grounding assumption and understanding through which Latter-day Saint women view their lives and the world, and this observation resonates to some degree with some of Gilligan's work on relationality.

Although notions of male-female interdependence and cooperation are indeed key aspects of the worldviews of many Latter-day Saint women, I suggest that a broader paradigm of non-oppressive connectedness is illuminating in evaluating the lives and choices of Latter-day Saints without white or male privilege. Whether the relationship is male-female, mother-child, friend-friend, individual-community, human-God, or any other type, non-oppressive connectedness is a theme and desire that surfaced in many of my interviews. Gilligan's work, which validates relationality, is particularly helpful because she suggests a framework in which women who value healthy connectedness and reject alienation can be evaluated in terms other than gender equality and autonomy, which center so much of feminist theory. At the same time, her work also acknowledges the importance of a justice orientation, one that is also present in the reflections and experiences of many Latter-day Saint women of color with whom I spoke. With the exception of the handful of feminist women I interviewed, this justice orientation often was not related to gender equality. Instead, it was located in critiques of abuse and rejections of racial and colonial oppressions.

Mormonism

To situate the perspectives and tensions of Latter-day Saint women of color, a very brief orientation to Mormon history is in order. Mormonism was founded in New York in 1830 by the young visionary Joseph Smith Jr. amid the religious fervor of the Second Great Awakening. According to Smith, as a teenager he experienced a vision of God the Father and Jesus Christ while praying for guidance as to which church he should join. These embodied divinities told him that he would have a key role to play in the coming restoration of the true Church of Christ. In subsequent years Smith said he experienced more visions, which led to him finding and translating the ancient document now known as the Book of Mormon. The institutional church was founded shortly after the Book of Mormon's publication. The religious movement grew rapidly in its first couple of decades but was dogged by persecutions in the late 1830s and 1840s due to its burgeoning numbers, distinctive beliefs, and practice of plural marriage.

After Smith was killed in 1844, his successor Brigham Young began making plans to leave Illinois and move the church members to the West. Nearly one-third of the members of the Church of Jesus Christ of Latter-day Saints decided to stay in Illinois, many of whom ultimately joined other Mormon sects, most notably the Reorganized Church of Jesus Christ of Latter Day Saints, headed by Joseph Smith's son, Joseph Smith III. Mormon followers of Brigham Young (known as Latter-day Saints, or LDS) began settling in the Salt Lake Valley in 1847, ultimately displacing Indigenous tribes already living there. In the shelter of this valley, beyond the reach of hostile Americans and the American government, Latter-day Saint leaders began to acknowledge their practice of plural marriage, which became an identity marker for members of the faith in the latter half of the nineteenth century. Other defining markers were the Mormon beliefs in authoritative living prophets and the mingling of religious and civil authority. After the church formally abandoned the practice of polygamy at the turn of the century, Mormonism underwent a period of assimilation into wider American culture, culminating in the 1950s when Mormon and wider American norms, with their postwar emphases on large nuclear families and clear gender roles, most fully converged.[25]

Since the mid-twentieth century the Church of Jesus Christ of Latter-day Saints has experienced significant growth outside the United States. During these years of global growth, there were also concerted efforts to centralize and consolidate Latter-day Saint teachings and so make the practices, doctrines, handbooks, and teaching manuals simple, clear, and available globally in several languages. This movement toward simplification and consolidation—known as "correlation"—resulted in many auxiliaries (including the official women's auxiliary of the church, the Relief Society) being brought firmly under the control of male priesthood leaders. The church saw rapid membership gains in many Latin American countries, but it was hampered in Brazil and Africa because of its policy of not ordaining people of African descent to the lay priesthood that was conferred on boys and men age twelve and older.[26] In 1978, however, the church removed this restriction, and it has since begun to see growth in more countries in the global South. Today, more than half of the members of the Church of Jesus Christ of Latter-day Saints reside outside the United States.[27] Mexico has the highest number of non-U.S. members, but some of the fastest growth is now occurring in various African countries. Retention in the global church remains a considerable problem, however, with only a quarter of members in Latin America and Asia attending church on Sundays.[28]

This very brief recounting of seminal moments in Mormon history foreshadows various tensions that are explored in this book. First, Mormonism carries within it an ongoing tension between personal revelation and agency, on one hand, and institutional and prophetic authority, on the other. Joseph Smith's experience of a God who poured down revelations upon him was foundational to his theological vision of the heavens being open and revelation accessible to everyone. Smith's teachings contain a profound respect for moral agency, free will, human potential, and the ability to communicate directly with God. As Terryl Givens states, it is therefore ironic that Smith founded "one of the most centralized, hierarchical, authoritarian churches in America to come out of the era famous for the 'democratization of religion.'"[29] Today some members of the church navigate the tension between institutional authority and personal revelation when these two sources of authority conflict with one another.

Second, tensions about the role of women characterized Mormonism from its earliest years. Smith instituted secret plural marriages as he developed his theology of individuals and families sealed together in a web of eternal relationships. Bound in this web sacralized by plural marital sealings, people would be exalted not individually, but with their families. In plural marriage sealings, Smith restored the biblical practice through which he could eternally bind himself to friends he dearly loved as he married their sisters, daughters, and wives.[30] As this new frontier religion bound many women in norm-violating plural marriages that clearly placed them as subordinate to men, it also offered Latter-day Saint women opportunities unavailable to women in polite society.[31] Joseph Smith's wife Emma Hale Smith was commanded in Latter-day Saint scripture to "exhort the church" and, moreover, to "expound scriptures," an activity associated at the time with clergy.[32] Women's roles were also expanded in Utah in the nineteenth century as plural wives learned to earn a living and make their own decisions, given the frequent absences of their husbands.[33]

Third, tension arises even today because of Mormonism's historic legacy of teachings about race and lineage, which prevented Latter-day Saint men of African descent from being ordained to the lay priesthood and Latter-day Saint women and men of African descent from participating in sacred temple rituals until 1978. This historic legacy also holds mixed messages for those of Indigenous American descent, as Joanna Brooks explains: "Beginning as early as 1830, early Mormon missionaries brought to the Sac and Fox, Delaware, Wyandot, Cattaraugus, and Shawnee nations a double message: first, that they were peoples of a sacred legacy and destiny that they could come to understand through the Book of Mormon, and second, that the disobedience of their ancestors was the source of their Indigeneity."[34] Pasifika people face a similar tension because church teachings include them in the cosmology of Mormonism as members of the house of Israel but sometimes also connect their dark skin to a curse from God.[35] Teachings about dark skin as a curse are no longer emphasized in the contemporary church, and other strands of Mormon thought reject racism and insist that "all are alike unto God."[36] Yet this legacy of racial exclusion haunts the experiences of some Latter-day Saints of color as they continue to see predominantly white men in Utah assume the highest positions of authority in the church.[37] For global members of color who are less aware of or less burdened by this historic legacy, tension might arise as cultural practices come into conflict with the church's prescriptions.[38]

Before proceeding further, a brief note about the terms *Mormon, Mormonism, LDS,* and *Latter-day Saint* is in order. The Church of Jesus Christ of Latter-day Saints is the largest denomination of the Mormon movement begun with Joseph Smith's publication of the Book of Mormon in 1830. Since the early days of the church members have referred to themselves as Mormons, and the term is commonly understood to refer to the Church of Jesus Christ of Latter-day Saints, though it can also refer to offshoot denominations including Mormon fundamentalist groups. In October 2018 Russell M. Nelson, president of the Utah-based church, discouraged the use of the terms *Mormon* and *LDS* when referring to the church and its members.[39] During the time when the oral histories discussed in this book were done (2015–2017), *Mormon* was a common moniker for the church and its members, and thus this term was prominent in these interviews. In the interest of specificity, I emphasize the term *Latter-day Saint* in much of my discussion, particularly when referring to church leaders and the institutional church. However, I employ "Mormon" as well, especially when I want to emphasize the broader religious culture surrounding the church. I also use the term *Mormonism*, as no other word encompasses the history, thought, theology, practice, and culture that have sprung from the movement begun by Joseph Smith. Because I do not focus at length on any other churches in this book, I refer to the Church of Jesus Christ of Latter-day Saints as "the church" throughout.

Gender and Mormonism

As mentioned above, Mormonism is filled with contradictions and paradoxes regarding women's status and roles. Scholarship centering on Mormonism and gender over the course of the past fifty years has been dominated by the histories, theologies, experiences, and critiques of white, middle-class, almost always American Latter-day Saint women. This scholarship has primarily had a historical focus as scholars like Jill Derr, Maureen Ursenbach Beecher, Lavina Fielding Anderson, Martha Bradley, and Claudia Bushman have delved into the lives and experiences of (often elite) early Latter-day Saint women.[40] They discovered that there was a greater flexibility in gender roles and conceptions in the early years of Mormonism, as Latter-day Saint women blessed and anointed others, claimed some form of priesthood, fought for suffrage, and ran their largely autonomous women's organization, the Relief Society. Linda King Newell, Dave Hall, Marie Cornwall, and Laura Vance document the slow tightening and narrowing of the Relief Society's vision and power in the twentieth century, as well as of Mormon ideas about proper gender roles, as the ideals of domesticity and full-time motherhood began to push out earlier support for wage earning and community involvement for Mormon women.[41]

Scholars who approach questions of gender from a theological standpoint have explored Mormon teachings for their liberatory and constraining potentials. Margaret Toscano and Janice Allred have worked to shatter the silence surrounding Mormonism's Heavenly Mother and raise her out of theological obscurity and into the Mormon godhead, while others have interrogated Mormonism's contemporary ontological positioning of women as mothers against men as priesthood holders.[42] Still others have examined the mixed or contradictory messages about the scriptural figure of Eve, whom Latter-day Saint leaders in the past several decades have celebrated as an exemplar of agency and wisdom for choosing to eat the fruit and thus propel humankind toward its cosmic destiny of godhood, but who is also paradoxically subordinated to Adam in spite of her righteous and wise decision.[43]

A central question for some scholars of Mormon theology, doctrine, history, and contemporary culture is the nature of patriarchy in the Church of Jesus Christ of Latter-day Saints. The *Concise Encyclopedia of Sociology* defines *patriarchy* in this way: "Originally used to describe autocratic rule by a male head of a family, patriarchy has been extended to describe a more general system in which power is secured in the hands of adult men."[44] By this definition, few would contest that the church's male-only priesthood and male-led institutional system are overtly patriarchal. Within the family realm, patriarchy reigned supreme in the early years of Mormonism as well. In this, the faith was not unusual—most Christian traditions upheld patriarchal practices and ideals in the nineteenth century. As B. Carmon Hardy points out, Mormon patriarchal ideology of that era, which embraced ideas of male superiority and female inferiority, found a powerful ally in the doctrine of polygamy, which was seen by several church leaders as a brace for male authority in the home.[45] Contemporary Latter-day Saint leaders, however, employ a dual discourse about male power in the home. On one hand, men are instructed to "preside" over their wives and children, and until 2019 wives ritually submitted to husbands in the endowment ceremony in Latter-day Saint temples.[46] On the other hand, contemporary Latter-day Saint leaders often emphasize in their sermons the importance of equal partnership and joint decision making. Contemporary Mormonism might be best described as a soft or benevolent patriarchy, in which men are strongly encouraged to treat women—whom they often describe as spiritual and moral superiors to men—with kindness and respect.[47] In this soft patriarchal system, complementarian gender roles are upheld as ideal, with men encouraged to be benevolent priesthood holders, primarily responsible for providing and protecting as well as presiding, while women are encouraged to be primarily responsible for nurturing children. The term *complementarian* describes a worldview in which women have complementary but different roles from men in society. Proponents of complementarianism believe that women are ontologically equal but functionally different. In practice, complementarianism generally results in decision-making power accruing to males as they take leadership roles in ecclesiastical, familial, or societal realms.[48] In Latter-day Saint complementarian discourse, however, mothers and fathers are to act as "equal partners" in the family, even as fathers simultaneously preside.[49]

The theologian Sheila Taylor uses different language to describe Mormon patriarchy, distinguishing between "fallen" patriarchy, which involves male tyranny and domineering authoritarianism, and "godly" patriarchy, which involves men presiding over the family yet also acting as equal partners. Taylor sees this godly version of patriarchy encapsulated in the Latter-day Saint scripture Doctrine and Covenants 121, which emphasizes gentleness, meekness, long-suffering, love, and persuasion as elements of righteous authority. Contemporary Latter-day Saint leaders, Taylor argues, reject fallen patriarchy but embrace godly patriarchy.[50] However defanged patriarchy might be in many Latter-day Saint homes, the institutional church remains a bastion of male power. As Colleen McDannell notes, in the contemporary church, males continue to dominate ecclesiastical administrative roles and the development of policy and doctrine, even as church leaders have worked to equalize marital power dynamics in the home.[51]

Much scholarly work on Latter-day Saint women has been historical and theological, but some scholars with sociological interests have explored the ways in which authoritative Latter-day Saint rhetoric concerning gender has shifted or not shifted over time, as well as how contemporary women have navigated the culturally conservative and patriarchal faith.[52] Lori Beaman, Amy Hoyt, and the authors of *Mormon Women Have Their Say: Essays from the Claremont Oral History Collection* all explore how mostly white American or Canadian Latter-day Saint women have articulated their experiences, understandings, struggles, and feelings of empowerment within Mormonism's gendered structure.[53] The edited volume *Mormon Feminism: Essential Writings* showcases the wide breadth of scholarly writings about Mormonism and gender since the 1970s.[54] It also contains pieces by Mormon feminists of color who examine issues of Mormonism and gender in their particular cultural and racial contexts. My project, likewise, seeks to contribute to the broadening and deepening of scholarship concerning Mormonism and gender by highlighting the voices of Latter-day Saint women of color in the United States and the global South. It also seeks to expand on the above-mentioned ethnographic and sociological work of scholars through an intersectional examination of the lived experiences of women of color navigating issues of gender, race, and class within a Mormon context.

Project Description, Methods, and Methodology

I conducted oral history interviews with Latter-day Saint women of color in Mexico, Botswana, and the United States, exploring the ways in which these women articulate their perspectives on contemporary questions of gender at the crossroads of race, religion, class, and culture. The overwhelming majority of my subjects were devout Latter-day Saints, highly committed to the church. I chose to focus one of my ethnographies on a location in Veracruz, Mexico, because this developing country has the largest population of church members outside the United States, numbering (according to church records) 1.48 million.[55] In addition, members of the church in Mexico overwhelmingly are of mixed Spanish and Indigenous descent (mestizo), and thus they navigate the Utah-led church as people of color with different cultural frameworks and contexts.[56] In fact, Mexico was the site of significant dissatisfaction with the centralized church hierarchy in the 1930s after church leaders appointed a white American to preside over the Mexican mission. Several Mexican church leaders, fueled by ethnic pride, desired a Mexican mission president, and the church's denial of this request led one-third of Latter-day Saints in that country to break away from the church. Many of these Latter-day Saints, known as Third Conventionists, ultimately returned to the church a decade later.[57] Mormonism's rich and long history in Mexico, which began in the nineteenth century as it became a refuge for American polygamists fleeing prosecution by the federal government, made it an ideal location for exploring issues of race, culture, and gender.

In contrast, the Church of Jesus Christ of Latter-day Saints in Botswana is very young; its first congregation was established in 1983. This landlocked country in southern Africa, located only a four-hour drive from the South African capital Johannesburg, has 3,653 members and fifteen congregations.[58] Because the church in Botswana is so new, nearly all members over the age of twenty-five are converts, and very little scholarly work has focused on its members. A former British protectorate, Botswana achieved independence in 1966, though it was able to retain some of its traditional structures and systems under British colonialism, which began in the late nineteenth century. Although racial discrimination against Black Africans influenced government policy in the late nineteenth and early twentieth centuries in terms of local amenities, public services, and facilities, in the mid-twentieth century "a culture of consultation between the colonial government and Batswana [people of Botswana] led to genuine attempts at eliminating official race discrimination in the territory, and peaceful decolonisation."[59] Thus, in Botswana racial tension between Blacks and whites is mild compared to that of its neighbor South Africa. Botswana's main ethnic groups are Tswana people (79 percent), Kalanga people (11 percent), and Basarwa, otherwise known as Bushmen or San people (3 percent).[60] People of European descent make up about 3 percent of the population. As oral histories attest, Batswana Latter-day Saint women carve out interesting and complex paths as they navigate elements of their traditional culture and their loyalty to their chosen faith.[61]

The United States, a Western industrialized country with gender norms that emphasize ideals of equal opportunities for women, is the location of my final case study. As residents of the birthplace of Mormonism and the site of considerable racial tension throughout its history, Latter-day Saint women of color in the United States sometimes feel the weight of America's—and the church's—troubled history with race. Unlike their counterparts in Mexico or Botswana, where local leaders are usually the same race as the vast majority of their congregants, Latter-day Saint women of color in America often experience their congregations as racial minorities. Questions about oppressive systems and patterns arise in the minds of some in this group, who navigate oppressions on multiple levels. Their everyday experiences of being minority women in a historically white patriarchal church bring to light issues of privilege unique to the United States, but these experiences also show the ways in which Mormonism gives these women resources to carve out more satisfactory lives.

The following questions drive my project: How do issues of gender register with women of color in the United States and the global South? How do women interpret the legacy of Mormon understandings of gender in their specific contexts and in parallel to third- and fourth-wave movements in global and intersectional feminism? What ethical imperatives do women of color, global and American, emphasize as they live their Latter-day Saint lives? Where are the sites of tension and resonance as they adopt and adapt Mormonism to their contexts? How do women enact a complex agency as they navigate their sometimes conflicting loyalties?

In order to investigate these questions, I employed a multi-method approach for studying communities of Latter-day Saint women in the United States, Botswana, and Mexico. The three methods were as follows:

Oral life histories. These reconstruct narrators' individual experiences and perspectives. This method is particularly valuable for capturing the voices of marginal groups, such as women, that historians often overlook.[62] Oral life histories allow researchers to glimpse the lives of everyday members of certain communities and allow narrators the opportunity to assess their own agency in relation to the structures (religious, social, and so on) that impact their lives. My approach to conducting oral histories was conversational and open-ended, giving narrators the opportunity to share the experiences and insights that were most important to them. Interviews were recorded and transcribed later, and each narrator had the opportunity to edit her oral history transcript in order to correct mistakes or clarify it. Interviews in Botswana and the United States were conducted in English, and interviews in Mexico were conducted in Spanish through my interpreter, Silvia Carlson, or by April Carlson, a Spanish-speaking colleague, except for two or three interviews that were conducted in English because the women were fluent English speakers. Narrators in Botswana were found through official church networks, facilitated by local leaders who embraced the project. Although this led to a certain level of homogeneity in interviewees (virtually all devout and practicing Latter-day Saints), colleagues and I were able to travel beyond the capital city of Gaborone to speak with women in rural districts. These women were often of a different socioeconomic class and thus brought a measure of breadth to the study. Colleagues and I collected a total of forty-eight oral life histories with Latter-day Saint women in Botswana.[63] Narrators in Mexico and the United States were found through informal networks (not official church networks) using purposive sampling and snowball sampling.[64] We collected twenty-nine oral life histories of Mexican women. In the United States, I conducted twenty-one oral life history interviews with Latter-day Saint women of color, some of whom were immigrants to the United States. For demographic information by country about the women interviewed (education level, marital status, birthyear, and age at baptism or affiliation), see appendix D.

Participant observation. As I interviewed participants, attended church meetings and other social gatherings, and sometimes visited them in their homes, I gathered data using the method of participant observation. As ethnographic scholars have noted, this method gives important insight into how people relate to each other and what the cultural parameters are.[65] It allows for richly detailed description and access to the "backstage culture."[66] In order to protect the privacy of individuals whom I observed and interviewed, I use pseudonyms throughout the book and sometimes alter minor details about their lives or appearances.

Textual sources. Most of my data were gathered via oral history interviews and, to a lesser extent, participant observation, but I also drew from articles, talks, books, blog posts, and podcasts that helped contextualize women's position, status, and experiences within Mormonism and within their specific geographical locations.

While these methods (particularly the first two) are meant to illuminate the thoughts, perspectives, and experiences of women who are often ignored in androcentric research and to position women as subjects worthy of careful study and analysis, they also have certain dangers. Whenever researchers engage in the practice of "representation," particularly of people with whom they have cultivated relationships in order to obtain information, there is potential for unethical use and exploitation by researchers more concerned with their own agendas and presentation of "objective" facts than with the ethical and careful treatment of their subjects. As the Indigenous researcher Linda Tuhiwai Smith has argued, anthropology has a long and troubled history of exoticized, demeaning, or ethnocentric representations of "native" or somehow "other" people.[67] She advocates for methodologies and methods, among them oral history, that "work with marginalized communities, that facilitate the expression of marginalized voices, and that attempt to re-present the experience of marginalization in genuine and authentic ways."[68] Smith delineates a number of decolonizing methods, methodologies, and projects that further the goals of ethical Indigenous research, which are "the survival of peoples, cultures, and languages; the struggle to become self-determining, the need to take back control of our destinies."[69] Among these projects are writing tribal and family histories, recording oral testimonies, documenting foundational stories of the community that communicate beliefs and values, celebrating survival and resistance to colonialism, and reframing the ways in which Indigenous issues and social problems are discussed.[70]

Although my white feminist paradigm of gender equality may have revealed itself in my choice of certain interview questions, I did consciously make a pronounced effort to carry out an ethical, sensitive, and non-imperialist or decolonizing project. In my analysis and in the writing of the chapters, I attempted to avoid isolated quotes from anonymous, non-contextualized women. Rather, I built the chapters around the stories of a small handful of women so that I could present their lives and perspectives in all their complexity. During my interviews, I also attempted to be ethical by deliberately giving the women opportunities to articulate their own specific themes, priorities, complex identities, and particular navigational strategies. Many of my questions were intentionally broad, focusing on their challenges and joys and on difficult decisions they had made in their lives. I invited them to discuss the ways in which their own cultures and identities melded with that of their chosen Latter-day Saint faith tradition. If women had stories they wanted to tell about their lives—be they stories of sorrow, achievement, joy in finding the church, or attitudes toward life—I tended to sit back and let them.[71]

Nevertheless, as feminist oral historians have emphasized, it is important to keep in mind that oral histories are ultimately co-created documents, shaped by both the narrator and the researcher asking the questions.[72] Thus, in some real sense, "the typical product of an interview is a text, not a reproduction of reality."[73] This cautionary reminder is particularly important given my insider/outsider status in relation to the women I interviewed. I may have been an insider in terms of my sex and church affiliation, but I was an outsider in terms of culture and race. Different perspectives and analyses could certainly emerge with a different scholar bringing her own unique positionality and experiences to the subject at hand. Indeed, there is every possibility that a researcher indigenous to the community studied would elicit different stories and produce different analyses.

Alongside the important work of Smith, other scholars have worked to develop methodologies that address the power imbalances between researcher and researched and to ensure more ethical and less ethnocentric treatment of subjects. Feminist approaches to research have been particularly attentive to issues of power, representation, and difference. In my research I utilized feminist frameworks and methodologies that work to redress such power imbalances, attend to differences between women, and explicitly locate the researcher within the production of knowledge. At their core, feminist research methodologies and approaches aim to empower women and other oppressed people, as well as create knowledge that is beneficial to women and to do so in ethical and reflexive ways that disrupt traditional hierarchies.[74] These research methodologies are based on the belief that "women can possess and share valuable knowledge and thus research can start from the perspective of women's lives."[75] As Sharlene Nagy Hesse-Biber, Patricia Leavy, and Michelle Yaiser explain, rather than assuming a subject-object split in which the researcher is the knowing party and the researched is the object, "feminists aim at *developing* knowledge *with* their research subjects who bring their own experiential knowledge, concerns, and emotions to the project."[76]

Feminist methodology also calls for researchers to be explicit about their positionality. Feminist researchers reject third-person "view from nowhere" objective scholarly accounts in favor of producing a "view from somewhere."[77] Explicitly revealing one's social location, questions, experiences, and ideology as a researcher helps readers assess the value and biases of the work.[78] Thus, throughout this volume I deliberately insert myself into the descriptions of my interviews with various women. The three ethnographic chapters and this introduction begin with a personal anecdote that locates me as a researcher.

These anecdotes may at times seem unnecessary, but I am committed to an explicit acknowledgment of my positionality as the filter through which my analyses and critiques emerge.

This Book's Contributions to the Field

This book helps fill certain gaps in the field of Mormon studies, while simultaneously furthering ongoing conversations in the field of women's studies in religion. First, it documents the lives of a group whose voices have been largely unheard and unanalyzed within the academy. The vast majority of academic work on Mormonism has focused on the institutional church, its theology, and institutionally powerful people (usually men) within it. With very few exceptions, little attention has been paid to Latter-day Saint women on the margins of Mormonism, far from the seats of institutional power.[79] These heretofore unheard voices document how the Utah-based church affects their lives and interacts with diverse cultures and contexts. This book's focus on Latter-day Saint women of color therefore decenters white North America in the emerging field of Mormon studies.

Second, this book attends to differences between Latter-day Saint women in ways that prior studies have not. As such, it is grounded in intersectional feminist and womanist frameworks, taking into account the ways in which race, class, gender, and culture interact to produce certain perspectives and experiences. As Elizabeth Spelman notes, many earlier feminists' "focus on women 'as women' has addressed only one group of women—namely white middle-class women of Western industrialized countries."[80] To speak of women as a monolith is now understood to be inadequate and to erase the experiences of women in different cultural, racial, and class contexts, who may not feel constrained or empowered by the same things that many Western white middle-class women do. In paying attention to issues of intersectionality—and in its utilization of womanist frameworks emphasizing the authority, wisdom, priorities, and stories of women of color—this project stands at the cutting edge of Mormon studies.

This volume also challenges and enriches feminist critiques of religion by broadening and complicating the way we think about women's agency at the intersection of race, colony, and class in the context of religion. While noting the moments of tension in which women resist or struggle with certain norms—a tension that has predominantly been associated with women's agency—this book also examines moments in which women embrace, creatively propagate, and support patriarchal norms. These agentive acts point to worldviews and values that anchor many of these women's lives.

Finally, this book also enriches feminist critiques of religion by suggesting an alternative interpretive paradigm through which to view the lives of traditional religious women. Whereas dominant feminist analytical frameworks valuing women's independence, autonomy, and equality are helpful in pointing to the ways religions empower or constrain women, I suggest that the interpretive framework of non-oppressive connectedness illuminates the choices of Latter-day Saint women of color around the world more fully and more fairly. As a paradigm that incorporates notions of liberation and notions of relationality, it acknowledges and honors the ethical imperatives that drive many of these women's decisions.

Structure of the Book

This introduction argues that the concept of gender equality, which has undergirded many of the most seminal works in the field of women's studies and religion, only takes us so far when studying religious women who choose to affiliate with an overtly patriarchal tradition such as Mormonism. I suggest that a fairer, more comprehensive, and more helpful paradigm for evaluating the lives and choices of Latter-day Saint women of color around the world is that of non-oppressive connectedness, human and divine. In considering the various intersections of identity that these women agentively navigate, intersectional feminist and womanist approaches are foundational.

Chapter 1 examines the experiences and perspectives of a group of Latter-day Saint women in Veracruz, Mexico. I argue that Mormonism, even with its patriarchal structure and theology, which bound women's actions, opens certain liberative spaces for Mexican women. These liberative spaces often include opportunities to find meaningful community and uplift themselves financially. For these women, liberation encompasses some notions of justice, independence, and self-development, but often it also involves chances to reject destructive patterns of infidelity, abuse, and alienation. Fostering connections that are sustaining, uplifting, and non-oppressive is a moral value that centers their lives.

Chapter 2 analyzes Batswana Latter-day Saint women's choices to affiliate with this American-born, historically white tradition and the ways these women agentively navigate their religious affiliation alongside loyalties to their cultures of origin. Examining four spaces of tension and confluence—chastity, adoption, bridewealth, and companionate marriage—I argue that Mormonism offers Batswana women spiritual and social connectedness in a society that has experienced deterioration of traditional ways of being in the past few decades. With Botswana's shift from a tribal village sociality and economy to a modern cash economy, Mormonism operates in some sense as a new village for Latter-day Saint women, giving them boundaries, responsibilities, and social ties that were more readily available to Batswana women in generations past. These boundaries and opportunities are framed by Western and patriarchal understandings, which Batswana women adopt or adapt to their own purposes. These purposes often center around creating non-oppressive connections with humans and God.

Chapter 3 examines the experiences of Latter-day Saint women of color in the United States. I argue that a dominant concern for these women is the rejection of oppressive relationships. These women have found within Mormonism, even with its gender complementarianism, resources for cultivating healthy relationships, thereby manifesting a moral orientation toward non-oppressive connectedness. At the same time, their accounts reveal how white and class privilege characterize some teachings within the church, teachings that these women carefully navigate. Thus, their oral narratives offer certain interventions and redirections in Mormon discourse, pointing to ways in which Mormon rhetoric could be more inclusive of women of color, who lack white, male, and sometimes class privilege. Finally, I analyze certain theological themes within Mormonism, such as personal revelation, which women of color in the United States find particularly ennobling.

Chapter 4 constructs a framework for a Mormon womanist theology of abundance, based on the theological reflections of the women I interviewed in Botswana, Mexico, and the United States. These theological reflections on abundance arise from these women's commitments to a loving personal God and to healthy relationships with themselves and others. Their ethical imperative of non-oppressive connectedness therefore emerges in their theologies as well as in their life choices. I explicate this theme of metaphysical abundance, which emerged in the interviews, describing how the theme takes on different nuances in different locations yet is connected by an expansive vision of human capacity and God's desire for human wholeness and well-being. Based on the methodology of womanist theology and ethics, I suggest other sources that could contribute to this theology of abundance, such as the writings of Latter-day Saint Relief Society leader Chieko Okazaki and the accounts of women in scripture such as Mary, the mother of Jesus.

By examining questions of gender at the crossroads of race, nationality, and class, this project uncovers new understandings of the Mormon tradition—its power, its potential, its challenges, and its shortcomings. Also elucidated are the complex, nuanced, and complicated perspectives of Latter-day Saint women of color, who adapt Mormonism to their contexts and for their purposes. In analyzing the oral life histories of these women on the borderlands of Mormonism, this volume ultimately suggests an important intervention in the field of women's studies in religion: that scholars pay attention to the ways in which marginalized women contest or nuance the preoccupations of white Western feminist scholars. By uncovering and honoring the paradigms that mark the lives and values of women in various global contexts, we can allow a fuller, richer, and more complete understanding of religion and religious adherents to emerge.

CHAPTER 1

Mexican Women, Agency, and Liberation

On a warm, sunny day in March 2015 I sat in a bedroom graciously offered to me as a place to conduct oral life history interviews with Latter-day Saint women in Veracruz, Mexico. The sights and sounds of urban Mexico filtered through the open windows: tortilla sellers on motorcycles announced their wares through loudspeakers, music from cars filtered up from the nearby street, and the light reflected off the bright pink house across the way. With my interpreter Silvia Carlson by my side, I sat in the room ready to interview Paloma, a woman in her sixties wearing sensible brown shoes, a brown skirt, a gray shirt, and a friendly expression. As I began to get my voice recorder ready, I asked her to complete a brief demographic questionnaire. While she filled out the sheet in careful writing, she asked Silvia, chuckling, "Can I put *mujeriego* [womanizer] as my husband's occupation?" Silvia and I laughed and assented, and she slowly wrote *mujeriego* on the line.

This moment comes back to me often. I had asked about occupations in the questionnaire in order to get a sense of the women's social location in society, but Paloma's humorous response highlighted the limitations of my project to conduct and analyze oral life histories of a community of Mexican Latter-day Saint women. I had embarked on the project to expand the archive of existing work on Mormon women beyond the borders of the United States, where the vast majority of such studies had taken place. I was convinced that it was neither adequate nor ethical to focus my attention mainly on white women in the United States since, as many intersectional feminist scholars have argued, women's experiences differ significantly along the intersecting lines of race, class, nationality, and more. Yet my interview questions were products of my own limited experience. Paloma's response signaled to me that several of my questions might not align with the stories the women wanted to tell me about their lives. I witnessed Paloma converting this interview into the story she wanted to tell: that of a difficult marriage, a brutal fight for the life of her sick child, and the horror of watching that child die.

This project filled me with excitement and considerable trepidation. I had spent weeks agonizing over the ethics of a privileged outsider gathering the stories and perspectives of devout Latter-day Saint women in Veracruz. I had only a semester of Spanish under my belt and thus would need to work alongside an interpreter and research colleague, and I worried about how I could fairly tell and analyze these devout women's stories given my feminist and white American positionality. While acknowledging to myself these complications, I hoped to do right by these women, who were giving me their trust and time. I ultimately proceeded with the project, hoping that despite our differences, these women would see these interviews as an opportunity to shape the stories they wanted to tell about their lives, as Paloma ultimately did.

A one- to two-hour interview can never capture the complexities, struggles, and triumphs of a woman's life, but these interviews did reveal many multifaceted glimpses of these women's experiences with Mormonism. A number of themes ultimately emerged in the twenty-nine oral history interviews we conducted during my eleven-day stay. First, many of the older women who had joined the church in previous decades converted in contexts of domestic violence, mujeriego husbands and fathers, and alcoholism. The move toward the Church of Jesus Christ of Latter-day Saints was a rejection of patterns of behavior they deemed damaging and harmful. Second, many women found in the church resources and skills that enabled them and their children to rise socially and economically. From gaining increased literacy through scripture reading to household production learned in Relief Society weekday meetings, these women were able to materially benefit from their association with Mormonism. Third, women who chose Mormonism found in the religion spiritual power. Before their conversions many had spiritual connections to the divine, but Mormonism, with its constant emphases on observance, scripture reading, and devotion, often enhanced their connection to God. The close personal relationships they developed with God as friend and companion as well as the ability they found to connect with God personally, often in dreams and visions, gave them a sense of a loving deity standing next to them in times of conflict and difficulty.[1] For many of these women, embracing the relatively strict and patriarchal Church of Jesus Christ of Latter-day Saints was a step toward a markedly better life because of its emphases on clean living, devoted families, skill acquisition, close community, and a loving and personal God.

That these women found in Mormonism uniquely appealing practices and teachings, given their particular contexts, is not surprising. As intersectional feminist scholars have discussed for decades, women are not a monolith and cannot be approached as a group with essential similarities and issues.[2] They have pointed out that women's lives and experiences must not be viewed only through the prism of gender but rather through prisms that illuminate the overlapping identities of gender, race, class, culture, sexual orientation, and more.[3] When one takes into account these other markers of experience, one sees that different concerns, challenges, and standpoints emerge. We even see that what is restrictive and problematic for one group of women can be liberating and ennobling for another, given their different contexts.[4]

In this chapter I elaborate on these and other themes, focusing on agency, self-development, and authority. In order to best honor their voices and stories, I center the chapter on the experiences of a handful of women that, in particular, elucidate themes I found important in the oral histories. I argue that Mormonism opens certain liberative spaces for Mexican women, even as its patriarchal structure and theology simultaneously bind women's actions. These liberative spaces include opportunities to reject destructive patterns of infidelity, abuse, and alcoholism, to construct vitalizing relationships with family members, the church community, and a personal and loving God, and to pursue self-development and socioeconomic advancement. Complementarian gender roles and patriarchal church structures undoubtedly permeate their Mormon lives, yet these women's primary moral concerns revolve around rejecting alienation, eliminating abuse, and building strong relationships and futures for themselves and their children. The paradigm of non-oppressive connectedness, which encompasses a focus on both vitalizing relationality and liberation, thus emerges as a particularly fruitful lens through which to analyze these Mexican Latter-day Saint women's lives.

Agency and Authority

On our first Sunday in Veracruz, my colleague April Carlson and I met Maria after attending Sacrament meeting, the weekly worship service of the Church of Jesus Christ of Latter-day Saints. The eighty or so people in the plain and serviceable chapel wore their Sunday best, the men in suits and the women in dresses or skirts. After this service, which featured two short sermons given by members of the congregation and the distribution of the

Lord's Supper, members of the congregation chatted with friends as they made their way to different rooms in the building for their other church meetings. Latter-day Saint Sunday meetings, at this time in 2015, consisted of three back-to-back meetings about one hour in length: the main worship service, various Sunday school classes (for children, adults, and youth), and separate men's and women's meetings featuring more lessons and discussions. The women's meeting and the women's organization that oversees these meetings are called Relief Society. All classes and activities are led by members of the congregation, who are given "callings" or assignments by the bishop (the leader of the congregation) to teach, provide music, arrange activities, and more.

As we made our way out of the chapel, women in the congregation, who had been informed of our oral history project, showed April and me to an empty room that we could use for our interview with Maria. She arrived a few minutes later, a small woman in her fifties with straight gray hair wearing plain clothing and eyeglasses. Her skin was lined, and her voice was low as she tearfully told us that she had not had a pretty life. April and I assured her that that was all right, that we appreciated any perspectives or experiences she was willing to share with us. What unfolded was an eye-opening interview for me. When we were done, I turned to April and said, "The LDS church for Maria is liberation. Liberation!" I had not expected that. Comfort, certainty, community—I had expected these given the many years I had spent practicing Mormonism and speaking with Latter-day Saint women. But a sense of liberation from a strict, patriarchal, highly centralized American-directed church was something of a surprise to me. What I later came to understand, after studying Maria's interview, was that the liberative sense that Maria described finding in Mormonism was primarily tied to the ways in which the tradition facilitated non-oppressive human and divine connectedness, rather than the elimination of gendered power dynamics.

Maria was raised in difficult circumstances by a mother who "hated everything. [She] had children with different men. She never loved anyone. Because I didn't fit in her world she was always against me. I feel like she hated me. I think that in my life, I've never had a worse enemy that would hate me so much as my own mother."[5] Maria grew up feeling utterly alone in a world where "children start drinking when they are little. When [boys] are ten, eleven, twelve years old they start dating women. In fact, parents are accustomed to taking them to prostitutes when very young so they become men, they say. But as long as I can remember, that was not right from my perspective. I hated that world."[6] Maria actively fought against this world, telling of one Christmas when, as an eight- or nine-year-old, she began throwing out the beer against her uncle's wishes.

The world that Maria described as being so damaging to her personally—she talked about crying continually and going without food for days—reflects some aspects of Latin American machismo culture well documented by scholars.[7] Bron Ingoldsby describes machismo as being characterized by male aggressiveness (verbal, physical, and in relation to alcohol) and hypersexuality.[8] Some scholars have noted that machismo is connected to colonialism and "conquest trauma," as men "displace their class antagonism onto gender relations."[9] Maria rejected and resisted this machismo world of promiscuity and rampant alcohol use in childhood and in adulthood. She married a man from whom she ultimately separated. She explained, "There was a bit of violence, but most of all irresponsibility. He was a womanizer. He hid it for a time. And he would economically and morally abandon the family."[10] Male abdication of familial responsibilities, Elizabeth Brusco writes, is a key element of machismo culture, and Maria refused to put up with it.[11]

The beginning of Maria's story is characterized by division, hostility, opposition, and resistance to the world in which she was living. Maria could not accept this culture and its expectation that she endure the behavior of her husband, an expectation that, Evelyn Stevens writes, is built into the female cultural counterpart to machismo, namely, marianismo. According to Stevens's classic (and controversial) article, marianismo is the cult of feminine spiritual superiority. In this framework, the ideal woman is characterized by

> moral superiority, and spiritual strength. This spiritual strength engenders abnegation, that is, an infinite capacity for humility and sacrifice. No self-denial is too great for the Latin American woman, no limit can be divined to her vast store of patience with the men in her world. . . . She is also submissive to the demands of the men: husbands, sons, fathers, brothers.[12]

Maria was fighting not only against the behavior of her mother, husband, and others in her world, but also against any sort of gendered expectation that she passively accept this behavior.

During the breakdown of her marriage, Maria came into contact with Latter-day Saint missionaries, whom her husband invited into their home to teach them. Her husband wanted to change his life and felt that joining the church would give him a new start. But because her husband was the one pushing for an association with Mormonism, Maria resisted the church. She felt, she said, as if the missionaries "were my husband's accomplices because I saw they understood each other very well. I lived on the offensive against the missionaries."[13] Maria attended church for the sake of her oldest daughter, who was accompanying her father to the Sunday services. Maria would sit in the back of the church and not talk to anyone. It was only after her husband gave up on going to church that Maria realized she missed it when she did not go. "I felt sad. I longed to go," she related.[14] Maria threw out her icons of Catholic saints, stopped attending mass, and began living the life the Church of Jesus Christ of Latter-day Saints advocated. It was not hard for her to change her life:

> I never liked living in that world—I never understood it. There was no room in it for me because I was going against everything; in that world there was never a place for me. I was always alone. I felt trampled on, sad, offended. And suddenly here where I was, now I felt peace, I felt good.[15]

Given her opposition to her cultural environment, it makes sense that Maria might feel comfort and peace within the church. Because of the church's strict norms against alcohol and infidelity, and because of its emphasis on involved, breadwinning fathers, Maria would have seen in Mormonism moral and behavioral teachings that would have resonated with her because they condemned certain oppressive male behaviors to which she was opposed. As Henri Gooren notes, conversion to Mormonism is one possible vehicle for men living in societies where machismo is prominent to abandon those practices. Mormonism and other strict denominations can provide an alternative whereby men can gain respect and standing through church service and leadership.[16]

Maria explained her initial attraction to the church as rooted in feelings of peace. However, Mormonism offered other appealing elements. Latter-day Saint teachings helped her son Pedro progress socially and economically. He is a returned missionary, has never drunk a drop of alcohol, and has completed his college education. Given that Maria herself only attended elementary school and has worked in low-paying job sectors such as domestic service and vending, her son's achievement is no small thing. Her two daughters, Imelda and Rosa, who have chosen at various periods of their lives to not practice Mormonism and who each had a child out of wedlock, have had harder lives. Imelda disliked school and therefore worked from the time she was a child. This resulted in her never having the opportunity to attend church on Sundays as a young person. Rosa had a baby with her boyfriend at fifteen. Although both daughters were attending church at the time of the interview and teaching in Primary (the church's Sunday school for children), they have struggled as single mothers. It would be difficult to definitively state the reasons behind the starkly different outcomes of Pedro and his sisters. It seems a strong possibility, however, that the church's strict behavioral standards and emphasis on goal setting, which Pedro embraced, helped him achieve a level of financial and personal security that Maria's daughters have not. That Mormonism has been attractive to Latin Americans because of its association with social mobility and middle-class values has been documented by several scholars.[17]

Another liberating element Maria found in Mormonism is the sense of a close, personal Father God:

> I've told [my children] that He will always be with us. Bad times may come . . . but that doesn't mean that we have been defeated because the Father will give us, will help us, and that's why I keep repeating to them every time I can. . . . And just like the scriptures state, the gates of hell may be opening their mouths upon us, but the Father will be there and He will lift us up.[18]

Life for Maria is still something of a battle. She used language of war and tribulation to describe her challenges, but within and alongside these trials, she described a personal loving God who knows her, cares for her, and stands with her.

Maria stated that she never read the scriptures when she was a Catholic, but now they have become a source of comfort and strength for her. She explained, "While reading the scriptures, I feel transported to something very real. Time passes and I don't want anyone to talk to me when I read the scriptures. It leaves a very good impression. I understand Father's love better."[19] Maria's experience of personally reading sacred texts has connected her to a benevolent and loving Father God. The scriptures also have provided figures to admire and to whom she can relate. She selected Job as one of her favorites. The story of Job might be a troubling text to some feminists because of the frightening image of God deliberately killing off innocents to test a man, but for Maria and the several other Veracruz women who mentioned Job as their favorite character from scripture, seeing their experiences of hardship and survival reflected in the life of this man overwhelmed any disturbing messages about God in the story.

While Maria loves reading the scriptures alone, she also has opportunities within the church to read them with others. When she served as a Sunday school teacher, Maria led discussions of stories and passages from the scriptures in a mixed group of adult males and females. Other scholars of Latin American religion and theology have spoken of the power of reading the Bible in the light of one's own situation and experiences, particularly for poor and marginalized populations. Maria Pilar Aquino discusses the transformational potential of ecclesial base communities in Latin America, where small groups of people (mainly women) come together to read the Bible in the context of their own lives and claim "their right to be the church and regarded as creative participants within it."[20] In a sense, Mormonism might to some extent be performing some of the functions of an ecclesial base community, since Latter-day Saint women and men take responsibility for ministering to each other and holding classes where they can read and discuss passages of scripture in light of their own lives. The church therefore offers members like Maria an active, participatory role within it, in contrast to some other religious traditions, in which interpretive authority and expertise lie solely in the hands of a priest or pastor.

One of the most fascinating questions that arises when I contemplate Maria's story is what role agency and authority play in her life. The extent (or mere existence) of women's agency in patriarchal religions has been a central issue for scholars of religion. Can women who choose to affiliate with conservative patriarchal religions be viewed as agents? Can they be agents when they insist on obeying their male church leaders? As mentioned in the introduction, scholars who embrace liberal Western notions of individualism and autonomy have often conceptualized agency as resistance to social norms and structures, and so ordinary women who uphold gender roles and religious injunctions received scant scholarly attention.[21] In recent years, however, several scholars have offered more nuanced analyses that explore the ways women have acted agentively within their traditions. Saba Mahmood, a pioneer in this reconceptualization of agency, argues that Western conceptions of agency must move beyond the notion that it means subversion of authority. She argues that agency is also present in actions that uphold norms, including patriarchal norms. Mahmood sees this agency in the women's mosque movement in Egypt, in which women gather to read the Qur'an and *hadith* and receive teachings from female preachers about piety, submissiveness, and modesty. "If the ability to effect change in the world and in oneself is historically and culturally specific . . . then the meaning and sense of agency cannot be fixed in advance," she argues, pointing out that agency can emerge in different forms in different places.[22] Thus, agency should be recognized not only in acts of resistance to norms but also in the various acts that support them. Catherine Brekus likewise argues for a new model of agency that acknowledges ordinary women's power to create change as well as the real structural constraints on their agency.[23] She argues that such a notion of agency should include ideas about agency as reproducing norms, not merely subverting them, and about agency being on a continuum between full freedom of action and complete constraint.

How does Maria function as an agent in her life? Before she joined the Church of Jesus Christ of Latter-day Saints, she fell well in line with predominant conceptions of women's agency as resistance to oppressive systems and individuals. Her life story is characterized by the tensions, sadness, loneliness, and hatred that being in constant opposition to one's family and society engenders. After she embraced Mormonism, however, she found belonging and community in this new world:

> Here [at church], I can have a very big problem with someone, because I have had them, and my rational thinking tells me, "leave," but my heart— that internal me that I have that's unexplainable—keeps me here. One day my children laughed a lot because I made a choice. I told them, "I would not leave even if nobody loved me, only if my bishop asked me not to come again." I do not leave the gospel just like that. For me that is the biggest thing the Lord has given me. And when I'm sad, depressed, defeated, I know I have a place in my Father's house.[24]

In this statement one can see some of the complexities of her agentive status, as it becomes clear that her agency indeed rests on a continuum between absolute freedom and absolute constraint. She has certainly retained her individual opinions and personality, if she has difficulties with some members. Yet we also glimpse elements of constraint in this brief passage. She has given primacy and a large amount of authority to her male priesthood leader, who alone, she said, has the moral authority with his words to keep her away from the church. While she continues to resist and push against certain people, she also chooses to uphold the patriarchal and hierarchical elements of Mormonism.

This willingness to support patriarchal authority is likewise present in Maria's God-language. She finds solace in her Father God, never mentioning Mormonism's Heavenly Mother. Robert Orsi's insights about some Catholic women's devotion to St. Jude may shed some light on the devotion of Maria and other Latter-day Saint women to their male God and male savior. Orsi describes Jude as stepping into the space vacated by absent, disengaged, or oppressive men in these women's lives. Their men might be undependable, but Jude is always there for them.[25] Maria likewise experiences her reliable, loving, and engaged Father God as comforting, perhaps particularly so given her experience with an absent father and disappointing husband. As she embraces the practice of reading the scriptures, God the Father satisfies her emotional needs in a way few of her male relatives were able to. Resistance to and accommodation of patriarchal norms thus characterize her narrative.

Her orientation toward non-oppressive connectedness determines which patriarchal norms she rejects (machismo because of its destructiveness to relationships) and which she embraces (God the Father, with whom she lovingly connects).

This same complexity regarding agency, resistance, and accommodation is present in a temple recommend interview with her priesthood leader, who encouraged her to discuss her problems with her mother. A temple recommend interview is a worthiness interview given by male priesthood leaders in the ward (congregation) or stake (similar to a diocese) to determine a member's worthiness to enter the temple. Only members who answer questions about belief and behavior adequately may be given a recommendation to attend the temple, where Latter-day Saints participate in sacred ceremonies. Sometimes, as was the case with Maria, these interviews offer opportunities to discuss troubles or problems. She said:

> I had interviews to enter the temple. They asked me about my feelings, and I told them that I didn't love my mother, so the leader who interviewed me helped me a lot. I am blessed to be an introvert—it's very rare and difficult for others to understand me—but I have the blessing to know that the words of my leaders are the law for me. So, for me it was easy to change my relationship or feelings with my mother. You can say that it improved because I started to understand her. I especially understood that only God has the right to judge her. I realized that I have the duty to forgive everyone.[26]

In this interview we see that the patriarchal power and deference to leaders that is encouraged within Mormon culture actually helped Maria overcome resentment toward her mother. Maria used her agency to comply with church authority and gained greater understanding, compassion, and the capacity to forgive. Yet this healing was at the behest of a male church leader whose words were "law" for her. For Maria, male priesthood authority in this situation was enabling rather than constrictive. In one of the most powerful moments in the interview, when I asked about her experiences with her male church leaders, she said, "My leaders have been my everything because they have helped me understand my life. I've had excellent leaders; if I can speak to you it's because of them. I used to not speak with anyone."[27]

In some sense, Maria's church leaders have, as feminists sometimes say, heard her to speech.[28] She was able to express the inexpressible with their help and encouragement. Throughout Maria's oral history we can see the complexities of her agentive status within Mormonism. Her leaders' words might be law for her, and they hold a moral and ecclesiastical authority which is extensive in the scope of its power, but when those words enable her to find her voice and tell her story, she experiences this male authority as a kind of power that facilitates personal, emotional, and spiritual growth and connection. Her leaders, who have listened to her, empathized with her, and helped her find insights, have functioned as the opposite of what she encountered as male authority in her childhood and marriage. We find in Maria's story a complicated form of agency in which her submission to and compliance with male church leaders leads to voice, power, connection, and healing in her life. Her worldview of non-oppressive connectedness orients her away from a critique of gendered power structures and toward behaviors that cultivate healing, sustaining, and ennobling relationships.

Maria's faith in her leaders and her relationships with them also give her moral support in her fight for justice. As many womanist and mujerista theologians have noted, a key moral concern for women of color is survival in contexts of oppression and injustice. The womanist theologian Delores Williams describes a God who does not always liberate exploited women from their oppression completely, but this God does care about their survival and helps them achieve a better quality of life.[29] Like many of the women upon whom womanist and mujerista theologians base their writings, Maria, too, has been affected by exploitation and injustice, and with the moral support of her leaders and the sustenance of her God, she has fought against it. She described how her daughter did hard physical work for an exploitative employer who would not hand over a house for which the daughter had paid him over the years. Desperate for help, Maria spoke to the stake president, the presiding priesthood leader over a group of congregations, about her problems. They prayed together, and Maria found ways to move forward legally to bring this employer to justice. She described praying to God about this matter "because only He can help us. The employer is very tough, and we ask the Lord that he will soften his heart and give him a bit of a thirst for *justicia*."[30] Mormonism gave Maria a sense of a personal God who hears her, answers prayers, and stands with her in her need for justice against exploitation. It also gave her a community, including men in authoritative positions, with which to sit, pray, articulate problems, and envision solutions.

From an early life characterized by pain, loneliness, opposition, and damaging behavior, Maria has found in Mormonism a strong community, a personal, benevolent God, opportunities to grow and contribute, and strict standards resonating with her own sense of rightness and justice. Conversion to this conservative patriarchal church has, according to Maria's narrative, enhanced her agentive status and enabled her to move forward productively with her life. In Mormonism she has found an agency which not only gives her the ability to resist machismo and the self-abnegation of marianismo but also gives her agentive scope and motivation to connect, grow, forgive, and find her voice.

Obedience, Abuse, and Change

Ana, a poised woman in her forties, elaborated in both English and Spanish on the power dynamics of an abusive Mormon marriage in her oral history. Raised by a practicing single Latter-day Saint mother, she described obedience as a characteristic she was taught as a child. When she was eighteen she met a forceful Latter-day Saint who had completed his two-year mission for the church and wanted to marry her. She was unsure. She related, "He had specific goals, and I wasn't ready to get married yet. I would see him and I would feel scared. But just like my mom, he would say, 'Everything I tell you is the best thing for you,' so I obeyed. It was always *obediencia*."[31] Despite her proclivity for the docility and obedience she had been taught as a child, Ana was undecided. She prayed continually. She said, "I asked the Father, 'Should I do this? Is he the right person?' . . . And I didn't feel answers."[32] Eventually, after talking with her stake president's wife, she came to understand that, as she said, "the Father wasn't going to tell me. The decision was mine. I mean, he's not going to take away my free agency by saying, 'Yes, it's him,' or 'No, this is not the one.' This was part of the decision that I had to make."[33] Respect for free agency—the Mormon concept that God has given humans the right to choose their paths in life—and the importance of prayerfully using one's own insight to navigate difficult situations characterize Ana's oral history. This understanding that she was responsible for making her life what she wanted it to be would ultimately give her the determination to work through what turned out to be an abusive marriage.

When asked about hardships in her life, Ana alluded to "big challenges" in her marriage: "Big challenges that I wasn't used to bearing. And I didn't know if they were correct or incorrect because I've never been in a situation like this. So they were really big challenges. Later I realized that most Mexican women have them, it's just [that] we keep quiet and no one says anything."[34] After she was asked if she was referring to abuse, she said, "Yes. We all experience it, but no one speaks about it. No one talks about it because, I don't know, out of fear."[35] The fact that spousal abuse is so widespread in Ana's experience is startling. This sense of the ubiquity of spousal abuse was seeded when, unsure of whether domestic violence was a normal part of marriage, she asked her Latter-day Saint mother-in-law about it, and the reply was, "It's normal. You have to endure it."[36] Years later, however, after she had three children with her husband, Ana ultimately understood that this behavior was unacceptable when her mother and three older Latter-day Saint brothers discovered the abuse. They were shocked and upset, advising her, "Get a divorce. Stay here. Don't go back."[37] Ana neither agreed nor disagreed with their advice, but once again prayed continually.

In the meantime, however, her mother, terribly upset over this discovery, had spoken to a lawyer who had grown up with Ana. The man was serving as a stake president in the area, and he arrived with divorce papers. Ana described their encounter:

> He asked me, "What do you want to do? Do you want to get divorced?" And I said, "No. No, he's a good man. He's a good member of the church; he just has this difficulty. . . . I need to help him until it goes away, but I don't know how. I don't have the ability to handle it, I don't know how to do it."[38]

The stake president then said a prayer with her and came up with a plan. He said, "Here are the divorce papers. Let's give them to him. If he signs, it's because he wants to change and it won't happen again, etc. If he doesn't sign, that means you shouldn't go back because he's not sure that he'll be able to do it [not beat you any more]."[39]

This anecdote reveals different ways in which Mormon masculinities can affect the life of a Latter-day Saint woman. On one hand, Ana's husband represents a domineering, abusive Mormon presence who expects obedience from his wife. On the other, we see the lawyer friend, a benevolent leader figure, emphasizing Ana's right to decide for herself what course to take and helping her come up with a plan enabling Ana to end the abuse but preserve the marriage—the outcome she preferred. His plan gave her significant leverage to stop the abuse.

When she presented her husband with the divorce papers to sign, she said, "He cried and cried and cried. . . . He asked me, 'Do you know what you're asking me to sign?' I said, 'Yeah.' And he said, 'I will sign. I will sign because I know that I can change, and I know that this won't happen again.'"[40] Ana described their life after this episode as a honeymoon. She said, "He totally changed. Everything changed. It was like starting a new marriage."[41] She then added:

> That's when I realized that we are the ones who have the answer to decide how to change our own husbands. We live with them more than their own mothers, and we end up educating them. . . . When things aren't being done right, it's only because we're afraid to do what we need to. Like any mother who is afraid to punish their child because you don't know if

the child will react well or not, so we don't do it. This is the reason things don't change—for fear.[42]

Unlike Maria, who never explicitly addressed the question of agency, Ana addressed it and clearly embraces the notions of agency, personal action, and personal responsibility. From her earlier realization that God wouldn't impinge on her agency by telling her whether to marry her husband—that it was up to her to figure it out—to this episode with the divorce papers, in which she realized that it is up to her and every other wife to forthrightly change damaging dynamics in their marriages, we can see that Ana values initiative and proactivity. Her belief that women can stem violence by literally choosing not to take it anymore is striking and implies an expansive sense of her own and other women's agency. Hers is a narrative of growth and development as she transformed from an obedient, docile, and scared figure to a woman insisting on her ability and right to make decisions herself, to enact change in her life, and to change her husband's behavior. Throughout this journey to a new self and better marriage, Ana described a God who has been a constant and benevolent companion through prayer but one who, like herself, values individuals' sometimes painful journeys toward growth and self-realization.

When asked about the scriptural figure she admires most, Ana named Joseph Smith's first wife, Emma Hale Smith, a woman who chose Joseph Smith and "knew what she wanted. Even though her parents disagreed, she was firm in what she wanted. And she was firm in bearing everything she was asked to bear."[43] Ana certainly manifested a similar strength of purpose and determination to find her way through her own trials. Though Ana herself never articulated this connection, Emma Smith is an intriguing figure for Ana to mention for another reason: both women resisted marital behavior they found damaging. Emma Smith ultimately rejected Joseph's practice of plural marriage, ridding their home of his plural wives and encouraging other women to spurn the practice. Similarly, Ana ultimately refused to acquiesce to her husband's harmful behavior. Although Ana's refusal to comply led to a more successful outcome than Emma's, these acts of resistance were turning points in the lives of both these women.[44] When reflecting on the challenges she endured, Ana said, "I needed to live a really challenging experience so I could have a strong character. My character was very weak."[45] Change from weakness to strength, from passivity to action, is a driving theme in her oral history.

Yet Ana's agency is on a continuum, as Brekus theorizes. Ana motivated her husband to change his abusive behavior, but it became clear later in the interview that she was not able to motivate him to change some of his authoritarian behavior. To obtain an outcome she desired, Ana had to carefully manage and finesse her husband. As she said, "We women have an ability and tremendous capacity to get the things we want without them [husbands] realizing. We let them believe it's them who are making the decision, but in reality, they're doing what we think is best."[46] When asked for an example of this, she described the remodeling of their home:

> He would always choose the furniture, he chose the color of the house, and I didn't like any of it. . . . I didn't have the negotiating skills to say, "I like this color," and "Look, I like this piece of furniture." So I started to think about how to tell him that I wanted the kitchen to be white and blue, and I said, "How do I explain this to him? How do I tell him? How do I choose my colors?" . . . One day we went to a friend's house who was renovating her kitchen and I liked it. . . . On the way back from their house, I commented on the good taste the husband had in choosing those colors. Later when I came [to our house], the same colors were in my kitchen.[47]

It is significant that Ana was able to achieve this outcome only by subtle finessing and not by forthright negotiation and declaration. She may have felt empowered as a change agent and a decision maker, and she was able to stop the physical abuse, but power dynamics are clearly such that she does not have the same hard decision-making power as her husband. For that reason, she resorted to a gentle manipulation. The ethicist Sarah Hoagland defines manipulation as "exercising (some) modicum of control from a position of subordination," and she describes it as a survival strategy that women have created in contexts of male domination.[48] In *God's Daughters*, R. Marie Griffith describes a similar dynamic in the marriages of evangelical women, whose submission to their husbands could be viewed as a "strategy of containment" that benefits both men and women, since women's submission helps "maintain domestic harmony as well as their own security."[49] Ana felt that in her marriage, even after the abuse had stopped, a strategy of gentle nudging and non-confrontation was the safe and productive route to achieving outcomes she desired. The carefully thought-out navigations and strategies she used in her marriage serve to highlight some of the limitations of female agency within a context of female subordination.

Patriarchy is a fact that Ana has learned to contend with in her marriage. One important question is the relationship between both abusive patriarchy and authoritarian (but nonviolent) patriarchy to Mormonism. Is Ana's husband's behavior tied to Latter-day Saint patriarchal teachings in any way? Does Mormonism open up space for men like Ana's husband to believe that they are within their rights to dominate, bully, and hit their wives—or if not, to nevertheless rule over them in other ways? As is made clear in other oral histories, and as Ana herself baldly asserted, domestic violence is everywhere. In the case of her husband, it is not possible from the oral history to ascertain whether his traditional patriarchal beliefs about power dynamics within marriage are tied to Mormon teachings or practices. Ana never told us that he justified his abusive behavior with claims of his right to preside in the home or her duty to obey him as her husband. Yet she painted a complicated and nuanced picture of the role the church plays in both discouraging and not discouraging such damaging male behavior.

A couple of incidents in Ana's oral history indicate that some church leaders actively discouraged domestic violence. In addition to the stake president friend who denounced her husband's abuse, we also see hints of discouragement of abuse at an institutional level. Ana told of how her stake in Mexico City arranged for fifteen women in each ward to attend a three-day program hosted by a Latter-day Saint woman formerly involved in the Miss America Pageant.[50] Ana described going to this program and hearing this successful Latter-day Saint woman speak about her own experience with domestic violence. Ana recounted the audience's reaction:

> Everyone was like, "Ah! I'm not the only one!" And we all started to write, and I turned around to look and saw everyone was writing [their experience with abuse] down. And we were just fifteen women from the ward, so what about the rest? That's when I realized it's not just here or there, it's everywhere.[51]

Ana described other focuses of the weekend program in Mexico City:

> They did fashion ideas with the sisters, they taught us the color wheel, how to put makeup on, which colors look good on us. We ended with a fashion show, modeling clothes, new haircuts, new looks. You leave with a different mentality. . . . [The weekend was about] your worth as a woman. . . . And most importantly that you don't have to stay silent.[52]

This program worked to countermand damaging dynamics of abuse and encourage women to speak about their experiences with violence. Doing so was remarkably empowering for women like Ana, who once again saw that she was not alone in having dealt with violence in her most intimate relationship. The program also made it clear that domestic violence was not an isolated or regional problem but one experienced in different parts of the world, and even by women who were educated, beautiful, and privileged. This was a liberating and empowering moment for Ana, who became determined to not bury her experience but speak openly about it.

Notably, this program also played into complementarian notions of women's worth and role, complete with a focus on female physical attractiveness. Ana, comfortable with notions of gender complementarity and gender roles, experienced this focus on beauty as self-esteem-building, rather than limiting. Stacilee Ford describes Latter-day Saint Filipina domestic workers in Hong Kong likewise feeling uplifted by church activities and expectations that involve beauty and fashion because they, at least in part, represent an opportunity to shed their weekday appearance and role, which could often be lonely and difficult.[53] For these domestic workers, and for domestic violence survivors like Ana, physical transformations can be symbolic reminders of inner transformations, and they have left women feeling new fortitude to carry on. Ultimately, this church-sponsored program for Latter-day Saint women in Mexico City indicates that there are strong currents within the church, coming from people with influence and power, against domestic violence, and at the same time, these currents are mixed with gender traditionalism and complementarianism.

Nonetheless, Ana felt that church leaders had not done enough to discourage domestic violence. She boldly stated, "The priesthood knows [about the problem of abuse]. What hurts me the most is that they don't. . . ."[54] She trailed off here in the interview, but then she continued:

> I think there should be more specific classes, or more specific trainings. Things that are more direct. Because when you say things out loud, things aren't left to the imagination. . . . So there need to be trained members of the church who speak directly. Because if there aren't, it can be counterproductive.[55]

Ana suggested to her stake president in Veracruz that they look for the American woman who ran the workshop in Mexico City and invite her to do a program in their region. It appears that her stake president never took her up on that suggestion. This exchange demonstrates how Latter-day Saint women can have considerable influence in local churches, but ultimately, most of the decision making rests with men such as bishops and stake presidents. Without the support of her stake president (or regional church leaders with more financial resources), hosting a program such as the one in Mexico City was impossible.[56] While this anecdote highlights the fact that women have limited structural power in the church, none of the women I interviewed explicitly acknowledged the systemic power differential between women and men in the structure of the church. For them, as for Ana, a sense of liberation and wholeness was more likely to be found in positive, non-abusive relationships than in the dissolution of patriarchy.

Ana's experiences with gendered power differentials reflect larger trends in the Church of Jesus Christ of Latter-day Saints. In other work, I reviewed the shift in church teachings about marriage, which emphasized stark male dominion in the nineteenth century but eventually softened in the late twentieth century to emphasize instead equal partnership in the home.[57] General church leaders, whose words are broadcast and translated for church members around the world, have also forthrightly condemned domestic violence, abuse of all kinds, and domineering behavior.[58] Simultaneously, however, teachings persist that designate the husband as the one who "presides" in the marriage, and sacred temple ceremonies until 2019 subordinated wives to husbands. Contemporary Latter-day Saint authorities envision husbands as presiding over their families through benevolent, proactive fatherhood and religious training, rather than outright decision-making power.[59]

Though Ana's husband embraces older notions of marital male decision-making power, it is notable that she described his proactivity with children and household tasks. She said that in her husband's family of origin, men "don't wash dishes, they don't wash clothes, they don't sweep, they hit. [My father-in-law] is a chauvinist. But [my husband] isn't. He always helped with the kids, he always washed bottles, washed diapers. He helps me with meals, with things. And he lets me work. He lets me have my money, spend my money."[60] Ana's husband embodies an evolving type of Mormon masculinity that retains older notions of male decision-making power but also produces helpful activity within the household and with children.[61] Ana experiences this male domestic proactivity as positive and liberating, and she experiences her own wage earning as similarly positive. She never expressed a desire to eliminate patriarchy or gender roles in her interview, but she has found happiness in a marriage in which domestic tasks are shared, violence is absent, and she has the freedom to pursue self-development and a career.

Ana's narrative is primarily one of liberation. This liberation takes the form not of gender equality but, rather, of transformation—in particular, her own transformation from abused passivity to agentive empowerment as she took action to end the violence in her home once and for all. In her quest to stop this abuse, certain elements within her Mormon framework became useful tools for enacting this change. Her Latter-day Saint family and friends gave her support and an effective strategy to end the abuse but preserve the relationship. In addition, the church-sponsored weekend that focused on domestic violence opened her eyes to the ubiquity of the problem and to the transformative importance of telling her story. Thus, as with Maria, finding one's voice and truth-telling are central components of Ana's sense of liberation. In her determination to help others likewise change their lives, she has encouraged her male church leaders to confront the problem of domestic violence within their stake boundaries. Ana, who operates within a largely unchallenged Mormon framework of gender roles and male hierarchy, has found in Mormonism such useful concepts as agency, change, community, and critiques of violence, which have unquestionably changed her life for the better and have enabled her to form healthier relationships with others. Ana's moral priority of raising her voice against violence and cultivating nonabusive relationships reveals her guiding paradigm of non-oppressive connectedness. For Ana, the ability to take action, change, and form better relationships is liberation. This liberation is not without its gendered constraints, which she must carefully navigate, but it is one that has opened her life to new and transformative possibilities.

Economic Empowerment and Male Domestication

In some ways, the oral history of Sofia, a thin woman in her late sixties with a soft voice, short gray hair, and anxious eyes, resonates with that of Maria, who found voice and liberation in the church, as well as that of Ana, who embraced her responsibility to change herself and motivate change in others. Sofia's story, however, also highlights important insights about other benefits the church delivers to women in oppressive circumstances—namely, the development of marketable skills and social uplift.

Sofia found the church as a young mother trying to cope with a miserable marriage. She said, "My husband drank a lot. He beat me. I was physically abused and I found refuge in the gospel."[62] This abuse was a reliving of childhood beatings from her stepfather. Her life with her stepfather was so filled with abuse and so deprived that at nine years of age, she said, "I turned myself in to a family so they would give me work and so I could have something to eat."[63] She even changed her first name after she left her family home because, as she said, "I wanted to be another person; I didn't want to be the same one."[64] She met and married her husband at sixteen, hopeful of a happier future. Yet some measure of happiness did not find her until she found the Church of Jesus Christ of Latter-day Saints and convinced her husband to be baptized along with her and the children. "I considered myself adopted by the church," she explained.[65] Her language of adoption is entirely appropriate; she embraced the church as a new family, full of supportive sisters and brothers who gave her moral support but also saw in her a woman with talent and the potential for leadership.

Within the church Sofia also found personal uplift, literacy, and increasing abilities and skills to support herself. She described some of her progress:

> I never went to school, I never got an education. I learned to read with the Book of Mormon, with the Bible, reading books, scriptures, and I started writing this way, too. I didn't take any classes. I now realize I can stand up and give a talk, give my opinion on certain things, talk and teach when it's expected of me as a leader in Relief Society. That helped me a lot inside and outside of the church. I've been very blessed.[66]

Sofia described a steady move away from violence and poverty and toward middle-class values of literacy, self-reliance, and social mobility after she joined the church, a pattern that Wesley Craig Jr. discusses in his analysis of the Church of Jesus Christ of Latter-day Saints in Latin America. He wrote that converts to the church there are often from underprivileged classes, with little education and money. Their first exposure to the church is usually in the form of two missionaries who appear to be middle-class: "[Converts] often see membership in this congregation as a social step upward. They anticipate that it will help their children to improve their own social position through education and leadership-skill development which might be converted into an improved socio-economic status in the broader society."[67] It is unclear that upward mobility was the initial attraction to Mormonism for Sofia, but it was certainly a result of her conversion. Because the church emphasizes the importance of personal scripture study and because it is a lay church with every member contributing by giving sermons, teaching lessons, and performing ministerial and organizational duties, Sofia developed literacy and skills that enriched her life. She has also, like Maria, found her voice within the church, which has given her a platform for speaking to audiences with a sense of authority and power. She said, "I share my testimony when the sisters have a very weak testimony, and they admire me a lot. I have very nice letters from the . . . sister missionaries, who were teaching the discussions to my brother so he could come out of the darkness. One of them who is from Guatemala told me, 'Sister, when I'm older I want to be like you.'"[68] In this way Sofia has received affirmation from church members for her willingness to raise her voice and speak her truth.

Mormonism has helped her develop other skills as well. When asked about how she has supported herself financially, Sofia said:

I've been a fighter. . . . I make and sell pies. . . . Before, when I was younger, I worked in homes as a housekeeper, but I would leave my children by themselves, so I decided to do sales and with that I've been able to subsist, helping my husband. But it's been thirteen years already that my husband became diabetic, so he doesn't work anymore, he depends on me and on my daughter. . . . I learned to make pies at church. Sister [Teresa] taught us.[69]

Sofia's brief statement reveals how important Relief Society weekday meetings have been for several women in this area. In these meetings women learned crafts and cooking skills that many turned into marketable ventures that have supported them and their families in times of need.[70] Natalia, a chic fifty-something middle-class woman, similarly talked about using these skills to provide financially for her family. She spoke of her husband being laid off and the family falling into greater and greater financial difficulties. Natalia, who had not been a wage earner during her marriage, described the inception of her business:

One day I said, "I don't do anything. I need to help my husband." My children were studying. Years before, I had taken a course in soy products organized by the church in Mexico [City] when I went to visit my daughter. I liked the course very much. Everything I know I've learned through the church. I said, "I know how to make soy milk so I can sell it and make products." I started selling and I still do today. . . . With this I can help my husband economically. I already have customers. I also know how to work with wheat, and non-members who are not familiar with this like it. They ask me where I learned it, and I always say, "I learned it at my church."[71]

Natalia later mentioned that one of the reasons she loves the church is that it taught her how to *do* things, unlike other churches that, she felt, did not teach practical skills. The church's focus on self-reliance, progress, skills, and development have materially benefited many women in this area who have supported or helped support their families with their earnings. The importance of this cannot be overstated. Whereas Latter-day Saint leaders have emphasized that fathers are to be breadwinners and mothers are to concentrate on childrearing (a message that various Mexican interviewees reported receiving in church classes), women like Sofia were simultaneously taught skills at church-sponsored events that they were then able to use to start small home-based businesses and alleviate their financial stress.[72] Given that so many of the (usually older) Mexican women I interviewed mentioned these classes, there seemed to be explicit recognition among local ward and stake leaderships that women needed to learn ways to either save or make money.[73] For some women, skills learned at church-sponsored meetings decades ago became life-changing opportunities to improve their material situations.

None of the women with home-based businesses manifested tension between their selling practices and traditional church teachings discouraging mothers from working for pay. The lack of tension may be due to Mormonism's embrace of the principle of self-reliance and to the fact that much of the work of informal vending takes place in the home and takes place according to the woman's schedule, rather than an employer's. Sofia was able to balance breadwinning with other duties such as childrearing and therefore could easily regard herself as fulfilling her primary role as a nurturer. The lack of tension for some women may also simply be due to an understanding of economic realities in Mexico. Eva, a woman in her thirties from a suburb of Mexico City, described working as something the vast majority of women in her area need to do, given the economic reality of the country:

> Even if church leaders tell us to stay at home, our reality is another. When the leaders speak to us, they speak from the U.S. reality. We live with poverty, unemployment, or really low wages—it's another reality. We try to adapt that to the direction from the leaders. Some women feel bad they have to work. Most of them see the reality, though. It's not optional—they need to work. . . . Eighty percent of the women worked outside the home in my old ward. It's a luxury to stay at home.[74]

Eva's comment points to the possibility of slightly altered discourses or understandings among these women about working, due to recognition of Mexico's economic situation. Indeed, Olivia, an educated career woman in her late thirties, explicitly told women in her Veracruz Relief Society that she supported mothers' working, despite occasional institutional messages to the contrary.[75] She said, "We do get messages about being stay-at-home moms here in Mexico. When I was Relief Society president, I would say that it doesn't matter if you choose to be at home or choose to work. You still have to go to school and study, you still have to know things because your kids will want to know things."[76] Another woman, a young mother, spoke of being encouraged by a priesthood leader in a private interview to stop working, a suggestion she politely declined due to her desire for greater financial security.[77] In many cases, for women who earn money outside the home or inside the home, a pragmatic understanding of economic realities and benefits of working often outweigh idealized institutional discourse about breadwinning as a male domain. Although the rhetoric of stay-at-home motherhood is alive and well in Veracruz, other discourses, particularly among women, are present that support working mothers.

Particularly striking, however, are the experiences of older women such as Sofia, for whom Relief Society cooking and crafting classes were transformative. These classes may have taught stereotypically feminine or domestic tasks, but through them, Latter-day Saint women expanded their economic opportunities. Anecdotes like Sofia's were evidence to me of the possibility of Mexican Saints "turning an imported religion to their own purposes."[78] Relief Society programs teaching domestic skills might have originated in the United States, but local Relief Society leaders in Veracruz were able to use this program in ways appropriate to their context, ways that expanded women's self-esteem and financial horizons. As such, their Mormon faith and community contributed to their agentive status.

One former stake Relief Society president's experience with these classes highlights the creativity that women in Latter-day Saint leadership positions could bring to their callings. When she was expecting her second child in the 1980s, Francisca quit her job as a chemical engineer, but she struggled with the confines of this domestic role. With the encouragement of her Latter-day Saint mother to find ways to use her skills, she became inspired to make household products (soaps, lotions, cleaning products) from such everyday food remnants as orange peels:

> I started to make formulas for products, [of] which, from 1984 to the present, there are one hundred and seventeen. At the beginning of the creation of the formulas I spoke with my stake president to ask his advice if we could teach the sisters in the organization [Relief Society]. His response was immediate and affirmative. This is how training began for all the sisters in all the wards of the . . . stake. Currently we continue in different states training the wards of the stakes.[79]

Francisca found within the structure of the patriarchal church space, time, and authoritative support to perform this self-sufficiency training for women. Her agentive scope in creating and carrying out this program was expansive, and her male church leader supportive. Notably, this program later expanded beyond the auspices of the church. She explained that she has offered these techniques and formulas to local and national government organizations as well as women's groups. This Latter-day Saint woman has become an important figure in the Mexican entrepreneurial and scientific community, winning in 2010 the national Better City Living Prize in the category of impact/innovation.

Sofia did not mention attending these particular Relief Society classes, but a similar sense of agency and possibility permeated her life story, filled though it was with difficulties and pain. We can see her faith enabling this sense of agency and self-expression when she discussed some of her struggles with her husband, who eventually was baptized. "My husband didn't change one hundred percent. Even being a member of the church, he drank. It took him a lot of work to change," she related.[80] She has clearly played an important role in this alteration of his behavior. When asked about her greatest challenges, she said, "The challenges I've had have been to confront my husband with his weakness."[81] She later described a confrontation with her husband:

> I tell him, "Your testimony is very weak." I speak to him, I read him the scriptures. I tell him, "If we are not right with the Lord, everything scares us. If you strengthen your testimony in Jesus Christ you will have the courage to face everything just like I've had to deal with so much."[82]

Her faith has given her a platform for critiquing her husband and encouraging him to change his behaviors and outlook. She has assumed the dominant spiritual role in the relationship and has spent much energy convincing him to fully embrace the church and its teachings. While spiritual strengths and benefits of conversion are major talking points for Sofia, scholarly work also has shown that husbands' conversion to strict Christian denominations has materially improved the lives of many Latin American wives. Brusco speaks specifically of Colombian evangelicalism as being something of a "strategic women's movement, because it serves to reform gender roles in a way that enhances female status as an antidote to machismo."[83] Given that a full conversion to the Church of Jesus Christ of Latter-day Saints, like a full conversion to certain other strict Christian denominations, would entail the abandonment of alcohol, infidelity, and familial abdication and would encourage active and helpful partnership in the home, one can understand why Sofia might continually assert to her husband the importance of embracing the gospel. These oral histories show that males who embraced Mormonism often became more involved and helpful husbands and fathers. Sofia never saw the full conversion she wished for in her husband, but she, like many others I interviewed, did see caring and involved fatherhood in the actions of the sons they raised in the church. Christian conversion leading to a kind of domestication of men turned out to be particularly true for men one generation removed from their mothers' conversion to the Church of Jesus Christ of Latter-day Saints.

Sophia's choice to join the church has led to expanded opportunities, self-development, and affirming community. In Mormonism she found the encouragement and opportunity to develop literacy, speaking, and leadership skills, as well as a marketable baking skill that has improved her financial situation. She has found a community that adopted her when her own family was abusive and violent. She has also found in the church a framework for encouraging loving and contributing male behavior in the home, a goal that she has seen realized in the lives of her sons. Moreover, it has provided her with strong spiritual experiences that have connected her to the divine and to her children.[84] For Sofia, as for many of the older and poorer women with whom we spoke, Mormonism was experienced as highly liberating because it provided pathways to stronger relationships and to economic and self-development. In pursuing opportunities to financially uplift their families, contribute to their communities, develop spiritually, and encourage benevolent and devout male behavior, these women's primary moral orientation toward non-oppressive connectedness emerges.

Gender, Race, and Mormonism: Intersectional Reflections on Limitations and Possibilities

Throughout the oral histories of Latter-day Saint women in Veracruz, Mexico, I saw myriad forms of agency emerge in the lives of these women. As they transformed themselves, nurtured self-expression, cultivated relationships, acquired skills, and communed with the divine, these women found hope, community, and power within the Church of Jesus Christ of Latter-day Saints. This power and agency are not unbounded, given the church's gendered power structure, but in these women's narratives, Mormonism was overwhelmingly characterized as more of an empowering and productive influence in their lives than a restrictive one.

When asked directly if they felt that women were treated equally or valued equally in the church, most women quickly said they did and chose not to elaborate. One or two oral histories, however, capture some of the mental grappling some women underwent as they confronted the limitations and possibilities of their roles as Latter-day Saint women. When Yvonne, a middle-aged adult convert, was doing some repairs on her roof, her Latter-day Saint husband told her to get down because she was a woman and should not be up there. She recounted:

> At that moment I didn't truly understand it, and for that reason it was difficult, because I had to lower myself to the level, the role, that is appropriate for me [as a woman]. To be a daughter of God, willing to be obedient, to be a good mother, good wife, good daughter, good neighbor. . . . So I've lowered myself from everything from that period, but only through the power of God.[85]

Though Yvonne indicated that it was not always easy to confine herself to her woman's role, she displayed no unhappiness with this new understanding when she later elaborated on it. In fact, she embraced it and felt fulfilled, complete, and important. Her repeated use of the verb meaning "lower," appropriate given its figurative and literal meaning in the anecdote, is striking. In one sense, she was acknowledging the constraints and submission that accepting this role entails and hinting at some of the accompanying struggles. But this lowering has led, she explained, to contentment and relief that she does not have to be all things for all people and can instead focus on certain areas of life. This gives rise to the possibility that for some women, having a delineated space and stewardship that feels valued and important by the community contributes to a sense of power and possibility in one's life. Some scholars have, in fact, noted that conservative women who inhabit defined female spaces often develop women-centered orientations and perspectives that might surprise Western liberal feminists.[86] Thus, Mormon gender roles for Yvonne, who is middle-class, are simultaneously and paradoxically lowering and liberating. For others, particularly those coming from less privileged circumstances, Mormonism is experienced as predominantly elevating for women.

These women's narratives reveal how social location affects the way women experience Mormonism. The circumstances from which one comes and the expectations and hopes born of those experiences matter. The church's teachings concerning gender roles, a personal God, and strict behavior standards were ennobling for many of my narrators, given their experiences with silence, exploitation, and abuse. As an outsider sensitive to structural inequities, I perceive some gendered constraints and boundaries in these women's lives, but these were not overriding issues for the women themselves. When we pay attention to particularities of location, nationality, class, and race, we can see that programs and processes that do not feel particularly liberating for white middle-class American women actually can be liberating for women in different parts of the world. As intersectional feminist scholars have pointed out, "gender can never be studied in isolation from race and class and related social conditions."[87]

One significant gap in this examination of Latter-day Saint women's gendered lives in Veracruz is a serious discussion of the ways race and American neocolonialism intersect with their experience of Mormonism.[88] I attempted to elicit perspectives on Mormonism, race, and structural inequities by asking them if they felt distanced from the church's prophet and apostles because they were white men living in Utah, and almost none of them said they felt any distance. They nearly always said that they felt connected to those leaders when they read the *Liahona* or watched General Conference.[89] Often there was a palpable shying away from the topic of race, and I surmised that part of the reason might be a sense of politeness or awkwardness, given the fact that I am a white American.

The one exception to the general avoidance of issues of race and American privilege was the 2013 closing of the Benemérito de las Américas boarding high school in Mexico City. This school, operated by the Church of Jesus Christ of Latter-day Saints, had educated more than twenty thousand students since its opening in the 1960s, but church leaders in Utah decided to convert the facility into a Missionary Training Center. Women in Veracruz, some of whom had attended or sent children to the school, mourned this loss. A couple of women articulated a suspicion that this closure was due to church authorities' willingness to cater to the desires of the rich white homeowners in Provo, Utah, who protested their local MTC's 2012 proposed expansion.[90] Hortensia said this about Benemérito's closing:

> It was very sad. We all felt sad because it was a place for our youth and now there is no place. The decision happened because they really needed an MTC, but I also know that the U.S. didn't allow it to be there, and for that reason they did it in Mexico. This was a disappointment because [people in Provo] defended themselves, and we were not allowed to defend the Benemérito. They imposed it on us. It was difficult and a big disappointment.[91]

The church's strong centralized structure, with correlated materials translated into Spanish and available for use by Mexican Latter-day Saints, proved to generally be seen as benign and helpful, yet the closing of Benemérito brought out poignant questions about race, power, and privilege within Mormonism.

As Gina Colvin and Joanna Brooks discuss, Mormonism can deliver significant benefits such as economic and educational opportunities and strong community to global adherents. However, Brooks and Colvin write, access to these benefits entails a cost in terms of the necessity of suppressing criticism or acceding to policies and decisions made by powerful American church leaders that contribute to loss and pain.[92] The authors describe this tradeoff—receiving benefits in exchange for bracketing critique—as a "compact" brokered by the twentieth-century church with its global members. The Latter-day Saint women of Veracruz never articulated their experience with the church in such terms, but certainly, in some sense, they had to bracket their pain and accept Benemérito's closure as a reality they could not change in order to move on with their lives as members of the church. Acceptance, however, did not entail silence for the women of Veracruz, who spoke among themselves and to me of their dismay and disappointment with this decision. Using the Colvin-Brooks framework, these women's vehement disagreement and their refusal to fully bracket or silence critique could be interpreted as rooted in a sense of betrayal of this unarticulated compact, as these women saw an important church-sponsored vehicle for social mobility and educational opportunity for their young people eliminated. The closure of the Benemérito is one striking example of a disconnect between Mexican members and church headquarters; further work is needed to explore the ways in which Mormonism's American hierarchy and racialized teachings impact Latter-day Saint women in Mexico.

Mexicans' experiences with Mormonism have been an understudied topic in Mormon studies, and work focusing on Mexican women's experiences is doubly rare. These oral histories, which have provided intimate glimpses of how and why these women have embraced Mormonism, help reframe issues of Mormonism and gender and decenter liberal feminist narratives and questions about gender equality. For the vast majority of interviewed women in Veracruz, gender equality was not a pressing concern. Far more important to them were principles and practices that encouraged positive connection, well-being, and self-development. In their orientation toward non-oppressive connectedness, alienation and violence were the prominent moral problems that they actively opposed, not gender roles and church systems that privilege male leadership.

Liberation may not be a term commonly associated with the Church of Jesus Christ of Latter-day Saints due to the tradition's conservative moral teachings, hierarchical structure, and general emphasis on personal righteousness rather than systemic oppression. Yet in this framework, Mexican women have described finding a real sense of liberation. Mormonism has given them a basis for developing better home lives, supportive communities, self-esteem, spiritual power, and economic uplift. This liberation is contained and regulated within a patriarchal, Americentric structure that sometimes constrains women's decision-making power, yet the women describe a significant amount of agency and self-determination within this framework. Ultimately, they have, as Brooks writes of Indigenous and global southern Latter-day Saints, claimed Mormonism for themselves and found in it a resource for imagining a different way of being in the world.[93]

This theme of liberation is but one dimension of global women's experiences with Mormonism, often born, in the case of these Mexican women, of their particular familial and social contexts. Mormonism gave them useful tools for fighting against familial and social conditions that led to their abuse, silence, and poverty. Latter-day Saint teachings and practices encouraging a personal relationship with God, community, skill acquisition, and benevolent masculinity coincided relatively neatly with their dominant moral paradigm of non-oppressive connectedness. In other locations in the world, however, particularly the non-Western peripheries of the tradition, tension can arise for Latter-day Saint women when church practices and teachings conflict with women's moral commitments to relationality, commitments born of their indigenous cultures and values.

CHAPTER 2

African-Born Women Navigating an American-Born Church

One cold evening in 2015 after a day of viewing wildlife in the Okavango Delta of Botswana, our group of women academics and oral historians from the United States gathered around a campfire to chat with our safari guides. We were on a brief break from our oral history work with Batswana women of various religious traditions. As the stars emerged in the cold, clear sky, we asked these three native Batswana men about tensions between Black and white people in Botswana and if they had experienced racism or oppression. Our main tour guide, Ollie, a large, bald man in his thirties, explained to us that Batswana (people of Botswana) have a different relationship to white people than do most other Black people in Africa. "We were protected by the British," he said. He continued, speaking with great emphasis, "Protected. Not colonized. We asked for the help of the British, and they did help us. So, we in Botswana feel differently towards white people than people in other parts of Africa do."

Ollie, of course, would have had good reason to downplay racial tension stemming from colonization and play up good feelings between Blacks and whites in Botswana as he sat surrounded by a group of mostly white, mostly American women who had hired him to manage this safari. Yet his understanding of the history of his country—and in particular the difference between the harsh colonialism experienced by many other African countries and the lighter hand Britain used as it made Botswana its protectorate—is echoed by many histories written about the country.

As Ollie mentioned, Botswana did indeed escape the worst ravages of colonialism in the nineteenth and twentieth centuries. In the face of encroachment by Zulus and Boers, Botswana, then known as Bechuanaland, was taken under the protection of Britain in 1885.[1] Because Botswana was believed by Britain to be economically unviable, Britain initially left the protectorate largely to itself, even instructing its skeletal staff to leave the native chiefs to rule as they had done previously.[2] In 1895 three Batswana chiefs, Kgosi Khama III, Kgosi Sechele I, and Kgosi Bathoen I, famously traveled to Britain to petition the government not to turn this protectorate over to South Africa or Rhodesia, as it had originally expected to do, places where white settlers were taking over the most desirable pieces of land and establishing racist regimes.[3] Their campaign was successful, and Botswana remained a protectorate of Britain until independence was won in 1966. Unlike many other African countries that suffered severely under colonialism and had most of their institutions decimated by colonial rule, Botswana was able to retain its leadership class and social structures, thus providing important continuity as it became independent.[4] Botswana, once considered one of the poorest of African nations, has become, against all odds, the longest-running and most stable democracy in sub-Saharan Africa, aided in part by wealth derived from diamond mines that opened shortly after its independence. With its traditional institutions in place to prevent dictators from seizing power and pillaging the country's wealth, Botswana was able to maintain a stable democratic state. It is now one of the wealthiest and least troubled African countries. As one of our cabdrivers said, driving us from the African Mall to our rooms at the University of Botswana in the capital city, Gaborone, "Peace. Peace is the best thing about my country Botswana."

Decades before it became a protectorate of Britain, European Christian missionaries from South Africa began to proselytize in Botswana. By the beginning of the twentieth century, Christianity had spread to the interior of the country and had become the official religion of five of the Tswana states. Today, more than 65 percent of Batswana claim Christianity as their faith tradition, with the majority of the rest engaged in Batswana Traditional Religion, which permeates every aspect of their lives, from planting to education to funerals. Of those that identify as Christian, many have been drawn since the 1960s to African Independent and Pentecostal churches, both of which emphasize healing, spiritual gifts, singing, and dancing.[5] Because Botswana's 1966 constitution assures freedom of worship, many religious groups, including "new churches" like the Church of Jesus Christ of Latter-day Saints, have been able to gain a foothold in the country.[6] Latter-day Saint missionaries entered the country in 1990, and today there are more than more than three thousand members and fifteen congregations.[7]

These Batswana converts to the Church of Jesus Christ of Latter-day Saints are part of a long history of Africans converting to Christianity in the face of concerted missionary efforts. Scholars have explored this phenomenon for the past two hundred years, finding that while conversion to Christianity entailed the loss or adaptation of some traditional ways of being in and seeing the world, it also opened up other avenues for them to connect to the spiritual world and claim authority.[8] Notably, many of the Christian traditions that have flourished in Africa—in particular, charismatic ones—have also welcomed local adaptation, so that Africans can meld their own culture with the tenets and principles of their new faiths, making these faiths, in some sense, uniquely theirs.[9]

Batswana women's conversion to the Church of Jesus Christ of Latter-day Saints is particularly interesting because the church's centralized male leadership in Utah makes indigenization or inculturation of the religion in the global South difficult. The United States–based church retains strong centralized control over worship practices, doctrine, and policies across the globe. In Botswana, leadership and teaching manuals originate in the United States, Western business attire is adopted for church attire (suits, white shirts, and ties for men, dresses and skirts for women), church services are conducted in English according to the pattern set in the United States, music comes from a hymnal produced in the United States, and General Conference, which is conducted biannually and available via satellite and other media, features predominantly white American men giving sermons.[10] As Walter E. A. van Beek explains in his article exploring some cultural tensions surrounding the growth of the church in Africa, "From hierarchical priesthood structures to meetinghouse plans, and from priesthood ordinances to Sunday School lessons, unity shines through, but always in the form of uniformity."[11] Latter-day Saint worship in Botswana felt very familiar to my white American eyes and ears, as I sang the same exact hymns that I have sung numerous times before in my California congregation—one exception being the noticeable lack of enthusiasm many Batswana congregants had for the solemn, slow European-type hymns. Yet despite the strong influence of Utah-based leadership on Latter-day Saint congregations throughout the world, this ward in Botswana was entirely Black-led and directed. On an everyday, practical level, many Batswana Latter-day Saints' experiences with the church probably have little overt connection to the white men in America running the institutional church. Nevertheless, with such a strong centralized church structure, there is little opportunity for members to bring into their worship traditional Setswana elements. This was also true of the Mexican ward I attended, where men wore Western business clothing, sang those same hymns, and worshipped in a building devoid of any traditionally Mexican décor. There was one important difference between the congregations in Mexico and Botswana in terms of cultural elements, however: in Mexico, church services were held in the members' mother tongue, Spanish.

Another reason why Batswana women's conversions to the church are interesting is the faith's mixed history with colonialism and racism. Most other Christian faith traditions also, of course, have mixed or less-than-salubrious histories with these issues, but Mormonism has a striking history in this regard. As Joanna Brooks points out, Mormonism has long been implicated in colonialist and racist projects, since it displaced natives in its move to the American West in the nineteenth century, spread throughout the world on the coattails of neocolonial ideologies in the twentieth, categorized Indigenous populations as people who might literally become "white and delightsome" with conversion and time, and deprived Black people of temple blessings and Black men of priesthood until 1978.[12] Yet despite this problematic past, Mormonism has simultaneously opened up space for some Indigenous people and people of color to come together in ethnic wards, work for the well-being and self-determination of their communities, and see themselves as an integral and honored part of Mormonism's cosmology as lost tribes of Israel or descendants of peoples promised to "flourish as a rose" in the Book of Mormon.[13] Thus Latter-day Saints in the global South convert in a context of mixed historical messages and actions concerning people of color.

How, then, do we understand Batswana women's choices to affiliate with this religion? Are they dupes of Western neocolonialism, playing into their own oppression by patriarchy and Western imperialism, as some earlier analyses of African women's conversion to Christianity suggest? Or are they agents carving out sites of power and finding ways to honor both their traditional culture and their new belief systems? Is it possible they are simultaneously agentive and constrained by structures that privilege Western ways of being? Why would these women choose to affiliate with this faith, and how do they navigate that affiliation alongside their loyalties to their cultures of origin and ways of being in the world? How do these women manifest and navigate a commitment to non-oppressive connectedness, particularly when this commitment puts them in conflict with practices in the church? This chapter addresses these questions.

My analysis is informed by postcolonial feminist scholars who have explored the complex positioning of women of formerly colonized countries, who, as Motswana (person of Botswana) scholar Musa Dube notes, live at the intersection of various patriarchal structures, both indigenous and colonial.[14] Attention to the structures that confine and determine women's options is crucial. Also important is attention to the ways Western discourses and understandings have unfairly characterized women of the global South. Chandra Talpade Mohanty, for example, decries Western feminists' tendencies to portray women from the developing world as victims of brown men and of their own traditional cultures. She advocates instead for a more complex analysis that explores how they, in culturally specific ways, are produced as subjects and act as agents within their societies.[15] I embrace Mohanty's approach, finding it most fair and most productive to listen closely to these women describe places of grappling, dissonance, and resonance as they carefully navigate their chosen religion and their cultures of origin. By letting the women indicate the places of tension and of resonance, we honor them as the subjects and experts of their own lives.

Although I feel that an agentive view of these women is most fruitful, some caution is in order. Gayatri Spivak, a prominent postcolonialist, writes that the subaltern—the dispossessed person in a colonial society—"in the context of colonial production . . . has no history and cannot speak, [and] the subaltern as female is even more deeply in shadow."[16] This statement has sparked much controversy among postcolonial scholars, and a careful reading of Spivak's theory indicates that the subaltern can indeed speak; the non-subaltern, however, cannot hear her. This disconnect between articulation and comprehension or interpretation exists because dominant systems of signification imposed in colonial or Eurocentric contexts are structurally predicated on binaries that associate women and the other with silence, even down to linguistic structures. These binaries privilege a coherent speaking subjectivity that colonialism is predicated on denying to the colonized. This results in the effective silencing of the subaltern, though as one scholar explains, "The silence of the female as subaltern is the result of a failure of interpretation and not a failure of articulation."[17] Spivak's point about the powerful structures that effectively render the subaltern silent is an important one. Therefore, caution is key when considering the many layers of filters (including my own, the Western feminist oral historian) and the variety of ways in which the voices of women of the global South have been misunderstood, impacted, and constrained by forces greater than themselves.

This question of agency, and how Batswana Latter-day Saint women find and create spaces for agentive action and complex negotiation, even within the patriarchal and Western strictures of the Church of Jesus Christ of Latter-day Saints, is an important focus of this chapter. I also explore the diverse realities of their particular context in Botswana, which at times make Latter-day Saint norms and strictures a difficult overlay onto this culture. This intersectional analysis extends previous explorations of women's agency by situating religious women's agency at the crossroads of colony, race, and class.[18] I find that a particular focus of agency and a particular moral center emerges in the lives and stories of these Batswana Latter-day Saint women:

that of creating and maintaining positive relationships and social ties. Like the Mexican women discussed in Chapter 1, a commitment to non-oppressive connectedness centers their moral lives. Yet that commitment manifests itself in practices unique to Setswana culture and results, at times, in tensions with Latter-day Saint church practices.

This analysis also points us toward *why* these women have chosen to convert to this American-born faith, despite these occasional tensions and the packaging of Mormonism in certain Western norms. These Batswana women Saints have found some liberatory elements in Mormonism, namely, the focus on loving, committed husbands and fathers and the sense of a caring God directing their lives. Highly devout and practicing Latter-day Saint women have also found social and personal benefits stemming from Mormonism's community structure and lay organization, which create space for women to teach, preach, minister, oversee certain programs, and attend congregational council meetings. The tradition's high level of individual involvement and moral strictures are sometimes challenging, but they can also be attractive to the most devout women, some of whom are drawn to clarity and boundaries different from those of permissive contemporary society in Botswana. Over the course of the past two or three generations its society has shifted from a tight-knit tribal village subsistence economy and sociality to a modernized cash economy and sociality that has seen some disintegration of the traditional ways of being, with younger generations having left the villages for work in the larger cities. Colleen McDannell states that for global Latter-day Saint women, especially those who have migrated, "wards are like a village where people develop friendships and networks."[19] This is true for many Batswana women. Mormonism, in some sense, functions as the new village, giving them responsibilities and social ties that were more readily available in traditional communities of generations past. This analysis highlights how these women adapt their religion to their particular culture, needs, and purposes. These needs and purposes, I find, have overwhelmingly centered on desires to create non-oppressive relationships. This moral imperative is sometimes satisfied in the Latter-day Saint congregational structure, which utilizes the skills and energy of all active and willing members, but it is also satisfied in doctrinal teachings about a loving, personal Father God and temple covenants that give Batswana hope that they will be bound to loved ones in the next life. Although these benefits of Mormonism accrue to Batswana women and enable certain agentive spaces and actions, these are bounded by patriarchal and Western strictures, which these women carefully negotiate.

I organize this chapter around the stories and reflections of a handful of Batswana women who describe the joys and challenges of embracing

Mormonism in Botswana. These sites of resonance and tension focus on a number of topics related to family, marriage, and motherhood. Their stories highlight why and how they thoughtfully adopt this faith tradition into their lives. Focusing on these women's agency and careful navigation of loyalties recontextualizes the church's teachings and policies concerning sexual morality, adoption, bridewealth, and companionate marriage in this global southern context.

Single Motherhood, Chastity, and Extended Family Structures

The Church of Jesus Christ of Latter-day Saints has gained a foothold mainly in the largest cities in Botswana, but some small congregations called branches survive in rural areas. I had the privilege of traveling to one of these towns during my first week in Botswana. As four colleagues and I drove out to this rural town, we passed field after field dotted with cattle, farms, and small homes. When we pulled into the tiny parking lot of the church in the dusty village, a church that consisted only of a few small rooms, I met Naomi, the first woman I interviewed in Botswana. She was in her thirties and wore a knee-length skirt and a white blouse. A colleague and I sat on folding chairs in a small room and thanked her for coming. We began with the usual questions about her childhood, but it was clear she had a particular story to tell.

Naomi grew up in this village as one of nine children. Her mother was a homemaker who grew the vegetables they needed to survive, and her father was a hospital messenger. She was initially raised in the Catholic Church and then joined the Dutch Reformed Church. As a teenager, Naomi was stalked and raped. Both she and the resulting baby acquired HIV. With the strong support of her mother, Naomi finished college and became a bursar at a school in another part of the country. Her mother was the primary caretaker of the baby, who caught meningitis as a newborn and suffered lasting developmental delays from the disease. Naomi visited her daughter as often as she could on weekends and holidays. While she was in the city where she worked, Naomi met her boyfriend and became pregnant with her son. Unfortunately, a shortage of 1,200 pula (about $100) while she was away on maternity leave led to her losing her job and destroyed her career as a bursar. She returned to her home village to live with her family and give birth to her son. To make money, Naomi opened up a tuck shop (a tiny grocery store) in her front yard. When her son was four, she met some Latter-day Saint missionaries in Gaborone and was impressed by their willingness to give two years of their lives to their missions. She had been attending a Pentecostal church but did not feel comfortable there. After two months of reading the Book of Mormon and feeling moved by the Spirit, she decided to join. Within a few short years, she accepted the request that she serve as Relief Society president, a calling that has enabled her to make connections with other women but has proved to be difficult given the high rate of inactivity in the branch.[20]

Naomi's oral history captures some of the realities of life for women in Botswana, in particular her experience with HIV/AIDS, which infects up to one in five people in the country, and her experience with single motherhood. Although HIV is an important and fascinating part of her story—it is striking that Naomi upends most institutional Mormon narratives about HIV, which position people with HIV as either having acquired this disease owing to sinful behavior or as objects needing Latter-day Saints' ministering help—I focus on single motherhood, which is a common phenomenon in Botswana.[21] One-third of the Latter-day Saint Batswana women I interviewed were single mothers.

Naomi described the way she initially managed single motherhood, given her job up north, and how she came to have her second child:

> My daughter was with my mom. Because she was going for review and tests, I couldn't take her to the hospital. But during school holidays she would be with me, and when I was on leave I would come straight home. I was transferred to a particular college. When I was there, that's when I met a boyfriend. This was in 2005. 2006 was when I had my second child, a boy.[22]

Naomi's description of how she initially managed single motherhood—giving her mother primary caretaker status as she earned money in another town—is not uncommon. Neither is it uncommon that Naomi had a baby with the boyfriend she met in the town up north. In Botswana many women have children out of wedlock. If they are employed in towns, mothers often send their children to their home villages to be raised by grandmothers or older village women. This arrangement, known sometimes as child fosterage, has a long tradition in Botswana, and it often works well for mothers who need to produce money in towns and for grandmothers who can use the help of grandchildren for chores and farming.[23]

Studies have noted that single motherhood and the decline of marriage are products of the rapid cultural and economic changes that the country has undergone in the past half century. According to David Suggs, large numbers of Batswana men migrated for work in the 1960s, 1970s, and 1980s due to the demands of a new cash economy in which subsistence farming was no longer viable. They often went to urban areas and mining centers in Botswana and in South Africa.[24] Wendy Izzard, who examined this issue in Botswana in the 1980s, explained the phenomenon of single motherhood in this way:

> The absence of men had a considerable impact on the role of women as wives and as mothers. [Out-migration] resulted in a reduction of the marriage rate . . . and an increase in the number of deserted wives. . . . There were concomitant adjustments in attitude toward marriage. . . . Women no longer saw marriage as the chief means with which to enhance their status in society. The role of mother assumed greater significance in the face of the declining importance of "the wife," and the two roles became isolated from each other.[25]

Suggs, in his study of a rural village in Botswana agrees, saying, "Today a woman need not marry to establish her own household provided she has the funds to build it, the experience to run it, and the will to do so. . . . There is today a decreased emphasis on marriage as a definitional characteristic of women."[26] Yet motherhood, he emphasized, is paramount for Batswana women. He summarized his findings on the topic of motherhood:

> The general opinion among both young and old women is that a woman is never complete and never happy without having children. Children are valued on several levels; as objects of love, as continuation of family, as extra hands while one is working, and as security in old age. As one person [a Motswana in the village] stated the importance of motherhood: "Only women can do this thing. Those who cannot are not wholly women. They work for nothing and die for nothing."[27]

Motherhood is such a prominent part of Batswana women's identities that childless women endure significant pressure from family members to have children, whether or not they are married. This is one of the greatest challenges single Latter-day Saint women face in Botswana: the overwhelming cultural expectation that they will provide grandchildren for their parents regardless of marital status. This, of course, becomes difficult when there is a dearth of Latter-day Saint men to marry, and marrying outside the faith is also difficult, given that Mormon values are markedly different from those of other Batswana, even other Christians, regarding sexual abstinence.[28] Scholars write that many Christian churches in southern Africa, while advocating for sexual abstinence until marriage, "have little control over premarital sexual relations," and it is very common for Tswana couples to form nonconjugal unions and for women to have children outside of marriage.[29] Naomi mentioned that a huge challenge for unmarried Latter-day Saint women was this pressure they feel to have children. She explained:

In our families, let's say I'm my age and don't have a child, my parents would keep encouraging me, "Hey, how can I have grandchildren if you don't have a child? Help us out, even if you are not married—you need a child." So parents will encourage us to have a child, believing that the more you grow old, the more difficulties you will have. So they encourage us to have a child. Especially after 30, they will encourage us to have a child. . . . They don't even look at getting married first. They just look at getting a child first. They want a child in the family. . . . People expect you to live with a boyfriend before marriage, so cohabitation is very common. Those are things that are very, very challenging in our lives.[30]

This is a fascinating example of the confluences and divergences of institutional Latter-day Saint and Batswana gender expectations, and it gives an interesting glimpse into the tensions that these women navigate. As many scholars have noted, motherhood and nurturing of children are primary roles and identity markers for Latter-day Saint women.[31] Latter-day Saint religious leaders have repeatedly emphasized the primary role and identity of mother-nurturer for women throughout the twentieth century, a role that became near-canon in the 1995 Proclamation on the Family.[32] So oft-repeated and prominent is this emphasis on motherhood and nurturing for women that this identity has even been extended to women who do not bear or raise children. General Relief Society counselor Sheri Dew noted that in Genesis Eve is named the "mother of all living" before she has children. She said, "Like Eve, our motherhood began before we were born. . . . It is the essence of who we are as women. It defines our very identity, our divine stature and nature, and the unique traits our Father gave us."[33] This conception of all women as ontological mothers echoes earlier twentieth-century church leaders' feelings about the main purpose and role of women. Latter-day Saint leader John Widtsoe claimed in 1939, "Woman has her gift of equal magnitude [to the priesthood]—motherhood," thus articulating what has become a common Mormon framework in which women's central role of mother parallels men's central role of priesthood holder.[34] Many Latter-day Saint women have embraced this identity of mother, finding power and fulfillment in this realm.[35]

This conception of Latter-day Saint women's identity as nurturers and mothers resonates well with many Batswana women, whose culture similarly assigns the primary identity category of mother to women. Therefore, it is entirely unsurprising that Naomi showed comfort with and appreciation for this role assigned to women in Mormonism. When asked to describe women's role in the church in Botswana, she stated, "The most important role is nurturing children. Taking care of children. That's a very, very important role for us women. Because if we don't teach our children the gospel, the world will teach them things that are contrary to our standards."[36]

For many Batswana women like Naomi, raising the next generation is a source of power and strength. Judith Van Allen's work on female political leaders in Botswana highlights just how central and powerful the role of mother is. She writes that female political leaders are able to "enter male-gendered political spaces as 'equal rights powerful mothers'—and as citizens, activists and leaders—and potentially transform their societies."[37] She points out that claiming and promoting their identities as mothers is a potent political strategy for them because of the long historical tradition of powerful mothers in Africa.[38] Van Allen insightfully puts her finger on the reason for many women's contemporary ambivalence toward wifehood: "A mother is someone to be taken seriously; a wife is someone who takes orders, serves and acts with deference toward men."[39] The female political leaders' deliberate merging of ideas of gender difference (emphasis on motherhood) with more Western liberal democratic ideas about equal rights is proving to be an effective basis for women's entry into political realms.[40]

It is also important to note that while motherhood is a central identity marker for women in Latter-day Saint rhetoric and in Setswana culture (culture of Botswana), there are different notions about how one mothers and nurtures. Western Latter-day Saint leaders' ideas of these tasks often have centered, particularly during the rise of the women's movement in the latter half of the twentieth century, on stay-at-home motherhood. In his famous 1987 talk titled "To the Mothers in Zion," President Ezra Taft Benson quoted President Spencer W. Kimball's injunction to women of the previous decade to "come home from the typewriter, the laundry, the nursing, come home from the factory, the cafe. No career approaches in importance that of wife, homemaker, mother—cooking meals, washing dishes, making beds for one's precious husband and children."[41] Although this emphasis on stay-at-home motherhood was prominent in the 1970s and into the 1980s, Laurence Iannaccone and Carrie Miles note that nonetheless church leaders' rhetoric did gradually shift toward becoming more conciliatory and accommodative to working women in the 1980s and beyond, especially in situations of financial need.[42] Church leaders have generally been more reluctant in the past several decades to critique working mothers, but there remains a kind of idealization of stay-at-home motherhood in authoritative Western Mormon rhetoric, with women advised to be primarily responsible for caretaking and men advised to be primarily responsible for breadwinning.[43] Scholars have argued that this division of labor has its roots in the Western industrial revolution, which introduced the phenomenon of men leaving the home for a separate workplace, unlike earlier familial constructions, which saw the home as the site of both nurture and production.[44]

Notions that motherhood should ideally preclude paid labor or breadwinning is something of a foreign construct to Batswana women, who associate motherhood not only with teaching and nurturing but also with production. Suggs notes that Batswana women "have both in the past and the present validated their status as women by their capacity for productive labor. And they value their labor most highly when it is put to the care and provisioning of their children."[45] Thus, what it means to mother in a Western capitalist middle-class conservative Mormon framework is different from what it means to mother in Botswana, which entered the capitalist economy only a couple of generations ago. For many Batswana women, a defining characteristic of a mother is laboring to provide for her children. Mothering may also involve active daily nurturing and caretaking, but it might not, given how common it is for women to send their children to relatives or friends to be raised so that these women can more easily earn funds for their children's upkeep. Motherhood is indeed a central identity marker for Western and Batswana Latter-day Saint women, but it is constructed differently for both groups.

While the Setswana and Latter-day Saint emphasis on women as mothers is in many ways a space of fortuitous cultural overlap for Batswana Saints, tension arises from Mormonism's emphasis on wifehood before motherhood.[46] As Izzard and Suggs explain, these two roles became separated in the latter half of the twentieth century in Botswana, as many men emigrated to other countries or regions. The Latter-day Saint emphasis on marriage, therefore, is in practice quite a challenge for Latter-day Saint Batswana women who would like to be mothers but for whom marriage seems unachievable due to gender imbalances in the church and different cultural expectations outside it. Naomi ended her oral history by speaking poignantly of her yearning to be married to a priesthood holder and sealed eternally as a family. (Sealing is a Latter-day Saint ordinance performed in temples that binds family members together in this life and the next.) She said:

> I know that maybe someday God will bless me with a husband who I will be sealed to. And it also keeps me strong. I remember this other time when I had a Family Home Evening with my son, and he said, "Mom, why are you not staying with dad?" I said, "We are not married." He said, "What if he marries another woman?" I said, "Yeah. Maybe I'll be married to another man also." He said, "No, maybe you won't get married. You need to make a way to reach out to him." I said, "The only way to do that is to put that into our prayer." Every night we pray for him and that we might

be one family. It just gave me the thought that even our children want to have that family united so that we can live as one strong family in this life and the next life.[47]

In this brief exchange, we can catch a glimpse of Naomi's reasoning for not having a relationship with her son's father ("We are not married") and her longing to form the sealed family that Mormonism promotes as ideal and eternal.

After her conversion to Mormonism, Naomi chose to end her intimate relationship with her son's father, thereby bringing about the end of her relationship entirely. She explained the phone conversation she had with him in which she made it clear that that part of their relationship would need to end:

When I joined the church in 2011, I called him and talked to him and told him that now I was joining this church and that I made a covenant with Heavenly Father that if I join this church, I would obey his commandments. I explained to him the law of chastity. He said, "We'll talk about it." He kept saying, "We'll talk about it." Since then, 2011, I didn't talk to him much. But I keep telling him about the baby. When the child does this or this, I just call him, though he's not that supportive at times.[48]

Naomi is not the only Latter-day Saint convert who has had to figure out how to navigate Mormon teachings regarding chastity (sexual relations only within heterosexual marriage) given the reality of an established intimate but nonmarital relationship. Naomi's choice was made slightly easier because of the physical distance separating her from her son's father, who lived in another part of the country, but other female converts have a far more immediate and painful choice to make. Neo, who was given HIV by a boyfriend who later died of it, joined the church while actively in a relationship with the father of her last two children. She had attended many churches in her life, but she never felt as if these churches could answer all her questions. She liked the fact that Latter-day Saint missionaries answered her questions, and when she converted, she had to decide how to handle this long-term boyfriend. Like Naomi, Neo is attempting to live the law of chastity. When asked how her boyfriend felt when she joined the church, she stated in her simple English, "He is upset . . . there are the laws we have to keep, like the law of chastity, I have to keep it *akere* [you know], he is drinking, I have to keep the law of wisdom, yes, but that one he can't force [me], he knows that this one, she keeps the law of wisdom. The problem is the law of chastity."[49] Neo has been able to draw the line with the Word of Wisdom and eschew alcohol and tea, but as she states, the notion of chastity is the real problem that she must navigate constantly with the father of her children.

On the surface the solution would seem simple: Why don't these women just convince their long-term boyfriends to marry them? I quickly learned that marriage is a complicated and difficult issue in Botswana. It traditionally involves bridewealth (*lobola*) on the part of the man because the wife's family requires money or cattle in order for a marriage to take place. This might take years for a man and his family to save up. In addition, the wedding is supposed to be an elaborate affair. These expectations mean that marriage is extremely costly. Charles, one of our safari guides, for example, told us that he had three children with his girlfriend and had been with her for eleven years, and he is still saving up money for the wedding and lobola. He wanted to marry her, but finances did not allow it at that time. Thus, quick and easy marriages are problematic options for Naomi and Neo, whose families would feel betrayed and offended if the couples eloped or married quietly without much family participation.[50]

Neo's and Naomi's choices to hold fast to Mormon notions of chastity (or at least try to) are poignant because they highlight one cost of membership in the Church of Jesus Christ of Latter-day Saints for some women in Botswana. Both have either ended or seriously jeopardized their romantic relationships in order to keep this principle. Some scholars have found such injunctions about chastity to be rife with patriarchal elements that impinge on women's agency to explore various types of relationships and enjoy physical intimacy, but other scholars studying religious women have pointed out how, in some cases, women find a sense of safety and protection in such frameworks. Jennifer Finlayson-Fife, who studies the sexual agency of American Latter-day Saint women, notes that "many LDS women, like cultural feminists, interpreted non-committal sexuality as male-defined and male-advantaging, and therefore undermining of their agency as it inherently served men's needs over their own."[51] Strong Mormon injunctions upholding chastity actually can give women a framework in which to demand commitment from romantic partners before engaging in sex, Finlayson-Fife explains. In this way, the conservative choice to embrace Mormon notions of chastity actually has the potential of creating a shelter for women against male demands and male abdication of responsibility.

Although this framework of chastity within Mormonism increases some American women's senses of safety and agency because it allows them to explore their erotic selves with committed husbands, it is important to note that the Latter-day Saint women in Botswana are not in a cultural context that would easily allow them to find committed partners who also embrace notions of chastity. As mentioned above, the gender ratios there are skewed female, making finding a Latter-day Saint husband difficult. Also difficult is finding non-Latter-day Saint men who would respect and honor demands for chastity until marriage, because unmarried coupling or cohabitation is the norm. Thus, whereas Mormon chastity norms have helped some Latter-day Saint women achieve what they want in a sexual relationship—commitment, trust, self-expression—and have made them feel agentive and powerful in their sexual lives, women in contexts like that of Botswana are less likely to benefit in the same way, given the gender gap and cultural expectation that they have children before marriage. Women like Naomi and Neo hold out hope for a marriage to a committed man who understands and respects Mormon sexuality norms and who takes responsibility for helping to rear children, but the likelihood of them finding that person is low. In Botswana the intersection of Mormonism, gender, and cultural context generates a situation in which some women pay a particularly high price for membership in the church.

Several single women with whom I spoke described chastity as a huge challenge in Botswana. Part of the challenge is the undesirable (in both Mormon and Setswana contexts) possibility of living a chaste, unpartnered single life until death, and part is the undesirable prospect of never having children. Women there deeply value maternal connections. Since motherhood is so essential to women's identities in Botswana, it is far preferable to many of them to become pregnant out of wedlock and raise the baby as a single mother than never to have a baby at all. Musa, a single woman who converted to the faith as a teenager, spoke to me about how even Latter-day Saint women would pull her aside and advise her to just get pregnant and then repent later, so essential is it to have at least one child in this culture.[52] With their choice to join the church and adhere to Mormon chastity standards, many face lifetimes without male partners and, more difficult for them, without children. Caught between a rock and a hard place, they live in tension with some of their deepest values and priorities: the establishment of maternal connections. Yet for Batswana women who do find husbands committed to their marriage and children, Mormon chastity norms and the ubiquitous emphasis on the importance of the family do help mold committed and present male partners, a highly desirable outcome for them. The final section of this chapter explores in more depth the way Latter-day Saint teachings engender more satisfactory male marital partners, even as these teachings reinforce patriarchal norms.

Although sacrificing romantic relationships is a significant challenge for unmarried Batswana Latter-day Saint women, these same women have often found within the church other areas that expand opportunities for agency and invite connection and relationality. This drive to create community and form enriching relationships with others, hallmarks of a worldview of non-oppressive connectedness, dovetails with what African scholars often call Ubuntu, a southern African notion of a communal self.[53] These scholars have pointed out that Western notions of the self—often more individualized, more focused on rights and autonomy—do not always translate well in non-Western contexts. In Africa, in particular, scholars have pointed out an entirely different worldview, one that privileges not the singular self and her goals but instead focuses on the community and communal becoming. John Mbiti famously coined a dictum to explain traditional African concepts of community and self: "I am, because we are; and since we are therefore I am."[54] Proverbs encapsulating this idea are found in many African languages, but for our purposes the Setswana proverb is "*Motho ke motho ka batho.*"[55] Mbiti considers this notion to be the hallmark of the traditional African worldview.[56] The self is thus inextricably combined with others, and many African scholars have echoed that this communal idea of the self is a distinguishing factor that separates African thought from Western thought. The African feminist ethicist Fainos Mangena describes the practical ramifications of an Ubuntu worldview: "In this intricate social network, the individual finds him or herself related almost to everybody else in the community as father, mother, uncle, cousin, niece, aunt, etc. Their well-being is supposed to be his or her well-being as well. Any misfortune that befalls any of them affects him or her as well. . . . His or her identity is caught up in the social identity."[57] Mangena argues that this Ubuntu idea, rooted in many southern African communities, pressures women to take in and nurse sick husbands or partners who have often given them AIDS, as well as other sick relatives and children in need of care. Mangena finds this problematic and potentially damaging to women, who feel compelled to perform intensive care tasks, often at the expense of their own health and well-being.

Mangena argues for a refined sense of Ubuntu, one that protects women's health and welfare but retains women's networks of care and relationality, especially with children, so that women can enculturate a new generation with less patriarchal ideas. In some ways the Latter-day Saint community in Botswana functions in this refined Ubuntu space as some women choose to turn aside from nonmarital romantic relationships and instead maintain and develop networks of care and friendship. Devout Latter-day Saint women participate together in the Relief Society, Young Women, and Primary organizations, assume stewardship over one another through the visiting teaching program (now called ministering), and teach various members of the congregation on Sundays.[58] This work of creating community within women's networks in the church is not easy given the high rates of inactivity, cultural resistance to programs like visiting teaching, and busy schedules that might prevent attendance at some ward activities. But women who persist within the Mormon framework do eventually create relationships and bonds that sustain. Naomi spoke of forming such bonds on a Relief Society trip to Johannesburg, her first time at the temple:

> It was quite amazing. When we got to the Johannesburg temple, we were sleeping in one room. . . . We didn't sleep that night. We were just sharing and talking. Some sisters were sharing with us how they met their spouses and some who belonged to the church longer were sharing experiences in the church. It was quite amazing, and you just feel the Spirit when you are with the sisters.[59]

Naomi ultimately became a Relief Society president and important minister and caretaker in her community, visiting non-practicing Latter-day Saint women and communing with them about the challenges of their lives. She said, "I got to know the sisters and got to love them. And if they are less active you learn why they are not coming to church. And at times you find out that some are having the very same challenges that you have."[60] Naomi also created these bonds of care as she served in the Young Women organization and as she attended Enrichment meetings. She spoke fondly of the latter, saying, "The Relief Society activities were so wonderful. We made a scripture bag. We designed cards for less active members. We designed—the most wonderful activity I enjoyed—we designed a book. Every sister would come with a different recipe, and we combined and bound them and made a book—mostly traditional food."[61] Naomi's narrative arc—finding the church at a low point in her life but then finding the space and confidence to rise within the Latter-day Saint community to become a leader, minister, and friend to other Latter-day Saints in her area—is striking. Within the church's patriarchal and Western frameworks and restrictive teachings concerning chastity, Naomi has embraced her new religious community and risen to the challenges of lay ministerial work, and in so doing, developed and deepened her connections with other Saints.

Naomi and Neo deeply internalize notions of care for children and community. They have channeled their focus of care away from expectations of boyfriends and have drawn lines that honor their new personal senses of morality and God's wishes for them, even if these lines are personally difficult, painful, and frustrating for them. The dilemma of whether to privilege the stability of personal romantic relationships over their newfound faith and convictions about God's law of chastity highlights them as agents who are deliberately negotiating their new paths in life. These are not passive women who simply went along with a religious tradition that was handed to them, as earlier depictions of Christianity among African women sometimes emphasized.[62] Rather, they actively fought for this new faith and life, and they embraced it, sometimes at great personal cost. As their romantic relationships are damaged, a distressing outcome given their drive to sustain and create connections, others are formed within the church. Not only do the highly committed develop strong networks of care with other members, but they also develop personal relationships with a loving God who, if they are faithful enough, will bind them together with their families forever.

Given the realities of navigating Mormon notions of chastity in a social context that does not understand or support this choice, it is important to note that local branches and wards are often loving and kind towards Latter-day Saint women who do not choose to abstain from sexual relationships outside of marriage. In the same branch as Neo, a woman named Kefilwe, who had held a calling in the Young Women program, spoke of the way they handle pregnancies of unmarried teenage girls in the branch:

> If a girl is pregnant, we started a group visiting this girl. And after we invite her to come to church with that baby. We will be supportive so when she comes she knows she is part of the Church. We encourage each other to be supportive if somebody falls pregnant, to know it is not the end of the world. We need to support her so that she can be able to come back to church and continue on the path of the gospel.[63]

In other words, these Latter-day Saint women and girls would collectively put their arms around these young women and wholeheartedly invite them to continue coming to church. Musa, a former Relief Society president, used to go to inactive sisters and say, "I don't care what you have done or what you are doing. Just come [to church]. We're not all perfect."[64] Limiting sexual relationships to marriage is such an unusual concept for Batswana that church members and leaders have, according to some of these oral histories, often showed understanding toward those who do not always live up to these standards.

Naomi's and Neo's experiences with attempting to live the law of chastity highlight the significant price some pay for church membership. Although that law is central to Mormon morality, one cannot help but wonder whether there is room in the church for possible accommodations for women like Naomi and Neo, so that they could have both their membership and their relationships intact. Anecdotal evidence from missionaries around the world suggests that Latter-day Saint mission presidents sometimes establish different rules on the subject of baptizing converts in common-law marriages, or marriage-like relationships that are unofficial but long-term, monogamous, and committed.[65] Because some countries make divorce almost impossible, common-law marriages are often widespread among people who have been previously married. This poses a real problem for missionaries who find families eager to convert, only to realize that couples are not legally married. In some cases, as in the Philippines recently, mission presidents allow couples to be baptized if they have lived together monogamously for five years.[66] Other mission presidents insist on baptism only for legally married couples.[67] In the case of Botswana, local church leaders appear to be adhering to a "legal marriage only" concept of chastity, but in practice, some church members and leaders on the ground are trying to make room for women who, like Neo, are in the very difficult position of trying to combine long-term relationships and Latter-day Saint activity. Long-term monogamous nonlegal relationships are a topic that church leaders wrestle with in different parts of the world, and they seem potentially open to considering adaptation depending on particular cultural and legal circumstances.

A concomitant issue that Latter-day Saint leaders and members must confront is how to assign a meaningful identity and space within Mormonism to women who are not mothers. With Mormonism positing such a strong stance against sexual relationships outside of marriage while at the same time closely intertwining women's identities with motherhood, unmarried Latter-day Saint women without children exist in a no-[wo]man's land, unable to fulfill either their faith's conception of womanhood or, in many cases around the world, their culture's conception of womanhood. They are left unable to create the maternal bonds that are one important aspect of their drive to form vitalizing and enduring connections, hallmarks of a worldview based on non-oppressive connectedness. It is therefore not surprising that so many single Latter-day Saint women in Botswana have trouble maintaining activity in the church.

Adoption

Given the strong cultural emphasis on motherhood, a number of Batswana Latter-day Saint women choose to have children outside of wedlock. As mentioned above, this familial and cultural pressure to have children is a product of larger ideological patterns and understandings of self, rooted in African traditional thought, that emphasize the community over the individual.[68] Naomi's parents pressure her to have children, even out of wedlock, because they see it as good for the community, good for the larger extended family, and good for Naomi personally. Choosing not to have children is seen as unwise (since children are caretakers of elderly parents) and possibly selfish in the more traditional worldview of Batswana. That some unmarried Latter-day Saint women therefore have children is not surprising, even in the face of strong institutional Latter-day Saint norms against doing so. This choice, however, brings into stark relief a tension between Latter-day Saint policies, which advocated adoption for babies born to unwed Latter-day Saint mothers, and Setswana culture, in which giving babies up is seen as untenable and unethical. The topic of adoption exemplifies issues of cultural accommodation, resistance, and agency within Mormonism, as well as the tensions that result when church teachings conflict with women's commitments to non-oppressive connectedness.

Musa, a devout member of the church, spoke of one such incident, in which an urban Relief Society as a whole vocally and forcefully rejected a certain practice they simply could not, as women of Botswana, embrace. She said:

> We were told that if a single sister falls pregnant, the advice or encouragement was for that sister to put that baby up for adoption. I didn't like that. I found the teaching hard to swallow. I still do, though I'm not sure what the stance of the church is anymore on that. One day our bishop came to Relief Society to tell the sisters about this principle coming from the First Presidency. Before the bishop even finished what he was delivering the sisters were up in arms, saying all sorts of things. They were like, "No!" I remember the bishop just walking out, without finishing what he had come to deliver. He just walked out. It was my first time seeing Saints, for that matter, women, opposing the prophet in such . . . a setting. Maybe our minds and hearts were not prepared. That's why it is such a hard saying to us. Or maybe we feel this way because we are Africans and we are taught that a child is a gift from God, and it doesn't matter if they come out of wedlock or not, that one has to treasure them and keep them. Because in Botswana, you fall pregnant, you might not be working, and relatives and siblings will pitch in and help here and there, and life goes on! That's how we're raised.[69]

This account reveals a dissonance between Setswana values and Latter-day Saint injunctions. In the first decade of the twenty-first century, when this incident took place, Latter-day Saint leaders advocated adoption for babies born to unwed mothers because they felt strongly that babies should be raised in nuclear two-parent families and sealed to these families. An unwed mother would be unable to provide either of these things, and thus adoption was strongly encouraged.[70] For these Batswana women, however, giving up their babies was unthinkable. It went against their culture, which has little experience with this practice. It went against their moral commitments, which center around fostering bonds and connections. In addition, it ignored the particular social practices of Batswana, who tend to have tight bonds of reciprocity and expectation between extended family members. As Musa said, family members are expected to help a new mother with childcare and funds.[71] The women in Relief Society therefore vocally rejected the message on adoption, actually driving the bishop out mid-message, because this practice was simply incompatible with their tradition, their sense of morality, and their conception of family responsibilities.

We can see in this incident a moment of hybrid identity. These Latter-day Saint women, who were attending Relief Society and actively embracing their new faith in many ways, asserted their rejection of a stance that seemed wrong to their conception of morality and unworkable in their society. As Rita Abrahamsen explained in her discussion of hybrid identities in postcolonial societies, "Hybridity is seen to signify the creative adaptation, interpretation and transformation of Western cultural symbols and practices, and shows that formerly colonized peoples are not simply passive victims in the face of an all-powerful Western culture."[72] Clearly, these women were willing and able to select which (Western) Mormon practices work for them and which simply do not. It is noteworthy that the official website of the Church of Jesus Christ of Latter-day Saints now features a far more nuanced discussion of women's options when they find themselves pregnant and unwed, compared to the clear directives from the first decade of the twenty-first century. The current directive ultimately encourages women to pray and find personal guidance as to how they should best deal with their situation.[73] One cannot help but wonder if the church's shift regarding this issue might be due in part to the negative reactions of non-American members, who simply could find no place for it in their worldview.[74]

Musa's story also highlights the active choices Latter-day Saint women in Botswana are making to comply with dictates originating from church headquarters, to resist them, or to do both simultaneously. It is notable that this one area of resistance that Musa noted—it was the first time she had ever seen Latter-day Saint women so clearly and wholeheartedly reject a church injunction—was that of how they should behave as single mothers. In the point of view of Batswana, motherhood and child rearing are arenas that are very much under the stewardship of women. Thus, men (and white American men at that) instructing these women to give their babies away was unpalatable. It struck at the heart of who these women were as mothers or potential mothers, but also who they were as Africans, raised to treasure every single child and to expect help from family members to raise their children, whether or not the children were products of a marriage. This bishop's message was seen as overstepping—not only by men telling women what to do with their babies, but also by Western church leaders who perhaps did not understand the tight bonds of extended family networks in Africa. We see in this incident a clear indication that the subject of adopting children out to strangers is one area in which Batswana women will rise up and forthrightly reject certain Western cultural practices that have little place within their more communal society.

Musa's story was striking in the way it highlighted a moment of resistance on the part of Relief Society women, but a careful reading of her words shows an attempt to balance her initial repugnance toward the idea with her faith and her loyalty to her church and her leaders. She mentioned the possibility that she and her sisters might have been wrong to feel as they did: "Maybe our minds and hearts were not prepared." She went on to wrestle with the idea more, trying to understand the church's position: "I mean, I understand that it's for the baby's best interest to be raised by two married parents and sealed and all of that. That makes perfect sense. But I think because of how I was raised . . . someone instilled in me this idea. Even if you are able to take care of your child—to just give it away?"[75] Musa is engaging in a complex grappling with the idea of adoption, wanting to honor and respect both her own culture's sense of morality and that of her chosen church. Although in the moment, Musa and her Relief Society sisters rose up and rejected the notion of adoption, Musa is actually struggling to come to terms with the church's position, trying to give it and church leaders the benefit of the doubt. She is attempting to accommodate both the church's and her culture's sense of morality and good in this situation. In some ways, Musa is displaying a kind of agency that not only resists authority—the kind of agency most feminist historians emphasize—but also accedes to authority at the same exact moment. Hoyt, who studied Latter-day Saint women in the United States, described this kind of agency that simultaneously resists and accedes to authority or social norms.[76] Musa vocally resisted the church's injunctions concerning adoption, but she simultaneously worked to honor and respect those injunctions and to find room for them in her moral framework. As such, this Mormon Motswana woman is engaging in a complex negotiation between different forms of morality, community, and family.

This story sheds further light on Hoyt's conception of simultaneous agency and the constant renegotiations between self and community because it brings into focus another realm of norms that converts to Mormonism from different countries must negotiate within a Latter-day Saint framework: that of loyalties to local communities and concepts of morality. Hoyt's study, which helpfully moves discourse about agency beyond dichotomous notions of either resistance to or support of norms, could not take into account the additional layers of loyalty and negotiation that are thrown into the mix when Latter-day Saint women's conceptions of morality and selfhood are formed in a non-Western culture in which the self is often thought to be tied inextricably to the community.[77] Musa is thus negotiating between multiple loyalties and conceptions of morality, including that of her Western-based church, that of her culture in Botswana, and her own visceral reaction, which, as she acknowledges, is probably deeply tied to moral conceptions of her home culture.

Musa's grappling and desire to honor and understand both the perspective of her American general church leaders and her Setswana sense of right exemplifies her development of a plural consciousness, which requires "understanding multiple, often opposing ideas and knowledges, and negotiating these knowledges."[78] Some scholars see this multiple consciousness as a source of strength because of the concomitant ability to transcend simple dualistic thinking and binaries.[79] This ability to inhabit a plural consciousness allows Musa to maintain loyalty to the culture that nurtured her *and* the church that has given her a sense of purpose, community, and a personal relationship with God.

This incident ultimately illuminates a multifaceted type of agency, one that not only incorporates plural consciousness and a complicated mix of accommodation and resistance but also points toward a constant and specific end result: connectedness. For these women, many of whom have emerged from fractured families and experienced separations from their ancestral villages and ties, their agentive actions are often geared toward nurturing human ties and relationality. Forming and maintaining relationships, a value that is central to both a worldview of non-oppressive connectedness and to Joseph Smith's theology, are constant features of their moral centers. Thus, the idea of severing the bond between a mother and a child born out of wedlock was ultimately seen as incompatible with their moral framework. Musa, however, was able to step back from her immediate repugnance and recognize that adoption, though it entailed the severing of certain bonds, enabled the creation of other bonds between a child and her adoptive parents.

This moral center focused on relationality helps explain why Batswana women such as Musa have chosen to make their faith home in the Church of Jesus Christ of Latter-day Saints. Specific issues such as adoption do not resonate with these women, but many aspects of Mormonism do. A glimpse of Musa's larger story helps illuminate this central moral focus on creating and maintaining relationships and why the church felt empowering to her. Musa was the product of a fractured marriage. As a young girl, her father took her and her sister to live with him in the city. Her mother stayed in the village with the other six children. She was raised in the Zion Christian Church, an African independent church that emphasizes faith healing and prophecy. As a teenager, however, she became dissatisfied with her church and began to look for a new religious community. She found Mormonism at eighteen and loved the community and the relationship she was able to develop with a God who saw her as a beloved daughter. These relationships were emotionally and spiritually fulfilling, particularly in the face of her father's eventual death from AIDS and two of her brothers' deaths. The vision and goals that were promoted in Mormonism—a loving and present God the Father, men who are present and helpful as husbands and fathers, families who could be sealed together in life or after death to cement these bonds—were hopeful and resonated with her desire to create the bonds that she had lacked to some degree as a child. She went on to serve a mission and served as a Relief Society president. She has taught Institute, been in countless ward council meetings, and more.[80] In this Latter-day Saint community she has found a new family and village, one in which to minister to others, assume certain clerical roles, give sermons, and teach adults. This community, so often in flux due to high rates of church inactivity, needs and appreciates her skills and devotion. She has found a place of belonging here in which to nurture her spiritual relationship with God and also her social relationships with other Latter-day Saints.

Of course, Musa's opportunities to grow and serve in the Latter-day Saint community are not limitless. As a woman, her authority is bounded within the congregation, and as an African, she must confront Western notions that creep into Mormon practice. Although she recognizes these challenges and has found agentive ways to navigate their complexities—including resisting, complying, and developing a plural consciousness—she feels she is ultimately more nurtured than constrained in her Mormon practice in Botswana. When asked about the all-male priesthood, she did not emphasize the limitations of her opportunities as a woman. Rather, she emphasized her capacity for action and the possibility of thinking and acting beyond limits and constraints: "I feel that half the time as women we don't really appreciate the powers and effect that we have in the church and in communities we live in. . . . I think if we understand that, then we'll be able to understand bigger things that Heavenly Father has in store for us."[81] Musa acknowledges that women do not have the same opportunities for leadership that men do, and that the lack of those opportunities sometimes leads women to have more passive attitudes, but she wants women to resist that. She said, "Women turn to sit at the back and not actively take part in issues that affect them, maybe with the fear of how they would be viewed. We don't have to always prove ourselves; we just have to be ourselves."[82] Mormonism, even with its patriarchal priesthood-led framework, which leads some women to assume a passive role, has given Musa a sense of possibility, capability, and space to be her authentic self as she agentively participates in the work of the congregation and develops relationships with her fellow congregants.

Bridewealth

Bridewealth, also known as bride price or lobola, is a traditional wedding practice of Botswana, as well as several other African countries, in which the groom gives money (or traditionally in Botswana, cattle) to the bride's family. Negotiations over bridewealth are typically conducted by the uncles of the bride and groom, and they might, as mentioned above, involve considerable time and effort. It might also take the groom and his family years to accrue an acceptable amount.

I first learned about just how difficult this issue of bridewealth is for some Batswana Latter-day Saints when I spoke with Warona one day in Gaborone after church. Warona, a confident and eloquent woman in her thirties, wore a colorful head-wrap and spoke in a melodic voice. She grew up attending a Congregational church, but sometimes she also attended a Catholic church, since she was trying to find a faith community that felt right to her. She converted to the Church of Jesus Christ of Latter-day Saints at fourteen and is deeply dedicated, having served in many leadership positions. Her relationship with God is strong and close: "One thing that won't change is that He loves me. I know that for sure."[83] She has needed that close relationship to cope with difficult decisions and experiences, in particular, the death of her newborn. Warona, a professional in the health sector, is ambitious and capable, a born leader in every way. Her leadership skills were recognized by her government when she became one of the first women in the country to be a captain in the military. She has thrived in this position, though it has taken some effort for her to balance her prestigious career with the needs of her husband and children.

Warona, the wife of a chief who later converted to Mormonism, spoke at length about the important role the church has played in her life as it has centered her throughout her career path and family formation. She has found the church and its teachings to be empowering and enabling, as is evidenced by this anecdote, in which she speaks about her intuitive and sensitive spiritual powers and her bishop's encouragement to use them:

I get so in tune that Heavenly Father reveals specifics to me in dreams.
. . . However, when I do that, sometimes I get scared because I think it's a
glimpse of what I just might be capable of. . . . The counseling my bishop
gave me at that time was: it doesn't matter who you are when you are spiritually in tune; your spiritual blessings come to the surface. And therefore it
was for me to learn not to be afraid to use them, or go back to my Heavenly
Father and say, "What would you like me to do with this information?"
Trust in the answer . . . therefore Heavenly Father has provided that I am
able to meet those needs of people that he has let me see.[84]

Mormonism has given Warona space to nurture a deep sense of her own
potential and powers—a sense so profound that she is sometimes afraid of
this spiritual power and intuition. Her bishop's counsel has enabled her to use
her gifts with confidence and assume responsibility for seeing to the needs
of others. Warona's dedication to the church is evident throughout her oral
history, and her ultimate wish is to one day be sealed to her husband and
children in the temple.

This dedication to the church, however, does not lead to a passive acceptance of all church policies and dictates. She pointed to lobola as an issue
she had to carefully navigate, given her loyalty to both her Setswana culture
and her Latter-day Saint church leaders:

I personally struggled the very first time it was said—the particular situation of the lobola. It happened to be done away with. This is the bride
price, my dear, where we take cows to get married. It's a very big part of my
culture. I'm going to use these words. I felt offended that somebody white,
somebody who doesn't understand why that has been institutionalized,
can say, "Do away with that."[85]

Warona explained that a white area authority from the church had recently
come to Botswana and told them that bridewealth practices should be
ended.[86] This was an enormous point of struggle for her.

Church leaders such as Dallin Oaks have critiqued lobola as one of a few
"negative cultural traditions" in Africa that they would like to see end.[87] After
praising "the strong African family culture," he explained that his objection to
lobola is based on the fact that it delays marriage for returned missionaries:
"When a young returned missionary must purchase his bride from her father
by a payment so large that it takes many years to accumulate, he is unable to
marry or cannot do so until he is middle-aged."[88] With celibacy before marriage such an important marker of Mormon morality and with marriage as a
central theological concept in Mormonism—men and women must be married and sealed in the temple to achieve the highest level of exaltation—it is

not surprising that Elder Oaks would find this practice problematic. It is also true that at least one interviewed convert was able to marry far more quickly and less expensively than expected because she and her husband decided to follow church leaders' advice and abandon traditional wedding practices, much to the consternation of some friends and family.[89] Thus, in some cases church leaders' condemnations of lobola have actually increased marital options.

Yet other members, like Warona, struggle greatly with the critiques and characterizations of this practice by white church leaders. Walter van Beek points to some of the troubling implications of Oaks's discussion of lobola, writing that such a critique is rooted in a "Deseret model of membership" that church leaders are thrusting onto people in cultures that differ significantly from the culture in which American Mormonism is enmeshed.[90] Van Beek argues that "a blanket condemnation of bridewealth is culturally uninformed, especially when coupled with admiration for the African family," since bridewealth in Africa is a symbol of the supreme importance of the family and of women's fertility.[91] Perhaps church leaders have come to understand that African members find critiques by outsiders of such important cultural elements at least somewhat problematic. In 2015 the church produced a short video that features Black African area authorities and leaders encouraging members to abandon lobola. Elder Oaks's words are also featured, and in fact are quite central to the video, but the very fact that so many African leaders are echoing Oaks's stance against lobola might make injunctions against the practice more palatable to some, since these African leaders clearly know and understand the cultures from which lobola springs.[92]

Oaks's description of a returned missionary needing to "purchase his bride" indicates a common Western understanding and critique of lobola. This practice has also been criticized by some feminists, both Western and African, as dehumanizing to women because it reduces them to the status of property. Caroline White's study gives support to this interpretation: some of her informants told her that lobola in South Africa leads men to think they own their wives and the products of their labor and gives them the right to beat their wives.[93] Recent scholarship concerning lobola and gender-based violence in Zimbabwe confirms the link between the two.[94] The Motswana feminist scholar Godisang Mookodi believes that the problem of male violence goes deeper than bridewealth, though it is part of the problem. She finds the view that the male must be the breadwinner, an ideology that developed with the advent of the capitalist economy in the 1960s and 1970s, to be the primary root of male violence and gender inequality. She argues that women's reduced access to resources contributes to the problem of male violence toward women in Botswana.[95]

The critique of lobola as a justification for domestic violence is a serious one that should not be lightly put aside. Yet it is also important, as many postcolonial feminist scholars have said, to interrogate Westerners' impulses to "save brown women from brown men," as Gayatri Spivak notes.[96] She and others in her field have pointed out that far too often, these impulses have been used to justify colonial interventions.[97] These interventions have often led to war, increased vulnerability for women, and cultural changes the women themselves were not seeking. Although lobola has in some situations led to the commodification of women and a sense of entitlement to domestic violence on the part of men, postcolonial scholars warn Westerners wanting to charge in and fix the situation that caution is in order. As is discussed later in this section, other approaches, such as letting communities devise adaptations that honor the best of cultural traditions, should be considered.

In addition, some postcolonial feminist scholars emphasize the importance of listening to and highlighting the voices of women of the global South and their perspectives on various cultural practices like lobola.[98] As Marnia Lazreg asks in her article about the ethnocentric and cultural imperialistic dangers of Westerners writing about these women, "Is it possible to do scholarly work on women in the Third World that goes beyond documenting existing stereotypes? How does one put an end to the fundamental dismissal of what Third World women say when they speak a nonstereotypical language?"[99] In other words, is it possible to hear and respect such women's voices and perspectives when their words don't resonate with Western or feminist worldviews? As intersectional feminist scholars have argued so cogently, what is dehumanizing to one group of women from a certain race, class, and nationality might not be dehumanizing to another, given their particular social location and unique experiences.[100] For Warona, and for Naomi as well, who also mentioned lobola in a positive way, bridewealth is not about dehumanizing or purchasing women. It is about respecting them and honoring them for the enormous contribution they make to families. It is also about forging strong bonds between extended families. As Warona explains:

> When a man and a woman decide to get married, when families decide to join through their children, a family is made one big main thing. Culturally, women used to plough fields, you know? So therefore, the strongest woman, not necessarily beautiful, the strongest, hard-working, the most obedient was the one who would be the first to get married—the hardworking one. The concept behind it would be, "She's going to plough our fields and bear our children, so we need her to be strong to do this." Two families could not equate how strong that would be. Therefore, they would give an appreciation in [the form of] those cows for the exchange of this

caliber of person who they were getting. The man's family gives the cows to the woman's family.

My thing is this. Lobola becomes offensive when a white person is explaining it to you . . . how they interpret it. For them, it is just bride price. For me, it's a connection of families, it's a token of appreciation. And it's who I am. I was married on the 21st of December, 2012. In the Philippines, in Utah and South Africa, anywhere in the world, someone in Africa, somebody shares that date as a marriage date, somebody in the States. But, what makes my marriage significant is that on that day, we saw that token of appreciation go from his family to my family. The relations we make, the sounds we make of joy, of appreciation, of gladness, makes my 21st of December, unique. I attach it to that. Therefore, it was different.[101]

To Warona, bridewealth is a beloved cultural tradition that symbolizes how very valuable women are in families. To not have this property change hands would actually have been an affront to her dignity and worth as a woman.[102] "The payment of *lobola* is what accords a woman the powers and respect of being a wife," explains McDannell.[103] Moreover, Warona believes that bridewealth brings two families together. For her, bridewealth is not about purchasing a wife. Rather, it is inextricably tied to the formation of bonds between the bride's and groom's families. Warona's sense of the importance of forging connections between families and within her own family (her desire to be sealed in the temple), hallmarks of her worldviews of non-oppressive connectedness, is a driving moral force, and it has led her to push back against Latter-day Saint leaders' injunctions to abandon the practice.

At the same time, Warona has worked hard to reconcile her deep loyalty to the church and church leaders with her personal experience that lobola honors women. An additional difficulty is her husband's role as chief, which obliges him to perpetuate Setswana cultural traditions. As she related:

Now I've prayed to Heavenly Father to soften my heart in obedience. That's the most important. The Prophet, whoever he sends, his servants, are the soldiers, the people who sit on the tower and watch for the enemy coming. I had to literally think that he's seeing and therefore, he's sounding the alarm. I cannot see that far. Can I just trust that?

Another dimension to our particular story—my husband is the Chief. He's very connected to his cultural past. He's the spokesperson of culture. I think he struggled a little more. He thought, "Honey, what am I going to say to the people?" I said to him, "I don't know, but maybe it comes to you because you are the Chief, and because you can stand here and your voice can reach a greater number of people." And I had to trust. And pray for wisdom. My husband listens to me, Sister Caroline. To be able to say,

"You need to trust the very Heavenly Father who gave that commandment and let us not see the white man before we see the commandment, the servant of God, who says this is right.[104]

Much like Musa, Warona had to navigate a middle path between her identity and loyalty as a Motswana and her identity and loyalty as a Latter-day Saint. Given Botswana's status as a former protectorate, she clearly is aware of Western imperialism and the issue of "the white man" asserting power over Black people. At the same time, she believes in church authority structures that have for the most part placed white men in positions of ultimate authority and power. She can also see how lobola can, in fact, be problematic at times. She explains, "The thing with lobola, it is so commercialized, Sister Caroline. These principles I'm teaching you matter to me, but not to everyone. Some people are going to look at it this way: my daughter does not have a child. She grew up in the church. She is CEO. She's student body president, so that makes her more expensive because your daughter is quiet, humble. So you are putting price tags on people."[105] Like Musa and her grappling with the issue of adoption, Warona is able to see lobola from the perspective of church leaders and others who are critical of it. She, too, has developed a plural consciousness that allows her to understand both perspectives.

After much effort and prayer (she mentioned discussing this with her husband continually for a week) she and her husband carved out a path forward regarding this issue. Her solution involved a complex negotiation between her various loyalties to church, community, culture, and self: "After the heated conversations that ended in the evening, the following week is when we told [our children] what we had decided. At eight years old, [my daughter] knows that if her husband can give the lobola, fine and good, but we're not going to stop them from going to the temple."[106] Lobola is therefore still a possibility if the prospective groom is able to pay it, but being sealed has become the paramount consideration for this Latter-day Saint woman. She has shifted her focus away from lobola and toward the temple, with that now standing as the most meaningful part of the wedding. Yet she is also open to (and probably hoping for) lobola to be paid because of the concomitant meaningful tradition of two families coming together, if the groom and his family can find a way to do so. She has therefore, as Hoyt explains in her concept of simultaneous agency, found a way to navigate between her own desires and understandings and those of her church leaders. This navigation is especially complicated because of the moral world of traditional Setswana culture that she is simultaneously working to honor. Rather than dichotomous frameworks of agency that highlight resistance or accommodation to authority, Warona is enacting a kind of agency that simultaneously upholds and pushes against the injunctions of her church leaders, just as it also entails both upholding and pushing against this cultural tradition of Botswana. In this complicated dance to make room for both sources of authority, Warona holds fast to a particular moral core: that of the centrality of creating bonds between individuals and families, or in other words, a commitment to non-oppressive connectedness. She treasures the traditional practice of lobola because it is meant to bring families together. Likewise, she treasures Mormon teachings that focus on the temple because of the sealing ordinances that bind families together eternally. This focus on the importance of creating and maintaining relational bonds grounds her navigation and decision making.

Warona's story highlights the active (and sometimes tense) meaning making and negotiation in which African Latter-day Saints engage as they navigate their loyalties to their chosen religion and their home cultures. It also highlights some of the additional burdens that Latter-day Saints in the rest of the world shoulder when the "gospel culture" they have been led to embrace springs from Western or American culture.[107] As van Beek mentions in his article about African Saints, the Church of Jesus Christ of Latter-day Saints must do careful work to "define what is core and what is periphery—in its doctrine, ritual, and life of the ecclesia. . . . It might well be that for any type of second harvest—or first in the African case—local cultures will have to be allowed in. . . . Cultural forms as a way to muster local agency have to be given their proper place."[108] Both Philip Jenkins and Jehu Hanciles argue that the church's resistance to inculturation, the absorption of local customs into church practice, has significantly slowed the church's growth globally.[109]

Similarly, feminist Mormons of color, who critique both colonialist and sexist tendencies in the institutional church, also suggest caution in promoting a gospel culture that could very well erase important elements of cultural identity among Latter-day Saints outside North America. Gina Colvin, a scholar of Maori descent, articulates the cost to some Latter-day Saints when notions of a (North American) gospel culture are promoted: "The idea of a 'gospel culture' . . . seems to require a suite of cultural losses for those at the borderlands. Living in a singular, transplanted gospel culture that imposes a laundry list of behavioral expectations that are recognizable to the metropole but are a burden on the margins involves an existential violence."[110] Colvin suggests that rather than calling Africans out on their traditional culture, a better course would be for church leaders to take a careful look at their own Western traditions, which may be out of step with the gospel of Jesus Christ.[111] It is also imperative, she notes, for Western Latter-day Saints to allow local Latter-day Saints to adapt their cultures as they find appropriate and meaningful. Colvin's vision of an inclusive Mormonism that is actively working to limit Western and first-world cultural imperialism includes empowering international Latter-day Saint communities "to draw on their own dialogues, rather than being dependent on Salt Lake City, to make sense of who they are and the limits and boundaries of their community engagements."[112] This inclusive Mormonism would also "involve American-born Mormons listening to unfamiliar voices, and being open to new ways of thinking, making sense of the world, and remaining open to critique from those at the margins."[113] Warona's voice is a prime example of a marginal voice expressing an understanding of the value of a cultural tradition that is foreign to Westerners. Creating space for her and others to interact with their cultures and live their values as they see fit might indeed strengthen the church and increase its reach, because these communities will see space for them to embrace their traditional identities as well as their Mormon ones.

With Mormonism's hierarchical structure and centralized teachings, it is inevitable that American culture and values are exported to international Latter-day Saints. To dismiss Mormonism as a whole as simply a vehicle for cultural imperialism, however, as some scholars have done with Christian missionary work in the global South, does not do justice to the complex negotiating and navigating that international Latter-day Saints do as they meld this new faith with their unique contexts and values. As Ryan Dunch argues, dismissing missionary efforts by Westerners in the developing world as simply cultural imperialism actually invalidates the agency of people in those cultures who deliberately choose these religions and grapple with their doctrines and policies.[114] These converts, like Warona, are well aware of the possibility that Western culture might encroach on them in the form of church dictates, and they work to hold space for their values and culture as they simultaneously adopt a new religious worldview.

Companionate Marriage

Although some Latter-day Saint Batswana women embrace certain cultural traditions in the face of church opposition, such as keeping babies born out of wedlock and lobola, these women were also willing to critique other cultural patterns in Botswana they that felt were not helpful or life-enhancing. One theme that arose repeatedly was the women's attraction to the companionate, romantic, unified marriage that they heard Latter-day Saint church leaders espouse. These Western conceptions of marriage were somewhat at odds with traditional African marriages, which they described as less affectionate and less unified. In their willingness to critique traditional marital patterns in Botswana, these women were engaging in what the Ghanaian theologian Mercy Amba Oduyoye describes as a cultural hermeneutics, a cautious approach to culture that sees both its possibilities as "a tool for domination" and its possibilities for sustaining and enhancing life.[115] Oduyoye sees her cultural hermeneutics as combining a hermeneutics of suspicion (toward dehumanizing cultural practices) with one of commitment (toward that which is uplifting and enhancing): "The cultural hermeneutics being proposed combines both, as it shows African women taking a critical stance on African culture as well as promoting its commitment to wholeness and enhancement of life in the community."[116] This cultural hermeneutics is thus a way of "taking seriously the issues of continuity and change."[117] In other words, it enables a re-visioning away from African practices that women find damaging, while holding fast to African myths, symbols, and ways of being that sustain life.

A cultural element that Batswana Latter-day Saint women were willing to critique was traditional Setswana marriage dynamics. These converts to Mormonism, with its Western emphasis on loving, companionate marriage, wanted to step away from cultural norms of less unified, less affectionate, and less egalitarian marriage. Scholars of gender roles in Botswana have noted that there are traditional elements in Botswana's culture that lead to inequitable marriages. In her study of traditional marriage advice ceremonies in Botswana, Sibonile Edith Ellece found that the counsel for women "constructs marriage, as experienced by a woman, as a series of duties that she has to perform and sacrifices she has to make."[118] In contrast, grooms receive advice "characterized by contradictions in that while the advisers may seek to promote partnership and equality, they still predominantly articulate 'male dominance' discourse which promotes male superiority at the expense of women."[119] These ceremonies therefore have both egalitarian and non-egalitarian elements, but for Ellece, they ultimately "generate unequal power relations between spouses."[120]

Latter-day Saint teachings about marriage contain a similar mixed messaging of equal partnership and male predominance, as is evident in the previously mentioned Proclamation on the Family, which enjoins men to "preside" over their families while they simultaneously act as "equal partners" with their wives.[121] At the time of these interviews, Latter-day Saint temple rituals also subordinated women to husbands, though this subordination was qualified by the husband's righteousness.[122] Despite vestiges of patriarchy that are part of Latter-day Saint marital rhetoric, church leaders' statements over the past several decades have drastically downplayed male decision making and emphasized instead unified, loving, equal partnership-oriented marriages.[123] The 2019 changes to sacred temple ceremonies, which removed the women's covenant to hearken to their husbands, exemplify this shift.[124]

Batswana women who converted to Mormonism tended to see Latter-day Saint discourses emphasizing marital affection, love, romance, and unity as positive messages that enhanced their marriages and improved their relationships. Such ideas of marriage are canonized in Latter-day Saint scripture. Doctrine and Covenants 42:22 states, "Thou shalt love thy wife with all thy heart, and shalt cleave unto her and none else," and many church authorities constantly emphasize the importance of building and maintaining strong, affectionate, and unified marriages. This has been emphasized in the twentieth century in particular, as the loving nuclear two-parent family rose to prominence and replaced earlier Mormon notions of polygamous marriage, grounded more in faith and obedience than in love and affection. President Spencer W. Kimball described such companionate marriage and love in this way: "The love of which the Lord speaks is not only physical attraction, but also faith, confidence, understanding, and partnership. It is devotion and companionship, parenthood, common ideals and standards."[125] Kimball's description from 1949 is still quoted generations later, for example, at a 2000 General Conference talk by Lynn G. Robbins and a 2015 *Deseret News* article.[126] This kind of marital partnership is a centerpiece of Latter-day Saint teachings, affecting not only how couples treat each other now but also how couples conceive of eternity. Mormon doctrine teaches that couples that are sealed for eternity through priesthood rituals will be able to maintain their marriages and families in this and the next life. Establishing strong, loving marital bonds is therefore an important step toward building a loving eternal family unit. Married Batswana Latter-day Saint women in general described such teachings as helping them create closer, more loving marital bonds and even more equitable and partnership-oriented relationships with their spouses. These teachings resonate with their ethical paradigm of nonoppressive connectedness.

Sasha was one Motswana woman who spoke at length about her Mormon marriage and the ways she sees church teachings affecting her relationship. Sasha was a stylish woman in her thirties living in the capital city. She had a child with a boyfriend in her early twenties after she dropped out of university, and she converted to the church only a few years before our interview.

Sasha found the church at a time when she was looking for a change in her life. "Ten years of my life were basically intoxicated," she told me as she described her twenties as filled with alcohol and marijuana.[127] She grew up in a nonreligious home, but in her twenties she came to be interested in Christianity and Scientology. Before she joined the church she had started to experience dark and malignant manifestations, and when she talked to the Latter-day Saint missionaries, she felt they had a kind of benevolent spiritual power. Baptism, when they explained it to her, felt exactly right: a new beginning in a strict church that emphasized chastity and abstinence from alcohol. She also found comfort in the Book of Mormon: "I had spent so many months of turmoil, spiritual, emotional, mental confusion of things around me happening that I couldn't talk to anybody else. . . . So when I was reading the Book of Mormon, I felt so much at peace. And I just felt . . . soothed. . . . Then I got to 2 Nephi where it talked about how having faith in Jesus Christ, how our faith makes us alive in Jesus Christ. And I just began to understand then."[128] This was the new path she was looking for, a complete change from the life she had led before.

After her conversion, Sasha met and married a Latter-day Saint man. She attributes the difficulties in their marriage to differences in their cultures. She explained, "By cultural differences, I am referring to the fact that I grew up in a Western lifestyle, because my father is Western [European]. He [my husband] grew up in an African lifestyle."[129] When asked about her expectations versus his expectations for the marriage, she said:

> I expected him to hold my hand and kiss me and tell me he loves me and look me in the eye and say thank you. Not to tell me that the food is not cooked properly. But I learned later that in his culture, that they do those type of things. I still think they are wrong. He expected me to cook, cook, cook, cook, cook. My father is the one who cooks at home. [My husband] expected me not to talk openly about my feelings. Also things like telephones. I wanted to know what was going on in his phone. I didn't care about him going into mine. Just little things like that. Money issues too.[130]

Sasha was hoping for a romantic, affectionate marriage in which she and he would make unified decisions regarding money and in which there would be little secrecy. He, however, had envisioned a less emotive and more separate relationship, the kind that was, according to Sasha, common among more traditionally African Batswana.

This clash of expectations was difficult, at one point leading her to think that she might have made a mistake in marrying him. But they have begun to find a better equilibrium. A major factor in this new equilibrium is church teachings, which have seemed to lead her husband to treat her with more affection:

> He's a very stubborn guy. Pretty controlling. When I was talking to the Stake President, he felt like it was probably because he was protecting himself from the previous disappointment. So he wants to be in control

so he doesn't experience that again. But something happened at some point. I remember it was a Tuesday. He was coming home from a [church] meeting. When he came home, he was different. The difference made me nervous. I was like, "I hope it's not a woman making him happy!" But he was different. And I tried to trace the difference—he came from a meeting. He came with a *Strengthening Marriage* manual from the meeting. So I've just been observing and praying. He's being easier to get along with. . . . I fear him less now. I got to a stage where I was afraid of him, saying anything, because he would blow at anything.[131]

Sasha found that Latter-day Saint teachings were having a softening effect on her husband. The meeting in which marriage evidently was discussed and he acquired the *Strengthening Marriage* church manual prompted him to be more affectionate and less angry with his wife. It is also notable that the Latter-day Saint ecclesiastical structure gave Sasha an acceptable place to turn to communicate her worries about her marriage. The Mormon practice of discussing difficult issues with church leaders therefore provided Sasha with a meaningful sounding board and hope that perhaps in time, her husband's behavior might change and become more affectionate.

Now Sasha is actively engaging in ways to foster this improved equilibrium in her marriage, an equilibrium in which she feels like an equal partner who is heard and respected. She found in church teachings support for a more egalitarian, more unified marriage, though other Latter-day Saint teachings also led her to put her husband first in a way that her husband does not always reciprocate. This lack of reciprocity became clear as Sasha spoke of temple covenants she has made to put her husband first. She said, "For me, I have covenants to keep. I know that I put my husband first. Whether he does it or not, whatever the Lord expects of him, it shouldn't affect me keeping the covenants I've made at the end of the day."[132] Although Sasha did not elaborate on which covenants she was referring to, it is possible that she had the principle of sacrifice at the forefront of her mind as she navigates difficult moments of her marriage.[133] She is willing to endure the marital challenges that are before her, if that is what God wants, but as she said, "I want it to be a confirmed thing that [the challenge] was from the Lord. Not just this guy thinking that he can just do whatever and put me second."[134] Thus, while Sasha understands that religious covenants emphasize her duty to, as she says, put her husband first, church teachings have also taught her that she can expect God to confirm to her that his treatment of her is right. She also finds comfort in scriptures about marriage that instruct "that nothing should come before [a wife]." Church teachings have led Sasha to believe that she should sacrifice for the sake of the marriage and prioritize the well-being of her husband, but they have simultaneously empowered her to expect similar sacrifice and prioritization on her husband's part, as well as divine confirmation that God does, indeed, want her to patiently endure her husband's troubling behavior. Ultimately, Sasha felt that equality, affection, and unity are what God wants for them. Sasha's connection to God and her sense of healthy relational reciprocity and affection are important checks on church and cultural traditions that emphasize the husband's preeminence in the family.

Sasha exemplifies an agentive, creative proactivity as she works to establish this more unified and egalitarian marriage, often using church teachings as evidence that such a union is ultimately in line with God's desire for them and their relationship. She explained:

> I believe in us being united in absolutely everything. I automatically think that our accounts should be joint. When he was difficult with money, I felt like going out to make money, but I felt like that wasn't going to solve what I knew was the right thing, which was for us to be united in everything. To be equal. To consult one another. To consider one another. So I felt, no, I'm not going to get out and get a job. We need to sort this out. So that when I do go and get a job it won't make things worse, make me more independent. So I managed somehow, I don't know how. It was inspired. We got a loan to get another car. He had to wait for my consent. There was that meeting with the bank, and I asked about joint accounts. I wasn't trapping him. It just came all of a sudden, and we got a joint account, and I got inspiration that the Lord will bless us when we are united, when we strive to live a celestial law. Unity, the law of consecration, it's not just for us out there at church. It starts in families and in marriages. When the prophet talks about [a] spiritual dimension, I'm just beginning to understand what he means about that, and how to apply it in every single way—not just as theory, not just as a canvas over a tent, but even the air inside that tent the gospel penetrates and impacts.[135]

Within Mormonism's patriarchal framework, Sasha has found gospel teachings to support her conviction about unity and egalitarianism in marriage. In particular, she has found in the principle of consecration inspiration to live a completely unified life with her husband, even to the point of making sure they have a joint bank account, thus giving this non-employed mother open access to their funds and ensuring open communication about expenditures in the marriage. It is noteworthy that she has also found in this ideal of marital unity a reason not to become a breadwinner, because she feels that unity is more likely to come if they together discuss and compromise over expenditures, rather than earning separate funds and maintaining separate bank accounts as many other couples in Botswana do. Sasha has a difficult road to navigate as a stay-at-home mother working for equal financial say and access in her marriage, but she has found in some church teachings support for creating this kind of companionate and equal partnership-oriented marriage.

Sasha's words, and those of other women I spoke with, give us a window into the ways Western Mormon familial expectations—stay-at-home mothers, breadwinner fathers, and affectionate, unified relationships with mostly egalitarian decision making—are not always easy to overlay on various African cultures. Sasha, who self-described as more Western than African, is working to make this Western conception of affectionate companionate marriage with her husband as primary breadwinner a reality in her life. Other women I spoke with articulated why the breadwinner father/stay-at-home mother model was uncommon among Batswana church members. Charity, a woman who converted to the faith as a teen and then became inactive and had a baby with a boyfriend, said this about why stay-at-home motherhood is not always ideal for African women:

> There is this fear. As African[s] we have an issue of women being abused and needing to be on their own and needing to work so they are seen as independent. That comes through working so we don't have to depend on [a man]. It seems if you talk to most women being a housewife is least desirable because of her circumstances. Work makes us independent, out of oppression, and self-reliant.[136]

Her words resonate with Mookodi's observation that male breadwinning notions, which began to come into play in Botswana when the country adopted a cash economy, have led more toward oppression than away from it, because they often put women in a dependent position and at the mercy of husbands who may not be benevolent.[137] Apart from worries about oppression in single-earner marriages, circumstances are also such that many Batswana Latter-day Saint families simply need two income earners in order to have a measure of security in their lives.

Pearl is a Motswana returned missionary in her thirties living in the capital city and married to a Latter-day Saint man. She works full-time because her family needs her income. It has been hard for her because she would prefer to be at home with her young son, but at this point in time that is not possible. Perhaps one reason Pearl feels comfortable with the idea of being a stay-at-home mother is the egalitarian relationship she and her husband have established. Unlike many other couples that separate finances and do not openly communicate about money, Pearl and her husband lay everything out on the table:

> You know, a friend of mine came to me and asked, "Pearl, how do you deal with finances in your house?" I'm like, "OK, when we met, I wasn't working. He was working. So every time he would put the money on the table, or his pay slip, and say, 'OK, this is it. Let's just do it.'" When I started working, that's what I learned. . . . We do that all the time. We've been doing it for 7 years now. A friend of mine came to me and said, "You know what, I just have a hard time with this." So I said to her, it's because you are separated with your finances. That's why you are fighting over finances. Put it together on the table. Because if you don't earn much, it's hard to expect your husband to go buy you a car.[138]

Pearl has also established an egalitarian relationship with her husband in other ways. When asked whether she feels as though she and her husband (also a returned missionary) are equal partners, she replied:

> This one is not the hardest part for us, despite me being African. I know people get shocked a lot with the things that we do in our family. Because my friends will come to me and ask, "How do you get him to do this?" I don't get him to do anything. He just does things for me. Because when I do laundry . . . before the mission, he wouldn't do it, now he will just put it in the machine and we come and fold it together. We'll clean together, we'll bathe the baby. We do everything together. Even yesterday, he was busy with the car, and I just came and helped. We were laughing about how much we do together. He has those parts where he has to be a man. He knows he is expected to be, especially in leading the family in the gospel way. . . . He tries. He's really soft, not loud. Even if he was to correct us in the home, we can clearly see, ok, we can separate our duties very well—as a mom and a father, and as a leader and presider in the home. At the same time we can clearly do things together.[139]

Though Mormonism has taught the couple that the husband is leader and presider in the home, they have in practice established a helpful, companionate relationship. Her husband's role as presider does not, in Pearl's experience, translate into an oppressive situation. Although Mormonism perpetuates gendered norms and hierarchies within marriage, particularly in its rhetoric about presiding, on a practical level it also encourages men to helpful investment and cooperative behavior in the home. It also, in Pearl's case, helps the couple choose unified approaches toward finances and goal setting.

Even within the overarching frameworks of cultural and ecclesiastical patriarchy, women like Pearl and Sasha are calling on and finding elements in Mormonism that they feel are leading them to establish more unified and cooperative marital relationships. These emotionally intimate and unified marriages may be perceived as more Western than traditionally African, but Pearl and Sasha feel little conflict in cultivating these marriage patterns, which they see as productive and more satisfying. It is telling that they tend to attribute more egalitarian elements of their relationships to church principles and attribute less egalitarian elements to cultural factors. This echoes the words of many other Batswana Latter-day Saints who were interviewed, one of whom explained cultural patriarchy and church teachings in this way: "Traditionally you accept everything [your husband] says with no questions. Gospel-wise that is not the case . . . I am not commanded to obey. Sometimes people use scripture to justify this behavior but that's not the way. Love is the way to lead your home. . . . I started to realize that we are true partners."[140] This interview, as well as those of Pearl and Sasha, indicate that Mormonism is often providing men with new forms of masculinity that empower them as leaders and priesthood holders but also direct that empowerment, ideally, to helpful, affectionate behavior toward their wives, children, and ward family. With colonialism and globalization having often ravaged traditional modes of masculinity, Mormonism seems to be providing Batswana men with a softer and more cooperative male leadership role to inhabit.[141] This coincides with research by Henri Gooren and Taunalyn Rutherford, who find that Mormonism's emphasis on benevolent masculinity and family harmony often tempers more extreme forms of male dominance in Central America and India, respectively.[142]

Although many Batswana women found in Mormonism support for establishing primarily egalitarian marriages with their priesthood-holding husbands, it is notable that sometimes church teachings lead Batswana women to assume clearly subordinate positions to men in the family. When asked if women and men are equal partners in Mormonism, Meldrad, a woman in her late fifties, responded: "I know [my sons] have the priesthood. They hold the priesthood, so as they are right now I know I have to listen to them. I know I have to listen to what they say. Because now they have the power I cannot have as a woman."[143] Meldrad's understanding of men's preeminence in the family—and women's subordination within it—stems, at least in part, from Mormon notions of priesthood as providing special and particular access to God's authority.[144] It is likely that patriarchal Setswana notions that promote deference to men have also contributed to her assuming this subordinate position in relation to her sons. That she is older than Pearl and Sasha may also be a factor in her more traditional attitude.[145] Regardless, Meldrad's reflections about women's role and position in the home provide a glimpse of the starkly male-dominated family dynamics that might result when Mormon notions of patriarchy are layered on African ones. In the double discourse that Mormonism employs regarding gender roles in the home (women are both partners and those presided over) there is space for women like Sasha and Pearl to work for greater partnership and shared power in the home. There is also space, however, for women like Meldrad to believe that their duty as women is centered on submission and deferral to the priesthood-holding men in their lives.

Mormonism and Women's Empowerment in Botswana

Studies of women in Africa done by Westerners have often emphasized women's victimhood and oppression at the hands of men.[146] This focus has been critiqued by female African scholars, who feel that such a focus on oppression ignores the important sources of creativity, strength, and flexibility that African women can call on as they uphold the elements of African culture that enhance life and critique those that do not. My analysis finds that Latter-day Saint women in Botswana are proactively grappling with both cultural and church norms. As these women negotiate between these two moral authorities, they often find ways to honor both Latter-day Saint teachings and their home culture.

This negotiation between (Western) church culture and home culture is complicated by the church's strong centralized control, which tends to discourage local adaptation. This aspect of Mormonism, a strong emphasis on authority and hierarchy, is paired simultaneously and paradoxically with another hallmark of the faith: a strong focus on agency.[147] While these women in Botswana embraced notions of priesthood authority, both in marriage and in church hierarchy, they also were passionately dedicated to concepts of agency and personal revelation. Again and again, women with whom I spoke emphasized that one of the most important things Mormonism has given them was a deep connection to the Spirit, which consistently helped them make choices in their lives. Although the Utah-based church hierarchy inarguably determines many aspects of Latter-day Saint worship and morality throughout the world, this tight control is balanced out by teachings that personally empower Saints to pray and figure out for themselves the best way to lead their lives. This personal revelation does not facilitate changes to church policy, but it does enable Batswana Saints to exercise a flexible agency that sometimes privileges church injunctions, sometimes upends them, and sometimes does both simultaneously. Warona, for example, left her husband and eight-month-old baby with her parents for nearly a year when she became convinced that pursuing officership in the military was right for her personally and right for her family. Thus, within Mormonism's gendered framework, which emphasizes nurturing duties for mothers and breadwinning leadership duties for fathers, she found space, through personal revelation, to do what was necessary to take her career in the direction she strongly felt it should go. This theological emphasis on personal revelation is an important counterweight to institutional focuses that impose Western or American understandings on these Saints. One of the most powerful moments in our research trip occurred when a teenage Latter-day Saint from a small village told her interviewer that she believes God has black skin like hers and that God speaks Setswana. Despite institutional Latter-day Saint artwork that routinely depicts God as a European bearded male, her personal spiritual connection to God, so emphasized and prized in Mormonism, gave her room to envision a God who looks and speaks as she does.[148]

Warona's determination to succeed both professionally and spiritually was mirrored by many other women with whom I spoke. Mormon Batswana women as a whole were strivers, eager to succeed professionally and personally. This may be due in part to the fact that Mormonism is primarily accessible to Batswana who have some degree of education, because church leaders have determined that meetings be conducted only in English. Thus, Batswana who live in more rural and traditional areas, without as much education in English, are not able to participate in the church easily. Upward social mobility was, therefore, a theme in some of my interviews, as women either developed greater English fluency, discipline, and leadership skills via church membership or as women who were already drawn to these traits were attracted to Mormonism. For example, when she first joined the church, Meldrad said, "My English was very poor." However, as she began to give talks, teach lessons, and work in various leadership capacities, she said, "I started to see myself being able to speak. My tongue was very loose now to speak."[149] Confidence and skills she gained through her church service translated to confidence and skills in her work. She described her coworkers' respect for and reliance on her; they now prefer to "wait for her to come and decide" when difficulties arise.[150] Given that many of her friends and family members gave her a hard time for her decision to join a "white people" church, she feels proud that this decision has given her not only a close sense of connection with a loving God but also skills to succeed professionally. As McDannell notes, Mormonism can open up opportunities for global women:

"From English lessons offered by visiting female missionaries, to pamphlets on family finances, to loans to support education and training, the centralized nature of the church provides distinct benefits."[151]

For many of these women, emphases on striving, development, and progression enhance not only their work lives but also their communities and relationships, a result that resonates with their moral commitments to non-oppressive connectedness. Some women have outward orientations and are determined to help their communities in various capacities. Naomi, for example, has led workshops for parents of children with HIV, and Mary, another woman I met in Naomi's rural village, became an adult educator. She believes strongly that the women in her village need to become empowered through education, and she dreams of running "a woman's empowerment center" in which women share their traditional knowledge about plants and trees with one another and "entrepreneur [this knowledge] into a sustainable project."[152] Mary sees church teachings as liberating for women: "The church has taught me that women don't have to be oppressed. And I've taught myself too, that I don't have to be oppressed. The exciting thing about being a Mormon woman is that you are able to express yourself."[153] Rather than being shut down by church systems that privilege male leadership, Mary experiences Latter-day Saint teachings and systems as empowering. This devout Latter-day Saint exhibits a woman-centered orientation and perspective that might surprise secular feminists. Paradoxical as it may sound, Mormonism, with its gendered theology and America-based organization, has given Mary space and inclination to devote herself to women's opportunities and uplift in the greater community. Laurel Thatcher Ulrich commented that women can often create powerful and far-seeing projects and institutions when they have separate female-led and female-focused spaces.[154] The contemporary Relief Society maintains such a female-focused space, though it lost much of its financial, directive, and curricular autonomy to male-led priesthood direction in the twentieth century.[155] It therefore makes sense that Mary has found in Relief Society the inspiration to work and advocate for women in her community but that this effort is taking place outside of church-sponsored forums.

Although many of the most devout Latter-day Saint women in Botswana have discovered in Mormonism an empowering sense of personal connection to God and the Spirit, as well as a community with which to gather and minister, they do constantly engage in a complex navigation of their Mormon identities and their cultural identities. As Africans who are familiar with the injustice of colonialism and white Europeans asserting their will over them, these women are wary of Western cultural elements intermingling with church teachings. As one Latter-day Saint Motswana said in her interview, "I look at how people want to change themselves and become little Americans [in the church]. It pains me. . . . I don't want to lose my identity because of the Church. I need to be seen as a Latter-day Saint of Botswana."[156] When confronted with church teachings that are in tension with certain cultural understandings or ways of being such as the issue of lobola and adoption, many of these women work to find ways to honor both their home cultures and church teachings. They also are willing to reject certain elements of their home cultures such as less unified and affectionate marriages in favor of Western concepts when they feel that the latter are healthier and create better connections. Driven by their commitment to non-oppressive connectedness, these women are far from passive pawns, hoodwinked by either traditional culture or Western authoritarian religion. Rather they are deliberate thinkers and actors, carefully weighing where their priorities lie and finding creative ways to combine those priorities.

Latter-day Saint Batswana women at times choose to either modify or reject what they consider to be Western cultural practices or understandings within the church, but it is clear that this negotiation takes place predominantly on a personal rather than an institutional level. As women who for the most part are outside decision-making structures above the congregational level, they have little opportunity to shape more culturally sensitive approaches and injunctions within the Latter-day Saint church organization. They may react to church teachings and injunctions in a variety of ways, from full acceptance to outright rejection, but the reality of a priesthood-led church structure places the shaping of most policy and doctrine in the hands of men. Much like wives who, as pre-2019 temple covenants indicated, had the space to determine whether they ought to hearken to the words of their husbands, Latter-day Saint women have the space to determine whether or how much to accede to the instructions of their church leaders. But the ability to set agendas remains firmly in the hands of men, particularly those above the congregational level. Thus, structural constraints that privilege men at every level cannot be ignored. In their Latter-day Saint marriages, however, despite the theoretical agenda-setting power of husbands, Batswana women are finding resources within church teachings to establish more egalitarian marital relationships. The overwhelming emphasis on the part of contemporary church leaders on cooperation, affection, and joint decision making within marriage creates a counternarrative to older patriarchal notions of marriage. Many couples are using that counternarrative to create stronger and more unified partnerships.

The creation of non-oppressive and vitalizing connections in marriage, motherhood, friendships, town, and church, as well as with the divine, is an undergirding theme in these Batswana women's oral histories. As these women engage in complicated navigations of various loyalties, moral authorities, and worldviews, their agentive choices often lead to the formation or maintenance of relational bonds. Senses of responsibility, love, and concern for others center these women's moral lives, and when Latter-day Saint church practices or policies enhance those bonds, the women work to embrace them. Ultimately, devout Batswana women have found in Mormonism, despite its Western worldviews, a framework that often supports their spiritual, social, and personal desires to create healthy bonds. Sometimes alterations, nuances, and resistance play a part in their interactions with that framework, but women who are able to maintain their church activity develop expansive senses of their own spiritual abilities as well as social connections within and without their Latter-day Saint communities. In the face of the rapid societal change of the past few decades, change that has weakened traditional practices and relational bonds, Latter-day Saint communities in Botswana can function as new villages, giving Batswana women connections, frameworks, purpose, and rootedness.

These women's moral paradigm of non-oppressive connectedness takes on a distinct quality. It is often born of indigenous values and traditions involving motherhood and extended family relationships, but it is enhanced by the church's emphasis on family, church community, and a benevolent God. In the next chapter we move away from the global southern margins of the church to the margins within the center: the voices and stories of women of color in the United States, who live their lives in contexts of white privilege as the outsiders within. Although positive personal relationships are prized by these women, their non-oppressive connectedness paradigm often takes on a different resonance than those already explored, one focused on broader systems, as whole vulnerable communities fall into the scope of their moral concern.

CHAPTER 3

Privilege, Complexity, and Women of Color in the United States

The blond woman said, "I'm sorry, but I am not a racist. I have Black friends. And all you women of color are just making yourselves victims by focusing on the ways you're being oppressed."

It was the summer of 2015, and I, along with a few dozen other Mormon feminists, had gathered in the mountains of Utah to discuss the issue of race in the church. White Mormon feminists had begun to grapple with feminist intersectionality, the idea that gender is only one of many oppressions that are inextricably linked in the lives of women of color. These white Mormon feminists had started to reach out and create bonds of trust with Mormon feminists of color, inviting them to write in blogs and publications about race and class in their lives. This meeting in the mountains, though dominated numerically by white feminists, included eight or nine women of color. We had just begun the conversation and were going over concepts of white privilege and racism as a system of oppression from which white people benefit. The moderators had asked about white people's unconscious privilege and how we could set out to be better allies to women of color.

That's when the blond woman spoke. Her words made my breath catch in my chest, and her defensiveness filled me with dread. One moderator, a woman of Pasifika heritage, spoke personally about how this dismissive comment made her feel as if her experiences and perspectives were not being heard. Yet the woman cut her off again and again, insisting that the whole premise of this conversation was flawed and that she herself was colorblind. Eventually an older Black woman demanded that the woman stop talking and listen, to no avail. What proceeded next was one of the most uncomfortable hours of my life as this white woman refused to listen to the perspectives of women of color.

In an extreme form, this incident reflects a common experience for women of color in the United States: the sense of not being heard by the privileged white majority. These feelings of invisibility take on an increased resonance for some American Latter-day Saint women of color, and in particular those who are sensitive to questions of structural power and privilege. These Saints not only observe women's exclusion from sites and circles of institutional Mormon power; they also see exclusion from those same seats of power because of race. They confront the reality of a double exclusion and disappearance within their faith communities because Mormonism's highest positions of power, those of prophets, seers, and revelators, remain overwhelmingly in the hands of white men.[1] But this concern about invisibility goes beyond current institutional church hierarchies. They extend into theological and cultural realms. As Janan Graham-Russell recounted, seeing Latter-day Saint depictions of fair-skinned Jesus surrounded by hordes of white angels makes her, a Black woman, feel invisible. "This is how my fellow saints see the eternities," Graham-Russell said. "I felt that my brothers and sisters didn't see me—not only on a cultural level but on a theological level."[2]

Black Latter-day Saint women such as Graham-Russell also confront the troubling history of the Church of Jesus Christ of Latter-day Saints with respect to race. Church founder Joseph Smith did ordain a handful of Black men to the priesthood before his death in 1844, but his successor Brigham Young in 1852 initiated a practice of denying ordination to Black men and access to crucial temple rites to Black women and men.[3] This policy remained in place until 1978, when what is commonly referred to as the priesthood ban was lifted. During that 126-year span, however, disturbing rationalizations for the ban made their way into Mormon discourse and writings.[4] These rationalizations often posited that Black people had been cursed as the "seed of Cain" or that they were less valiant than people of other races in their pre-earth life.[5] The church has only recently, and with little fanfare, repudiated these teachings on its official website, and it has never apologized for them.[6] Thus Black members even today might be confronted with these troubling justifications for the ban, which live on in old but popular Mormon-authored books and in the minds of some church members.[7]

Much has been written about Blacks and the priesthood in the church, the vast majority focusing on the ban for Black men. In recent years, many Black American Latter-day Saint women have emphasized that this ban did not only affect men; under its edict all Blacks, male and female, were banned from attending the temple, denying them essential rites and blessings that cut them off from exaltation in Mormonism's highest heavenly realm.[8] One writer suggests that constant references to the priesthood ban make invisible the suffering of Black women under this policy. She suggests renaming it the "priesthood-temple ban" or the "exaltation exclusion" in order to reflect the breadth of exclusion fostered by this policy.[9]

Although Black American Latter-day Saint women have a particularly heavy burden to carry, other women of color in America, including those of Indigenous American descent, sometimes also feel the weight of Mormon history as well, which saw nineteenth-century white Mormon expansion into Native American territories. Notably, the church did offer those of American Indigenous descent a place in Mormonism's cosmology as a branch of the house of Jacob known as the Lamanites, whose skins were turned dark in their unrighteousness.[10] In earlier times Latter-day Saints tended to believe that all people of American Indigenous descent sprang from this branch of Jacob, and many Native American, Mexican, and other Central and South American Latter-day Saints embraced the promises given to the Lamanites in the Doctrine and Covenants, namely, that they would ultimately "blossom as the rose."[11] The Book of Mormon also gave them stories of noble ancient Lamanites to hold up as exemplars. Mormonism's theological perspective on Indigenous Americans therefore has both empowering and disempowering aspects.

This mixed history regarding Mormonism and race is reflected in the mixed experiences of people of color in American Latter-day Saint congregations. For non-white people who attend predominantly white wards, questions of power and privilege might arise if people of color are not fully embraced and incorporated into ward leadership and fellowship. People of color who attend wards based on language or ethnicity, however, often find space to combine ethnic pride and Mormon beliefs as they see people of color take leadership positions and find opportunities to foster and perpetuate their native languages and some elements of their culture.[12]

Latter-day Saints of color may find elements of Mormonism's mixed history and theology that are troubling, but they also find elements which empower. The Book of Mormon asserts that "all are alike unto God," and Latter-day Saint scripture holds up as ideal a Zion community characterized by unity and righteousness with "no poor among them."[13] For some of these women, however, questions about all being alike unto God present themselves when they see that the most revered and powerful general leaders are white males. Separated by gender as well as by race, these women sometimes wonder if they have a valued and honored place in the church. Many Latter-day Saint women of color nonetheless persist in their church activity, finding certain social and theological elements of the church so compelling or transformative that they downplay questions of race and gender.

This chapter explores the intellectual and spiritual navigation that Latter-day Saint women of color in the United States perform as they find ways and reasons to embrace this historically white Mormon tradition as their own.[14] It also explores the ways in which Mormon teachings, particularly those focusing on gender and race, impact these women. As many intersectional feminist scholars have pointed out, policies and emphases that affect middle- or upper-class white women in one way might have different impacts on women of color, who often must navigate racial and class oppressions, as well as those relating to gender.[15] Patricia Hill Collins describes the interlocking nature of oppression, noting that "oppression cannot be reduced to one fundamental type and that oppressions work together in producing injustice."[16] This chapter considers the intersecting forms of oppression that Latter-day Saint women of color in the United States have faced and how the church helps or hinders female members navigating lives without white or class privilege.

Using the twenty-one oral life histories conducted in the United States, as well as other published narratives of Latter-day Saint women of color, I argue that a dominant focus of their worldview of non-oppressive connectedness is the elimination of oppression rather than the promotion of a type of gender equality that emphasizes the importance of women and men assuming the same roles in society—though gender equality is also a concern for some, especially those who identify as feminists. Many of those I interviewed—some American, some new to the United States, representing a variety of ethnic and racial backgrounds—have found in the Church of Jesus Christ of Latter-day Saints spiritual, theological, and social resources for resisting oppression. Others, however, have found that the church has at times contributed to oppressive rhetoric, ideology, and practices. As these women discuss race, class, and gender, they describe the ways in which church rhetoric and policies affect them differently than their white brothers and sisters, thus underscoring the issue of white and class privilege that inevitably undergirds some Latter-day Saint discourse. A key coping mechanism for many is to reject black-and-white thinking, embrace ambivalence, and affirm the humanity and fallibility of church leaders. Another is to prioritize their own spirituality and divine connectedness, which may at times lead them away from typical Mormon understandings or practices. For them, the Mormon concept of personal revelation is paramount.

When compared with their sisters in the global South, these women's worldview of non-oppressive connectedness takes on a slightly different dimension. Like women around the world, women in the United States discuss interpersonal abuse and the ways Mormonism both helps and hinders the creation of strong, ennobling relationships with others. But many also emphasize larger issues and articulate concerns with systems that disempower the vulnerable. We therefore see in these women's stories a new layer in this moral paradigm, as women push against structural oppression as well as personal oppression.

Privileging Freedom from Oppression Over Gender Equality

On a cold November evening in New England in 2016, I stopped by Samantha's apartment to interview her. She was a member of the same small ward I attended during my five-month stay on the East Coast. Her apartment was tidy but happily chaotic as her two-year-old ran around, sometimes with no diaper on, and her husband wrangled the boy to finish his dinner while also juggling their newborn daughter. Originally from Cape Town, South Africa, Samantha and her husband Thomas had been in the United States for several years while he earned his graduate degree. Samantha is what is known as Cape Coloured, a person of mixed African, white, and Asian descent. She grew up in the Church of Jesus Christ of Latter-day Saints because her mother converted when Samantha was a small child. Thomas is a white South African who, after years of investigating the church and dating Samantha, joined the church before their marriage.

A dominant theme in Samantha's oral history is her experience of and concern with oppressive societal structures—no surprise given South Africa's brutal past as an Apartheid government. She returned to this theme repeatedly. As she discussed her parents' lives in Apartheid and post-Apartheid South Africa, she noted the societal inequities that kept her parents poor: "They worked very hard their whole lives but they will always be poor because they were born at a distinct disadvantage. No amount of hard work will ever make up for those huge disparities and structural inequalities."[17] For her mother, joining the church in the 1980s was an act of self-determination. She had felt that other churches were not a good match for her, but Latter-day Saint missionaries' lessons gave her a sense of peace and authenticity that she had not experienced for a long time. That the missionaries were both white was not a problem, particularly since the tiny branch was filled with Coloured people. The family's move to an area where the local ward included white people brought more challenges. Though most white Latter-day Saints were kind, the family could sense the preference for white people, and tellingly, the ward leadership was almost always white.[18] This dynamic led at times to situations in which the congregants felt misunderstood, unappreciated, or not heard by the leadership when Black or Coloured people would talk about some issue they were struggling with. Samantha mentioned that her mother's affiliation with the church was not always easy. She said, "There were periods where she didn't take us [to church]. I can see now that racial tension was definitely one of the issues, especially when we moved from the Coloured ward into the mixed ward."[19] Samantha has lived most of her life in a context of racial prejudice, both inside and outside the church, and she freely acknowledges the negative effects it has had on her and other Black or Coloured people. She places great hope in the younger generation: "I'm so thrilled by the 30 years and youngers who are . . . calling it [racism] for what it is. They are seeing it and they are acknowledging it. They are saying this happened. This is a real thing. Let's stop not talking about it. This is very encouraging. We are moving in the right direction."[20]

At the time of our interview, Samantha's dedication to her Mormon faith and her desire for less oppression in the world did not produce much tension for her. She found Mormonism "quite liberal, compared to other Christian faiths. And other faiths in general too."[21] She located this liberality in much of the way gender is approached in the church. She explained, "In Mormonism, generally speaking, men and women have the same dress standards, the same modesty standards, same chastity standards. So I like that. That's kind of liberating."[22] She spoke from experience; she spent months dating a Hare Krishna who wore sweat pants and sneakers to their religious meetings while she wore formal saris and jewels, in accordance with dress expectations for women.

But more than anything, Samantha found Mormonism's focus on a strong nuclear family hopeful, liberating, and likely to lead to a less oppressive situation for women. Coming from a context of poverty and systemic racism in which state policies affected the ability of people of color to form stable families, Samantha sees how male abdication and unwed teenage pregnancies mar the lives of both mothers and children:

> Growing up I've seen many single-parent families. Within my own extended family, I've seen people having babies when they are teenagers, not getting married, not staying married. I've just seen so many discarded children. I've seen so many children without a place. I've seen so many women so overwhelmed by their responsibilities of having to do family life all by themselves. So many. Especially in my extended family. These children often they get raised by granny, and mom drops out of school more times than not. . . .

These moms are stuck because they need to stay near their own mothers to help raise the children. So they end up just never being able to go and find their own way, their own path. I feel like there's freedom in marriage relationships in that . . . when you have the burden to share it, it frees each other up to do more than just the children. I see the wisdom in that. I know it's not always possible. We're talking about an ideal here. I know it's not always possible. And I know in some cases it's not always the best choice to be married just for the sake of marriage. But I do see the wisdom and the freedom that having that permanent shared responsibility gives to both the parents. I see the wisdom in children having a strong sense of roots and knowing who they belong to.[23]

She is keenly aware of the suffering that often arises when parents abdicate their responsibilities. Both her parents were "discarded children" who suffered as a result of not having invested parents looking out for their children's well-being.

Samantha's words about women finding freedom in stable marriages reflect the point that many intersectional and postcolonial feminists make: that oppression and liberation are experienced differently by women because of their particular positionality and experiences. Samantha's sense of liberation in her strong marriage is born of her specific context, in which she saw women trapped when they did not have a helpful male partner dedicated to raising children. This experience mirrors those of women in other contexts where poverty and male abdication are common. Colombian women whose husbands converted to charismatic evangelicalism, for example, reported a distinct increase in their quality of life as men became far more invested in the welfare of the family.[24] For Samantha, the Mormon emphasis on strong, involved, loving husbands and fathers leads to more freedom and possibility for women. This stay-at-home mother might be inundated with caretaking tasks, but she knows the day will come when her children will be in school and she can pursue her dream to be a choral conductor. As she said, a good marriage in which two people are dedicated to the well-being of the children gives mothers the opportunity to dream big and pursue their personal goals. She is determined to restart her musical career, and she has utter confidence that her husband will support her in that goal: "I know that when this [raising small children] is done he will fully support me doing whatever I need to do, whatever that is, whatever that might look like. So it's okay. There will be an end."[25] Single parenthood, on the other hand, is, in her experience, an oppressive situation that stifles women's dreams and opportunities.

Critiquing oppression and finding liberation, even in institutions such as marriage that sometimes are not viewed as liberating, is an overriding theme in Samantha's oral history. She has worked to ensure that her marriage is non-oppressive, even as she embraces the theoretical Latter-day Saint positioning of husband as presider over his wife and children. For Samantha, this position has nothing to do with ultimate decision making; rather, it is related to ultimate responsibility before God:

> I don't find the man presiding as a threat to me. It doesn't threaten my authority in the home. It does not mean he has ultimate decision-making power in our marriage. I have heard him say that he doesn't have the ultimate say in everything. But he feels like he's going to have to answer for things in a different way than I will have to. He feels like his stewardship is slightly different, that the way he's going to be held responsible for us is different than the way I will be held responsible for us. . . . I can see that.[26]

Samantha explained that she felt that her husband's responsibility to preside entails his needing to ensure her personal happiness, as well as that of the children, while her main stewardship role is the children's well-being. In that way, Samantha interprets her Mormon marriage with a male presider as egalitarian in practice, with the presiding aspect a primarily theoretical idea of greater responsibility before God for the entire family's success.

Samantha does not love traditional Mormon gender roles, but she understands that they, as set forth in the Proclamation on the Family, "are most likely to bring the most benefit to society."[27] And she finds a certain amount of flexibility in these gender roles. She believes that they do not (or should not) constrain or limit women's abilities and potential. She said, "Fathers providing for the physical needs of the family first and foremost and spiritual leadership, that does not feel like an absolute to me, not even slightly. Nope. My mother was a spiritual leader in my home growing up, so I have grown up with an example of a spiritual leader being the woman in the home."[28] Mormon gender roles position men as providers and spiritual leaders, but Samantha sees flexibility built into that system, and she also sees men as being highly capable nurturers, saying that nurturing is not "exclusively a woman thing. Not even remotely."[29]

Some ambivalence is apparent in her discussion of gender roles—a certainty that the husband's presiding does not infringe on her prerogatives, but also a clear desire for flexibility in the way those roles are performed. But one clear takeaway from our discussion is her commitment to critiquing oppression, while believing that liberation can be present in situations in which men and women do not have the exact same roles and opportunities. Her commitment to non-oppressive connectedness is embodied in both her critique of racist systems as well as her reflections on her partnership-oriented marriage.

This particular moral orientation—the focus on freedom from oppression rather than the dissolution of gender roles—was echoed by Claire, an American woman of African and European descent. I met Claire, a bubbly stay-at-home mother of four young children, during my stay on the East Coast. She grew up in Southern California in a troubled family. Her Mormon Samoan stepfather, who introduced her and her mother to the church when she was very young, was physically abusive at times. He also prevented her from acknowledging her African American heritage: "I was told my whole life to be Samoan, act Samoan, and tell everybody I was Samoan. And I was never allowed to be who I was."[30] It was a rocky childhood, but she now sees the good in this man who, at twenty-two, married a woman with three children. As she said, "He has this huge heart, a huge willingness to love, but the reality of it was he was twenty-two and he married a whole family. His parents were very physical and their parents were very physical and there were nine siblings in his family. Of them he was the least physical, the kindest, and the gentlest."[31] "Physical" is Claire's euphemism for physically violent.

Coming as she did from a difficult situation that was oppressive in its violence and in its insistence that she bury her African American heritage, Claire has found happiness and a feeling of liberation in her marriage to a nice, reliable Latter-day Saint man. She said, "It's been a phenomenal marriage. Every dream came true. He is old Mormon stock. He is really unexciting to the outside person, but he has this huge wonderful heart. People didn't understand how I could marry such a boring guy. But he is everything I never had—stable, peaceful, loving, supportive, kind. He's just an incredible friend and partner."[32] In her traditional marriage, in which she has assumed the caretaking role and he the provider role, she feels respected, appreciated, and nurtured by her husband. She related that he "does everything I do at home. Laundry, dishes, etc. He respects the lifestyle I lead at home. There's nothing that is above him. There's nothing that he doesn't encourage me in. I'm part of a gourmet cooking group; he encourages me to get out. I do yoga at night. He sends me out the door. He's totally supportive and helpful with the kids."[33]

Given her very happy marriage, Claire has no problem with the familial and ecclesiastical male leadership roles laid out by the church, so long as they are performed with love and benevolence. She likewise has no problem with the idea that women should be the primary nurturers. This arrangement has given her family peace and balance. The desire for women's equality, defined as men and women having the same breadwinning and ecclesiastical roles, does not resonate with her. She said, "I know some people really have issues that women aren't the bishops or aren't the stake presidents or aren't the financial clerks or whatever. I think they are fully capable of all those things. I think, just like the scriptures we have, it's a patriarchal society."[34] Claire accepts this fact and stated that she is more interested in balance than equality. "I don't think we need to do everything they do to feel—I surely don't, maybe some people do—to feel appreciated and fulfilled and sustained. I think that we do have different roles. I think we do have different strengths and talents and I think we enjoy doing different things. . . . So I think it's not so much equalness as balance that's important to me. And uplifting each other."[35] Within Claire's gender complementarian framework, which privileges men with types of leadership that are unavailable to women, is ample space for her to reject oppression and violence. She rejects a world in which people put down other people because of their identity, race, or gender. As she said at the end of her interview, intolerance or verbally "bashing" others is totally unacceptable. She has profound respect for two gay men who stepped in and took care of her sister's children when her sister was going through a rough time in her life. Claire explained, "In my eyes they are more kind and loving and they have incredibly good nonjudgmental Christ-like souls, and I don't understand why people need to gay bash or race bash or any bash. . . . People are allowed to have their own ideas and feelings and own lives and are allowed to be who they want to be. That's why we're here. We're here to choose our own path."[36] Tolerance, the importance of authenticity, and a rejection of abuse or oppression center her oral history, alongside her belief that true partnership and power sharing can exist in complementarian marriage.

The complexity of Claire's positioning with regard to gender roles became evident when she discussed her dreams for her future. She envisions someday working with an empowerment organization for girls. She had recently discovered the Girls Rule Foundation, and she loves their vision and activities: "They teach them about a lot of important women in history and what they did. They teach them self-affirmation, how to build yourself up when people are putting you down, how to own who you are and how to embrace it. They have an entrepreneur class as well—how to make a plan and follow it through. It sounds really awesome."[37] Claire may embrace traditional Mormon gender roles in her home and church, but her allegiance to those roles and that ideology has not prevented her from embracing feminist-friendly organizations that uplift, empower, mentor, and encourage girls to become leaders in the community. Claire's enthusiasm for this organization is undergirded by her commitment to reject oppressive situations and work against them. Organizations such as this one align with her convictions. Notably, Claire, who is clearly aware of oppression and abuse in families and in society, does not experience Mormonism's gendered practices as oppressive. Rather than focusing on issues of power and equal opportunities for women in the church, she emphasized the way the church has helped her build uplifting and cooperative relationships. As with the women I spoke with in Mexico and Botswana, Claire's moral priority is to foster non-oppressive connectedness. In her loving and supportive marriage she has experienced a freedom, happiness, and stability that she had never known before.

Beth, a woman I also met in my East Coast ward, likewise emphasized her concern with and experience of oppression. Beth is a Black woman in her sixties who is considered a well-loved matriarch in the ward. I interviewed her one Sunday after church, as we sequestered ourselves away in the Family History room of the ward building while her adopted teenage children chatted with friends and played in the hallway. Beth came to the United States in 1990 from the Caribbean, where she experienced a devastatingly abusive marriage. She said, "[My husband] used to beat me up. Once he punched me in my stomach. I was pregnant and I lost the baby."[38] The abuse became so awful that at one point, she recalled, "This thought came to my head: feed him rat poison. And when that came into my thoughts, that's when I realized I needed to get down on my knees and pray. I wasn't going to let him kill me. I was going to kill him first."[39] She did not use the rat poison, but on the next day she did determine once and for all to escape the marriage. She explained,

> I was sitting on the couch and he just called my name. You know when you are afraid of someone? He called my name and I was sitting on the couch, and I jumped so hard that the baby went up in the air so I had to catch the baby. With that I turned around and put the baby on the couch, and then I kneeled down and prayed. I just prayed and prayed. When I got up I knew I had to leave because this calm came over me and the Spirit said, "You have to go." So I started packing up things, things he wouldn't notice.[40]

Beth soon ran away from her husband. She then moved to the United States to become a domestic worker for a wealthy family.

Beth found the Church of Jesus Christ of Latter-day Saints in the early 2000s. It was not an easy conversion because she had grown up attending Methodist, Seventh-day Adventist, and Pentecostal churches on the islands and had a difficult time believing everything that was being taught to her about Joseph Smith. Yet a dream convinced her that she needed to be baptized despite some of her reservations. What she appreciates most about the church, she said, is "how simple it is. You can tell the leaders love Jesus Christ and Heavenly Father so much. But they are not loud about it. They are not boastful about it. It's just the way they carry themselves and the ways they speak. If you listen to General Conference, they are so humble. So much humility. For example, Brother Eyring. Since I joined the church, I don't think he has spoken once without crying."[41] One of her primary attractions to the church, in addition to the peace and the presence of the Spirit she feels inside the church building, is the demeanor of its male leaders, whom she sees as gentle, humble, and loving. Given her experience with her domineering and violent husband, these Latter-day Saint men strike her as the opposite of oppressive and cruel—in touch with their feelings, concerned about kindness, and Christ-centered in their convictions. Like Claire, freedom from oppression and violence, as well as the freedom to be herself, were dominant moral concerns: "I always say that you have to be yourself. I don't want to change who God made me. I want to be exactly what He made me."[42] In her ward, dominated at the leadership level by white men, she has found space to embrace her authentic self and to feel God's love. Gender roles and race are not factors that concern her. As she said when asked about being Black in the church, "You don't come to serve the church. You come to serve Jesus Christ."[43] For Beth, power structures and hierarchies within the church were secondary to developing that connection with Jesus.

Beth's, Claire's, and Samantha's focus on rejecting various forms of oppression in homes and societies, rather than fixating on gender equality, is a priority that womanist scholars have long promoted. In 1983 Alice Walker coined the term *womanist* to describe a Black feminist or feminist of color.[44] Rather than embracing the term *Black feminist*, womanists such as Walker wanted a term that would allow them to define and articulate goals particular to the experiences and priorities of women of color. A key element of womanism is its commitment to the well-being, uplift, and survival of "entire people, male *and* female."[45] This concern for both men and women in communities of color and the desire to oppose "all oppression based on race, sex, class, sexual preference, physical ability, and caste" necessarily involve focusing not simply on gender-based inequities but on all the varieties of oppression that characterize the lives of women of color.[46] This sweeping focus on various oppressions and the desire to resist them are likewise echoed in Katie Cannon's description of her womanist writings, which are "a call for action wherein the individual social-self as well as the larger collective community can break out of brutal cycles of misery and violence."[47] In its dual emphasis on building community and critiquing oppression, womanist thought has some resonances with a paradigm of non-oppressive connectedness.

Breaking out of cycles of misery and violence is a theme in the oral histories I conducted with women of color in the United States, and it is also a theme in the writings and speeches of American Latter-day Saint women of color who have spoken publicly about their primary moral concerns. Catherine Stokes, a Black woman who joined the church in 1979 in Chicago, believes that racial violence is a more critical issue than gender exclusion. In her opinion, racial violence must stop in order for women and men to rise together as a community. The journalist Peggy Fletcher Stack quotes Stokes in her article about these women's thoughts about racism and sexism: "The war on young black men is 'documented by dead bodies,' Stokes says. 'And if black men are not free, then we—men and women—are not free.'"[48] Stokes went on to say that comparisons between the way Latter-day Saint women are treated in the church and the way Black people were treated including "lynching, the rape of the black women from the time they got off slave ships, burning crosses, the death of [those] who were struggling for the rights of black people" is "deeply hurtful." As Stack concludes, "racism is a greater priority" for Black Latter-day Saints such as Stokes.[49] Moreover, white feminists who compare their experience of marginalization and inequality in the church with the experiences of Black people, according to Stokes, miss the mark.[50] For her, as for many of the women I interviewed, oppression and violence take primacy over gender role constraints.

In my interviews, Latter-day Saint women of color often described mixed feelings about working for gender equality within the church. The issue of oppression and violence tended to be more pressing for them, though the handful of feminists I interviewed were committed to gender equality along-side the elimination of other oppressions. Women such as Claire and Beth worked to eliminate and escape from oppression, but their gazes tend to be more focused on the level of personal relationships than on the societal level. They feel that Mormonism, with its gendered teachings and policies, gives them tools on the personal level to reject oppression and expect or require non-oppressive interactions with men in their lives. Samantha also appreci-ates these tools within Mormonism for fostering equal partnership with her husband, but she pointed to some larger structural issues in both society and church that lead to some oppressive situations. Thus, as Paulette Payne discusses in her work on a community of Black Latter-day Saint women in the South, Mormonism has pros and cons for women of color.[51] It promotes an intense if solemn religiosity, gives women their own space to enact that religiosity, and supports strong families. Yet as Payne points out, contem-porary Mormon practice and rhetoric tend to not emphasize the larger is-sues of social justice and the elimination of structural oppression, a moral focus that some Black women missed.[52] Ultimately, these women's stories and perspectives serve as important checks on white Mormon feminists who focus on gender equality to the detriment of more comprehensive analyses of oppression.[53] They also demonstrate a slightly different emphasis within the paradigm of non-oppressive connectedness. Forming good relationships is still a priority, one which Mormonism often helps them foster, but many of these women's discussions also reveal an awareness of larger systems that harm whole communities. Their reflections on vulnerable communities brings the issue of structural oppression into their moral framework.

Privilege and Standpoint

Although many women of color in the United States spoke of the ways in which Mormonism gave them tools for rejecting oppression and helping foster healthy connections, some also spoke about the times when Mormon discourse led to feelings of marginalization and alienation. Often, these moments centered on recognition that their realities were not acknowledged in the discourse of their fellow Latter-day Saints and that embedded in that dominant discourse were privileged assumptions. Paying attention to these moments and stories is valuable, since they illuminate the particular vulnerabilities that Latter-day Saint women of color face in homes, wards, and the larger society, vulnerabilities that might not be immediately obvious to many white church members, leaders, and feminists. The stories and insights of women of color uncover the privilege, race-based and class-based, that sometimes underscores contemporary Mormon gender discourse. This section explores some of the ways institutional Latter-day Saint rhetoric, particularly gender rhetoric, falls short for some women of color in America as they navigate diverse racial and class landscapes.

According to Peggy McIntosh, white privilege is "the invisible package of unearned assets" of which white people are often unaware.[54] These are unearned privileges extended to white people beyond what is extended to non-white people in similar political circumstances. These privileges include things such as expectations of seeing people of one's own race represented in textbooks, not needing to coach children about systemic racism to protect their lives, and entrance into better schools. In the early twentieth century W. E. B. Du Bois noted the phenomenon of white privilege, calling whiteness "a sort of public and psychological wage" that accrued to white people.[55] This wage, largely unrecognized (by white people), was a set of advantages they enjoyed because of their race, including expectations of courtesy and admittance to all public functions.[56]

Other forms of privilege, including class, nondisabled, and heterosexual privilege, have also received attention in the past several decades. As the sociologist Allen Johnson writes, whatever its form, privilege "allows people to define reality and to have prevailing mainstream views fit their own experience. Privilege means being able to decide who gets taken seriously, who gets attention, who is accountable to whom and for what."[57] Because privilege has often made people in positions of power less aware of the realities of people in vulnerable positions, feminist standpoint theorists point out the importance of listening to marginalized voices. Abigail Brooks writes, "Building knowledge from women's [particularly marginalized women's] actual, or concrete, life experience is acutely important . . . if we hope to repair the historical trend of women's misrepresentation and exclusion from the dominant knowledge canons. And only by making women's concrete, life experiences the primary source of our investigations can we succeed in constructing knowledge that accurately reflects and represents women."[58]

Learning about the experiences Latter-day Saint women of color must navigate, coming as they do from diverse and often less advantaged contexts, does indeed highlight issues that are less likely to affect privileged Latter-day Saint women and men. As the following stories illustrate, their experiences, insights, and strategies for navigating teachings and advice that do not represent their reality give a glimpse into some limitations of traditional Mormon discourse and teachings. They also point toward new ways of thinking about race and gender within Mormonism, ways that are expansive in their scope and often more resonant with the lives of women on the margins.

On one frigid day on the East Coast, I met Bianca, a woman to whom Claire had referred me. I waited in the church hallway as Bianca finished teaching her youth Sunday School class and then went inside to introduce myself as she gathered her materials and erased the chalkboards. Bianca had long, straight black hair and wore a bright pink professional dress. She was in her early thirties and spoke with what I originally thought was a Spanish accent, but it turned out to be Portuguese. We found a quiet corner outside and I turned on my recorder, asking her to tell me about her background and life experiences.

Bianca is originally from Cape Verde, a country in Africa colonized by the Portuguese in the nineteenth century, and she was brought up in the Catholic Church. She explained to me that she is ethnically mixed. Her father was of Middle Eastern descent, and her mother was part Asian and part Portuguese, among other things. Bianca came from a middle-class background, but some of her father's business pursuits failed when she was a child. That financial crisis, along with the dissolution of her parents' marriage, prompted her father to bring her to the United States when she was fifteen years old. She thought the stay was temporary, but actually, her father had planned to leave her there permanently with his brother.

Living with an uncle and aunt who were not excited about having this teenager thrust upon them was difficult. From the moment her father left her in the United States, she had to take care of herself: "I was on my own. Just so you have an idea, I went in and got myself enrolled in high school. No one enrolled me. I took the bus—good thing I learned English in Cape Verde. . . . [I] went in and said, 'I need to enroll in high school.' They gave me a paper, and I took it back to my uncle to sign. . . . Then I had to get my vaccines. They told me to go to this clinic. I did everything alone."[59] Self-sufficiency and proactivity are the hallmark traits of Bianca, who figured out how to navigate a new country without much help from her aunt or uncle.

One crucial resource for Bianca was the Church of Jesus Christ of Latter-day Saints. She had joined the church as a twelve-year-old in Cape Verde, and the Portuguese branch in the United States was her main support system. She said, "So the Portuguese branch was essentially my life. They were my family basically."[60] She needed their support when she graduated from high school with high grades and was offered several scholarships. As she told me, "I was able to take none of [the scholarships] because when I was applying for college, I realized I had no documents. Now I'm not undocumented, but back then I was. I was like, 'What do you mean?' They said, 'You need a social security number and green card.' I had no idea what that meant. It was devastating for me."[61]

Bianca eventually obtained documents when she married her husband, also originally from Cape Verde. But it has been a struggle to survive and thrive in the United States, separated as they are from the support of family. Bianca worked continually to find ways to obtain a college education so that she could get a job to help support her family. Because she did not have parental financial support when she graduated from high school and because her husband works for the government and does not earn a high salary, Bianca has always worked. She said, "I've worked all along. I've been working since eighteen, and I've never stopped working."[62] The fact that this mother of young children works full-time sometimes causes tension for her when gender roles are discussed in a Mormon context. As mentioned above, in the 1970s and 1980s Latter-day Saint leaders encouraged women to be full-time mothers and avoid paid employment. Since then, church leaders have significantly diminished their critiques of working mothers, choosing instead to emphasize the relatively vague concept of mothers as nurturers.[63] Nevertheless, critiques of working motherhood have taken root in many Mormon communities, impacting the psyches, decisions, and self-perceptions of Latter-day Saint women.

Bianca sheds light on the class privilege that these traditional Mormon gender role prescriptions assume:

> I had such a conflict because [teachings about mothers staying home] gave me a guilt trip. I felt, ok, I've always had to work for survival. I always thought that it was wrong for someone to just completely stay home with kids. I'm not judging those who do that, it's great if you can do it, but the reason I feel this way I guess is because my reality is different. I don't have a support mechanism. If my husband and I get divorced, where do I go? I have no education and I have nowhere to go? Why would I leave my job? I've met women who have dedicated their whole lives to their husbands and families and then at the end of it when they are fifty or sixty, the husband takes off and gets a young woman and she's left without much. She can't even retire because she has nothing. Since I was a kid, I had to figure out how to survive on my own. So it's very hard for me to just say, "Oh, now I will just stay home, and my husband will take care of it, and I'm going to trust that everything will be ok." It's very hard for me. But there were times that I was willing to do it, but we couldn't afford it even if we wanted to. My husband is a social worker. He doesn't make enough. So it's always been that my salary was important for the survival of the family. There's no way I can just stay home. If you just put it on the paper, it's not going to work. Right now it's a struggle. Imagine if I'm not working.
>
> Another strong reason I work is for my children. They don't have $20,000 sitting somewhere from a great-grandparent. Most of my American friends, their parents will give them $50,000 or a car or let them live in the home for a year to save money. I don't have any of that. So, if I don't work, my kids won't have any of that. If I don't work my kids will not be able to go to good schools. So it's a different reality.[64]

Bianca pinpoints the class assumptions inherent in the rhetoric about stay-at-home mothers that is common among Latter-day Saints. As an immigrant to this country with no close family here, she has no parents or siblings to help her financially if the marriage fails. She must be her own support mechanism and backup plan. Her concern for her children's future is paramount because there is no nest egg or cushion from grandparents for them. In order for her children to go to a good Catholic school in the neighborhood they live in, she must work in order to pay the fees. She also wants to save money so that her children will never be as vulnerable as she has been. As she stated, after her years as an undocumented immigrant scrambling to find work and gain an education, her reality is different. She has none of the structural privilege that many more established American families have, and moreover, none of the deep roots and family support waiting in the wings to help her out. She and her husband alone are working to carve out some security for their children. In her discussion of her financial vulnerability as an immigrant, she never once mentioned the church as a possible support mechanism in the wake of a failed marriage. This is because Latter-day Saint congregations excel at helping on a short-term basis with family disasters (death, disease, emergency financial help) but are not structured to help with long-term need or assistance.

Bianca's decision to work, in part due to concerns about her future and that of her children, shows her resisting cultural pressure to trust that her husband can find a way to fully support the family financially. Because Bianca has lived without a strong economic support system and understands the worry and concern that that engenders, she refuses to put herself in a position where she is "one man away from welfare." She is actively resisting a system in which, as mujerista Ada Maria Isasi-Diaz says, women's "economic status and privileges are, in great part, determined by whose daughters, sisters, and wives [they] are."[65] Bianca is determined not to place herself or her children at the mercy of other people, who may or may not be able to support or help her in times of crisis.

Bianca did express her understanding as to why church leaders promote stay-at-home motherhood, even if it does not fit her reality:

> I understand why they counsel a mom to stay home because it's hard for a woman to do everything. It's like beyond hard. To fulfill your work responsibilities and then take your work hat off and put your family hat on and then still be happy for your husband—it doesn't work like that. It's very hard and stressful. So, I understand why the church encourages moms to stay home if they can because it would make everything much easier. In some ways. Because I can also see it the other way where a mother will feel like, "Ok, who am I? All I am is for my family."[66]

Bianca spoke from the context of her own reality, which is a standpoint of less structural privilege than that of many white Americans. She recognizes value in a gendered division of family labor, but she also recognizes that that value does not map well onto her life. But she is still able, as the quotation above shows, to see the issue from the perspective of Mormonism's generally affluent American church leaders. These leaders see the gendered division of family labor as ideal because it allows women the time to concentrate on the home and encourages men to contribute materially to the family. Much like women in Botswana who manifest a "plural consciousness," Bianca has the ability to understand the issue from both her own viewpoint and that of her church leaders. Feminist standpoint theorists call this a "double consciousness," which is a "working, active consciousness of both perspectives."[67] It is an "awareness not only of their own lives but of the lives of the dominant group . . . as well."[68] Scholars speak of this double consciousness as helping vulnerable women protect themselves and ensure their survival because understanding the perspective of the dominant actors helps them to navigate their positions of less structural privilege.[69] In Bianca's case, her double consciousness allows her to view the traditional gendered counsel of privileged Latter-day Saint leaders as based in their own reality, and she can thus view them with compassion, for in their context they experience the ease and sense of bifurcated gender roles. Her life, however, has produced its own truth, and she knows that such a division of labor for her family could very well be disastrous, particularly for her children. Both staying at home and working incur costs for women such as Bianca, but on the whole, she sees greater safety and a better outcome in having a dual-income family. Bianca's poignant reflections provide an understanding of the risks that women, particularly less privileged women, face when they eschew the workplace.

Bianca's double consciousness gives her a unique lens through which to view the still-relevant topic of stay-at-home versus working motherhood. It also may, as Brooks argues, enable the more marginalized actors in society to see and understand certain realities "from which others [white or male] are obscured."[70] Latter-day Saint leaders have in recent decades articulated that there is moral space for mothers to work in cases of financial need, an important development that nuanced earlier discourse on the topic.[71] But Bianca's reflections show that concerns beyond the immediate feeding and clothing of her children drive her decisions—and that those concerns are born of trying to ensure her family's long-term survival in a system in which she has few means of financial recourse. Ultimately, her reflections highlight the hidden assumptions of class privilege that undergird some traditional Mormon cultural attitudes toward gender roles. They also provide a glimpse of one way in which a paradigm of non-oppressive connectedness plays out for women in relatively vulnerable positions who choose to work because of their commitment to the long-term well-being and safety of their children.

White privilege embedded in certain Mormon practices and discourses involving gender and family became apparent to me when I interviewed Sita, a woman who was born to a white Latter-day Saint mother and a Tongan Latter-day Saint father. Sita was a single mother of five children. She divorced her husband after he went back to prison for the second time. Her Mormon community has been a support to her throughout these tough years, giving her a few hours of child care each week and in general embracing her as an individual.

However, her life has been severely and negatively impacted by old Latter-day Saint teachings that discouraged interracial marriage. These teachings and their concomitant disparagement of people of African ancestry are nearly as old as Mormonism itself. Joseph Smith feared Black-white miscegenation, and the second president and prophet of the church, Brigham Young, vociferously condemned the union of Black and white people, saying in 1863, "Shall I tell you the law of God in regard to the African race? If the white man who belongs to the chosen seed mixes his blood with the seed of Cain, the penalty under the law of God is death on the spot. This will always be so."[72] Like many American Protestants at the time, Latter-day Saints believed that the "curse of Cain" or "mark of Cain" mentioned in the Bible meant the black skin of those of African descent. Such teachings persisted into the twentieth century, becoming near-canonized in Bruce R. McConkie's *Mormon Doctrine*, a book often considered by members to be authoritative. McConkie stated, "The whole negro race have been cursed with a black skin, the mark of Cain, so they can be identified as a caste apart, a people with whom the other descendants of Adam should not intermarry."[73] Statements by church presidents in the 1960s and 1970s discouraged any kind of interracial marriage, and these quotations crop up at times in more recent church teaching manuals.[74] Because such authoritative sources in the past have denounced interracial marriage and because current Latter-day Saint leaders have not widely refuted these old statements, opposition to interracial marriage lives on in the minds of some church members. Women such as Sita, themselves products of interracial unions, feel as if they still suffer from these teachings, because they are viewed by their male peers as less desirable marriage partners. She described these teachings as causing pain and tension in her life:

> I think the thing that has most impacted my life tension-wise about the church is that I remember being taught that we were not supposed to marry outside of our race. As a biracial person, hearing that meant to me that no matter who I married, it wouldn't be pleasing to God because I'm bringing that into the marriage no matter what. So that's something I struggled with. . . . When I got to college, I had four different relationships within about a six-year period that were all fairly long—like eight months to a couple of years. And they were all with Polynesian men. And all four of them after that long period within the next few months ended up marrying white women or full Polynesian women. So it felt to me at that time like they don't want you because you're neither. So that was a really hard thing for

me to deal with and for me to try to grapple with because I felt like I was unmarriageable. And it wasn't something I could correct.

I hate it when people are like, "It's not that big a deal that they are teaching outdated material." But it is. Because it directly impacted my understanding of myself. I felt like it directly impacted my marriage choice. Part of why I married my ex—I don't think it was a conscious decision and I've done a lot of counseling to try to get past a lot of this stuff, but I do remember telling my therapist, "You know, I feel like I can go into a room and there will be a room full of guys that are moderately interested in me, and I will pick out the one with the most baggage. And be like, 'That's the guy for me.'" And he was like, "Yeah, because their baggage makes yours feel ok." I really thought about that and I feel like that's accurate. So it makes a difference in people's lives when they hear things like that.[75]

Sita stated that Mormon teachings against interracial marriage led to pain, self-doubt, displacement, and ultimately her choice to marry a troubled man. Sita's oral history shows us how past racist Mormon teachings, which so infamously affected Black people by denying them ordination and temple blessings, also affect a whole other subset of Latter-day Saints: biracial women. Like all other youth, they are taught from childhood about the importance of marrying. In a competitive Mormon marriage market, past teachings against interracial marriage put these women, as well as other women of color, at a disadvantage. For Sita this played out in painful ways, and she hopes for a healthier community where women of color are not made to doubt their worth.

Although the contemporary church condemns racism, it generally avoids condemning past racist statements and teachings of church leaders, preferring instead to let the old ideas slip away into the past. The clearest refutation of racist teachings occurred in the 2013 Gospel Topics essay, available on the church's website, which states, "Today, the Church disavows the theories advanced in the past that black skin is a sign of divine disfavor or curse, or that it reflects unrighteous actions in a premortal life; that mixed-race marriages are a sin; or that blacks or people of any other race or ethnicity are inferior in any way to anyone else. Church leaders today unequivocally condemn all racism, past and present, in any form."[76] This disavowal was limited in power and scope, however, since it appeared online with little fanfare and was not read over the pulpit at General Conference or in local wards, the ways in which important pronouncements are made public in the Church of Jesus Christ of Latter-day Saints. Recently, however, some efforts have been made to raise awareness of these Gospel Topics essays, including incorporating links to them in online Sunday School manuals.[77] It is therefore probable that with time, more Saints will become aware of the church's disavowal of past racist teachings through familiarity with these essays. Moreover, it is probable that younger Latter-day Saints will become increasingly less familiar with older Mormon ideas about race as books such as McConkie's *Mormon Doctrine* become less widely available.[78] While Sita has felt the far-reaching tentacles of these old teachings in her life, perhaps her children will not experience similar feelings of displacement and marginality, given these recent efforts by the church.

Sita's story is a testament to the fact that old teachings about the inappropriateness of interracial marriage can have grave consequences for the self-worth and sense of belonging of contemporary Latter-day Saint women of color. Her story illustrates the inadequacy of "the past is the past" rhetoric that some church leaders have employed when asked about such outdated teachings.[79] The past had the power to make Sita doubt her worth, positioned as she was without white privilege and thus without the privilege of not being personally affected by these teachings. Happily, church leaders have made important strides toward clearly refuting these old ideas.

The experiences of women of color in the United States also offer important interventions in the church's emphasis on and understandings of agency. Moral agency, or free agency in typical Mormon parlance, has been a central concept in Mormon cosmology throughout the church's history. Terryl Givens writes that according to Mormon theology, "in God's conception of human existence, moral agency is the bedrock value, and the capacity for independent virtuous activity is a crucial part of eternal moral development."[80] Latter-day Saints celebrate this agency and often feel a profound sense of ability to carve out their paths in life. In Mormon thought, the ability to choose can reap outstanding rewards, as righteous choices lead to exaltation and divine potential in the next life, while poor choices lead inevitably to negative consequences such as unhappiness and stagnation in moral development. As Givens states, in this cosmology "choices are allowed, inexorably, to bear their own fruit."[81] Because the idea of choice is so central there is in Mormon discourse an underlying confidence that humans have a great deal of power in determining their futures. Societal structures that constrain choice and the determination of one's path (poverty, racism, sexism) are not typically emphasized in Mormon rhetoric.

The reflections of Samantha, the woman originally from South Africa, offer some important nuance to the Mormon discussion of agency. In her experience, this profound confidence in self-determination has led to a lack of understanding and distance between privileged white leadership and ward members of color. Reflecting on her experiences in South African wards, she stated:

> So pretty much all of our leadership was white and pretty much all the people coming to the ward were not white. There had been quite a few instances where there was a lack of understanding between people, and I think it's sometimes been hard for leadership to empathize with people properly because they honestly don't have a frame of reference for where black people and coloured people are coming from. They have no idea of the conditions in which they live. They have no idea about the schools the children go to. It's much easier for a bishop to say, "You've got to pull yourself up by your bootstraps and get to work and get yourself out there and find a job." It's like, "Yes, but you from your privileged private high school that you went to during Apartheid years, you've benefited from that. You can just do that. You have no idea what these people [of color] have dealt with."[82]

Samantha did not explicitly use the word *agency*, but the attitude of the bishop she was describing—his confidence that people can choose their course and improve their material well-being—is tied theologically to the Mormon emphasis on agency and choice in life. When in a privileged position unimpeded by structural inequities, life and its possibilities may indeed seem expansive. But when trying to carve out a life in a regime of rampant racism that has systematically prevented people of color from obtaining good educations and finding good jobs, the "pull yourself up by your bootstraps" mentality does not work as well. The American womanist Graham-Russell and the Maori womanist Colvin, in a podcast devoted to the topic of Mormonism and womanist theology, likewise noted that the Mormon emphasis on agency might sometimes negatively affect marginalized people working within systems of oppression. Graham-Russell believes that discussions of agency in Mormonism need to be better nuanced: "We [Latter-day Saints] talk about agency like it's the next fashion trend. If you are in this [negative] situation, it's something you chose and did and came to yourself. But that's a gross misunderstanding of how oppression and homophobia work."[83] Graham-Russell, like Samantha, points to the idea that contemporary Mormon discourse concerning agency, which is often tied to one's ability to choose and shape one's life, tends to not adequately recognize societal constraints and oppressions that impact choice and opportunity for vulnerable populations. A reworking of this key Mormon concept is in order, these women believe. A more robust acknowledgment of societal oppressions, rather than the emphatic focus on personal sin and righteousness that generally permeates Mormon discourse, might bridge some of the distance people of color may feel when Mormon discourse does not represent their distinct realities.

The experiences and standpoints of Bianca, Sita, and Samantha illuminate the ways in which Mormon discourse sometimes inadequately represents the realities of Latter-day Saint women of color and weakens their sense of self-worth and belonging in the church. For these women in the United States, as for women in Mexico and Botswana, non-oppressive connectedness, personal and societal, is a valued moral paradigm. When privileged assumptions are embedded in Mormon discourse, assumptions that do not reflect these women's experiences, feelings of alienation and marginalization can arise. Discourses of privilege result in fissures in the vitalizing connections they seek within the church.

Surviving and Thriving in the United States as a Latter-day Saint Woman of Color

When Nadine agreed to speak with me, I was elated. A fifty-something Black lawyer in the South, Nadine had experienced significant overt racism, and I was very interested in hearing her discuss her decision to join the Church of Jesus Christ of Latter-day Saints. Nadine was a relatively recent convert to the church, having found it in 2008 after seeing singer Gladys Knight bear her testimony on BYUtv. Mormon theology made sense for this religious woman who had never found satisfactory answers to some of her questions in her Baptist faith. Getting answers to questions she had always had—such as "What happened to Enoch?"—was, she said, "like a Claritin commercial. You know the commercial where before you take it there's like a film over everything and you can see it and see parts of it, but then when you peel back the film, you can see clearly. That's what it felt like to me."[84]

Despite that clarity, choosing Mormonism was not easy. As a proud feminist Black woman, Nadine had serious issues with two aspects of the church: the priesthood-temple ban and polygamy. These practices, which she found disturbing, were serious impediments to her deciding to join the church. She eventually, however, made peace with them after she received personal revelation:

> What I eventually used was the principle of personal revelation, which I had believed as a Baptist and which was key to me in looking at the LDS faith. I prayed and the answer I received was that neither the priesthood ban and the temple ban nor polygamy had been of God. So I was like, ok. . . . There was a quote from Joseph Smith. He was asked one time to explain

our religion. He said the key part of our religion is the atoning sacrifice of Jesus Christ. And that everything else—everything else—was all just appendages to that key tenet. And I was like, I can go for that. And you know, all these other things, they are appendages, so I don't really have to worry my head about that. I had already received clear revelation to me that the priesthood ban and the temple ban and polygamy were not of God—so I could join the church.[85]

This understanding ultimately gave Nadine the peace of mind that enabled her to be baptized and join the church. Nadine could accept that fallible humans could devise practices that were oppressive and harmful. Her up-bringing as a poor Black girl in the South was a living testament to that truth. What she could not have accepted is the idea that these oppressive practices were desired and authored by God.

Nadine's experience with personal revelation allowed her to bypass the multitude of explanations and rationales for these practices, some as disturb-ing as the practices themselves, that have been offered by Latter-day Saints over the course of the past century and a half. Using personal revelation, which she had embraced as a Baptist and continued to embrace as a prospec-tive Latter-day Saint, she was able to cull problematic teachings, embrace the good things the church was offering her, and choose membership in the church. This process—rejecting certain aspects of Mormonism in order to ultimately embrace it—flies in the face of the way many Latter-day Saints think of membership and belief. Undergirding this process, however, is a paradigm of non-oppressive connectedness. Her connection to the divine realm enabled her formal connection to this religious tradition, which she found compelling on many levels.

This willingness to be led by the Spirit through personal revelation, even if it leads to beliefs or behaviors not supported by the institutional church and its leaders, is a strategy that has allowed Latter-day Saint women of color to survive and often thrive in the Church of Jesus Christ of Latter-day Saints. Personal revelation provides an important counterweight to the church's au-thority. Latter-day Saints tend to have a profound respect for religious author-ity and hierarchy because they have been taught that God and Jesus Christ directly lead the church via communication with the fifteen male prophets and revelators of the church. The institution headed by these fifteen men exerts considerable power over individual Latter-day Saint congregations, and these leaders claim the privilege of receiving revelation for the church from God. Yet personal revelation is also a revered concept in the faith. Members believe that God can personally communicate with individuals and provide specific direction for their lives. The emphasis on both personal revelation from God and the centralized hierarchical and authoritarian structure of the church is a paradox that many members grapple with.[86]

Many Latter-day Saint women of color call upon personal revelation and their own connection to God and the Spirit to sustain them and guide them within a religious culture that does not always reflect their most pressing concerns and values. In this way, they are able to bypass male mediators proclaiming things they find problematic or irrelevant and find inspiration by going directly to God. As Nadine said of Latter-day Saint church leadership, "They are men. They put their pants on one leg at a time, so I sustain the prophet, sustain the members of the First Presidency, I sustain the Quorum of the Twelve Apostles. But I don't, as part of sustaining them, give up my ability to ask or to claim the promise of personal revelation and to ask God, 'Is this true?' And receive an answer for myself."[87]

This ability to reject all-or-nothing thinking is a hallmark of the women of color in the United States with whom I spoke and is a survival strategy, as well. They have learned to embrace ambiguity in the form of a church that offers what they acknowledge as problematic history, current policies, or culture but which simultaneously inspires them, connects them to God and others, and gives them a profound sense of their own power and worth. Linda, a left-leaning salty-tongued musician of Japanese descent in her forties, embodies this ambiguity. She has had a rocky and complicated faith journey—raped by a fellow ward member in her teens, asked in her twenties not to come to church by an overwhelmed bishop, and, after a ten-year break from the church, coming back to embrace the best of Mormonism and reject that which does not resonate with her. Like Nadine, Linda rejects a black-and-white approach to the church, and she recognizes the humanity of leaders who are bound to make mistakes in their stewardship. She told me, "This is how I manage the church. I take this here, I take that there, and I don't feel like I have to hold onto that over here."[88] Although this style of "cafeteria Mormonism" has been frowned on by church leadership as showing laziness or a lack of commitment, there is nothing easy or convenient in the ways these women exercise faith to navigate the minefields of privilege and patriarchy.

Nowhere is her ability to embrace ambivalence and ambiguity more apparent than in Linda's attitude toward the Latter-day Saint temple. When I first got in touch with Linda via email, she wrote, "I might say that my time away from the church was some of the best . . . for my spirit. Except . . . I can't live without the temple."[89] She loves the temple, and the experiences she has had there have grounded her in Mormonism, despite her struggles with the church's position on LGBTQ issues and women's issues:

The thing that has been the most interesting has been that truly, every single time I've been in the temple, it has changed who I have been. It has, in a certain way, erased the person going in and cleared whatever was going on in the brain so that I can actually see ahead how to progress. It's been really amazing to have that sense. I never thought that sitting through a couple hours of whatever was going to ever do that for me. But the more I've gone, it's been such a way of dealing with stuff. It's been really amazing. Recently I haven't gone as much. I used to go every week.

I've been trying to figure out what is so powerful about the temple because it's been clawing at me. What is it? I was talking to a friend of mine who is a career coach. He was saying how our bodies are set up so that when we sleep, we are restoring our bodies so that we can function again. When we go to the temple, it's kind of like we're going to sleep and then restoring our spiritual selves.[90]

In addition to a sense of vision, peace, and rejuvenation, Linda has had profound experiences with the divine that have connected her to a different spiritual realm. At the end of our interview, she said, "I sometimes feel like God responds when I pray. . . . It's weird, but I'm really in tune with beings. Anytime I'm in the temple, I see people [who have passed on]. I think, 'Ok, what's up with you?'"[91] Mormonism has opened up space for Linda to develop a mystical worldview in which it is possible to have interactions with the spiritual realm. Her faith not only connects her directly to God but also opens up a world in which the transcendent and the divine are present in her daily life. The temple plays an important part in enabling her access to this realm of connectedness beyond the mortal sphere.

Simultaneously, however, Linda acknowledged aspects of the temple that she finds damaging to women. Specifically, she mentioned the ritual subordination that women experienced in the temple at the time of her interview, which entailed promising to hearken unto their husbands as their husbands hearken unto God.[92] She dealt with these aspects by relegating them to the cultural and historical context in which these ceremonies arose. She said, "You've got a whole bunch of . . . backward thinking about women—that was the norm for the [nineteenth-century]. That's how I deal with the hearken covenant."[93] Thus, Linda brushed aside this covenant as a product of its sexist time, confident that it is, as Nadine would say, "not of God." This ability to mentally disregard rituals or teachings she has found problematic has enabled her to remain affiliated with the church and devoted to the parts of it that do uplift and feed her soul.

Linda lives with her ambivalent feelings about the church, feeling simultaneously nourished and excluded by it. Mary Bednarowski has elaborated on women's religious ambivalence, which she describes as "grounded in a deep sense of belonging, familiarity, and commitment and an equally strong sense of alienation and distrust. This distrust is not so much of their traditions' most central insights, but the traditions' failings particularly in regard to women."[94] Linda did not describe her ambivalence as distrust exactly, but she did readily ascribe human failings and shortcomings to church leaders, who sometimes promulgate decisions and policies that inevitably lead the organization as a whole to fall short in its treatment of not only women but also of people of color and LGBTQ persons.

Bednarowski theorizes that religious ambivalence is actually a virtue to be cultivated because "there is a vitalizing quality to its manifestations." This willed ambivalence "requires women always to be vigilant, always to be critical of their communities' inclinations toward exclusion and distortion and at the same time to be open to new possibilities to hold up and reform or transform or dig up, from wherever they have been hiding, their traditions' most liberating and healing insights."[95] Bednarowski sees creative thought and practice arising from this ambivalence as women work to sort out their contradictory experiences within the faith. Certainly, for Linda, her ambivalence has led to creative theologizing about Mormonism's Heavenly Mother, who is reputed to be the consort and equal of God the Father but who is paradoxically absent from the almost all official Latter-day Saint discourse about God and totally absent from all Latter-day Saint liturgy and ritual.

Note how Linda describes her Mother in Heaven and the expansive sense of women's potential that she connects with the Mother. Mormonism might produce rhetoric and practices that sideline women, but Linda finds power in Mormonism's nearly buried feminine divine:

> My thought is that we can't handle the power of the Goddess. You've got women who bring life into this world. The kind of power that female humans have is extraordinary. I am not sure that we could even handle that power, that level of deity, of the Heavenly Mother. That idea that God is protecting her from people badmouthing her—oh, eff off!! She don't need no protecting! . . . It's not to say that men aren't strong—they have their own strengths and their own things—but if you look, time and time again, you see women of every culture being totally squished to the core, and yet how do they prevail? It's the most inspiring thing to see how over time, women have been able to kick ass. I can only imagine what the power of women could be if they didn't have a foot on top of them.[96]

Here Linda overturns folk doctrinal explanations for Heavenly Mother's invisibility in Mormon discourse and worship, which characterizes her as needing protection from the curses and insults that humans might direct her way.[97] Instead, Linda envisions the Mother as so supremely powerful and awesome that humans cannot "even handle that power, that level of deity." In seeing such power in the Mother, she sees extraordinary power in Her daughters as well, who prevail despite patriarchal culture putting "a foot on top of them" and "squish[ing] them to the core." Within the context of patriarchal Latter-day Saint practice and teachings Linda has developed a profound sense of female capacity and authority. She has incorporated into her belief system aspects of Mormon thought that can empower women—a focus on divine nature and divine potential for all humans, a feminine divine, a close relationship with a personal deity who loves, guides, and directs—while rejecting the aspects that she finds disempowering.

Moreover, Linda has rejected traditional restrictions on women's healing and blessing outside the temple. When she went to the temple for the first time, she recalled, "It made 100% sense to me that women were doing blessings [in the temple]. I didn't ever have any doubts that that was the way it was supposed to be. I have given blessings [outside the temple]. I have done healings and all sorts of things."[98] She later explained that the temple and patriarchal blessing taught her that she had both the gift to heal and the priesthood power with which to bless others' lives:

> I feel that with the power given to me in the temple, I have power to utilize my priesthood in daily life, which I do. So I will bless my family because I am the priesthood holder in my house. I will uphold the priesthood in my home because I am the priesthood holder in the house. So in that way, I am probably not your typical woman in the church. But if [church leaders] are not going to give me the power, then don't expect me to toe the line. I was thrilled to receive the blessing to heal, and if I have this blessing then I need to be able to use it. I have, definitely.[99]

Linda's spirituality and closeness to God and divine power, nurtured in her by her upbringing in the Church of Jesus Christ of Latter-day Saints, have enabled her to transcend some of its gender-based constraints, limitations that posit priesthood as well as blessing and healing as the province of men, not women. She sees some Latter-day Saint women as "torn away from their own roots, from their own power, stripped of identity, stripped of dignity."[100]

But for the Latter-day Saint woman "who steps into the power and does, does, does," Linda sees enormous ability and potential.[101] She described such women in this way:

> They know themselves to be powerful women. They just get it. They so get it. And they don't need men to say, "You are allowed to do this. You are

not allowed to do that." They will just . . . do it anyway. Because they know their own strength, they know their own power, and they know what it's about. They know it's their own choice. There is something called choice and accountability that is the very baseline fundamental root of the entire religion, and these women exercise it.[102]

These women of color who have found power in Mormonism have been able to develop a strong sense of confidence in themselves, their own power, their own divine nature, and their own connection to God. Like many women in Christian history, from medieval Catholic mystics to female American preachers of the nineteenth century, they recognize the church's authority but also develop a self-confidence and authority grounded in personal revelation and their connection to God.[103] This self-authorization sometimes puts women at odds with male ecclesiastical authority, as the Black preacher Julia Foote found in the 1800s, but God's call often outweighs their society's expectations of women's compliance and silence.[104] Latter-day Saint women who are publicly outspoken about gender also at times face punishment for challenging male authority and asserting the primacy of their conscience and spiritual connection.[105] But more common are women such as Linda who quietly authorize themselves to move forward in their religious and private lives as they see fit. Because as Linda indicated, they do not ask for permission to bless, heal, and more, they can often stay under the radar of male leaders. Mormonism might restrict women's opportunities and promote specific gender roles for them, but it also simultaneously teaches these women that their eternal potential is limitless and that they have the right and responsibility to commune with God personally about the great questions in their lives.

The voices of Latter-day Saint women of color in the United States illuminate specific priorities, vulnerabilities, and realities that are sometimes not reflected in institutional Latter-day Saint and Mormon feminist discourse. Their stories, which often reveal a moral orientation toward vitalizing, nonoppressive connectedness to the divine, introduce important interventions into both of these discourses. In the past five years Mormon feminist writing and thought have become noticeably more intersectional. However, further shifts in emphasis toward denouncing all oppressions—and recognizing the ways in which Mormonism does create some liberating spaces for different groups of women—would foster a more inclusive and robust Mormon feminist movement. Likewise, attention to systemic injustice could offer institutional Latter-day Saint discourse productive avenues for discussing agency, sin, and race in nuanced ways that could resonate with the experiences of people of color in particular.

These women's experiences of race and gender in the Mormon context also bring to light the issue of privilege, which at times leads to institutional discourse that does not reflect their experience and results in feelings of marginalization. Despite the challenges of navigating membership in the church for some women of color, however, many have been able to thrive within the tradition and embrace it as their own. Their strategies of rejecting all-or-nothing thinking, embracing ambivalence, and developing their own intimate connections with the divine offer a potential model for all Latter-day Saints who grapple with historical, social, and theological issues within the tradition. Their stories therefore add another layer to the paradigm of non-oppressive connectedness. As with Mexican and Batswana women, positive, uplifting divine and human connections are vital, but many of these women in the United States emphasize the eradication of dynamics that harm vulnerable groups. Their vision of vitalizing relationality often extends beyond the personal and toward larger systems, discourses, and practices that hinder the development of a unified Zion community.

The paradigm of non-oppressive connectedness illuminates the experiences, choices, and practices of women in Botswana, Mexico, and the United States. It sheds light on these women's decisions to affiliate with the church, their sense of finding liberation there, and their struggles with it. It also, as the next chapter details, undergirds one particular aspect of their religious imaginations and understandings of how God works in the world. Not only is non-oppressive connectedness a personal moral imperative they find compelling; it also, as we see in their theological musings on abundance, is an important aspect of God's hopes and wishes for humanity.

CHAPTER 4

Toward a Mormon Womanist Theology of Abundance

Latter-day Saint women have always produced theological discourses about the power of divinity and the nature and capacity of humanity. Since the church's inception they have discussed the characteristics of a virtuous and godly life, expounded on scripture, and related religious concepts to their own experiences. Yet because of the church's hierarchical priesthood-led structure, which privileges the voices of (white) men, women have had far fewer opportunities to expound theologically in a way that reaches large swaths of church members.[1] Much of their God-talk, often voiced in local church meetings, has not survived the test of time because it has not been preserved in historical records or disseminated broadly. As Margaret Toscano points out, the church's power structure can have profound ramifications for the nature of theological discourse within the tradition. Androcentric power structures, she argues, lead to androcentric theologies and a dearth of women's perspectives, and this limits Latter-day Saints' theological imaginations. This concept applies to power structures that privilege whiteness as well, Toscano writes.[2]

A few Latter-day Saint women have nonetheless produced theological discourses that have found a wider audience among church members. In the early years of the church, women often turned to forums outside the formal church structure to circulate their ideas. In a newspaper called *Times and Seasons*, Eliza R. Snow famously theologized about Heavenly Mother, thus near-canonizing the idea of this divine feminine personage, in her poem-turned-hymn "Invocation, or the Eternal Father and Mother."[3] Another newspaper, the *Woman's Exponent* (1872–1914), whose masthead slogan read, "The Rights of the Women of Zion, and the Rights of the Women of All Nations," featured various commentaries on scripture and Mormon thought, often from a first-wave feminist perspective.[4] In the twentieth century, Latter-day Saint women interpreted scripture and spoke of deity in General Relief Society meetings and other auxiliary conferences. Since 1994, in the general sessions of General Conference, broadcast around the world, two women have been routinely numbered among the thirty or so male general authorities sermonizing on various topics. Women outside the church hierarchy have also produced theology. Of particular note are Janice Allred and Margaret Toscano, who were both excommunicated, at least in part because of their refusal to stop publishing theological works about Heavenly Mother.[5]

Although religious discourse by such women has variously reaffirmed standard Mormon doctrine, gently stretched Mormon teachings to include or take into consideration women in innovative ways, or advocated for a theological revolution that would impel Heavenly Mother into the Godhead, all these discourses share the almost entirely non-diverse positionality of their producers. These Latter-day Saint women have with very few exceptions been white, middle-class, and often closely connected to the elite men of the church. One notable exception to this pattern is the widely beloved general Relief Society presidency member Chieko Okazaki, who in the 1990s and 2000s wrote and theologized from the viewpoint of her own life and experiences, often drawing on her Japanese Buddhist upbringing. Apart from Okazaki, there is a dearth of theological discourse produced and published by Latter-day Saint women of color in the United States and around the world. The God-talk of women navigating Mormonism at the crossroads of race, class, and culture has overwhelmingly remained buried, unheard, or forgotten.[6]

The oral history interviews I conducted with Latter-day Saint women of color from Mexico, southern Africa, and the United States, however, begin to fill this gap. The theological priorities and imperatives of female Saints outside the privileged center emerged in these interviews as women discussed their religious values and conceptions of God and humanity. Though there was wide variation in the responses, I highlight in this chapter one thread that ran through several women's oral histories. This theological vision centered on a worldview in which God's love was vast and abundant, spiritual powers could be highly developed, and the opportunity to connect with God personally was unbounded and took on varying forms. As in earlier chapters, non-oppressive, vitalizing connectedness to God and others characterizes this worldview, but in this chapter, particular attention is also paid to women's connections to their own authentic and best selves. In their religious imaginations, they saw an abundance of female ability and strength in themselves and others, and they advocated operating within a framework of abundance rather than one of scarcity. Moreover, God inhabits a moral framework of non-oppressive connectedness in these women's theological musings on abundance, as they depict God as a source of inestimable generosity and grace who has endowed each of God's children with profound potential and wills them toward just and loving relationships with one another. In contrast to this perspective, fear, competition, and exclusivity were the byproducts of a misunderstanding of optimal humanity and God's structuring of the world. Based on these reflections by the women interviewed for this book, this chapter examines various iterations of a theological perspective that could be formulated into a Mormon theology of abundance.

The second half of the chapter discusses possibilities for further directions and development for such a theology based on the methodology of womanist theologians. Womanist theology is my primary inspiration in setting out this framework for a theology of abundance, given that it is based on the complex lived realities of women of color, privileges their experiences of God and theological reflections, and challenges the multiple forces of oppression that characterize their lives.[7] As such, this theological project is also an intersectional one because it moves the voices of the marginalized to the center and employs a lens that explores the impact of intersecting gender, racial, and cultural identities on women's theological formulations. Ultimately, this chapter begins to build a womanist theology of abundance from the ground up, based on the religious insights of global Latter-day Saint women of color. In their reflections, often born of the complexity of their positionalities, these women offer an expansive Mormon theological vision, robust and flexible enough to feed their spirits, excite their religious imaginations, inspire them to seek justice, and affirm their own strengths and identities. These theological reflections offer lessons for the wider church as they point toward an ethical, broad-based faith that relates to everyday struggles and that resonates with core Latter-day Saint values. It is this kind of Mormonism—rather than white, middle-class Mormonism—that attracts and inspires these Saints and helps keep them in the fold.

It is important to note at the outset that this theology of abundance is distinct from prosperity theology, which has swept across various Christian charismatic and evangelical communities in the United States and, more recently, around the world in the past half century. Prosperity theology promotes the idea that wealth, health, and success are divine gifts from a God who wants his people to prosper materially. It holds that if people express their faith in certain ways, they can overcome poverty and ill health.[8] This theology has its roots in early twentieth-century ideas about the power of individuals' minds to change their circumstances, often called the New

Thought Movement. The combination of this movement with American ideas of individualism and upward mobility and with Pentecostalism resulted in the emergence of the prosperity gospel in the late twentieth century, when television personalities and megachurches started to arise.[9] Oral Roberts and Pat Robertson are notable prosperity preachers who have inspired countless Christians to adopt this worldview. In 2017, when United States President Donald Trump was inaugurated, two of the six religious leaders he invited to pray were advocates of the prosperity gospel.[10]

Although Mormonism has within it resources for its own development of a form of prosperity theology—in particular, Book of Mormon promises that people would "prosper in the land" if they obeyed God's commandments—Latter-day Saint women of color tended to not play up the connections among wealth, health, and righteousness.[11] Certainly, Mormon teachings about self-reliance, financial providence, and clean living might in fact lead to members improving their finances and health, but the interviewees seldom conflated wealth and health with righteousness. These women, many of whom have personally experienced structural inequities that disadvantage racially or economically marginalized people, were not comfortable with simple equations of financial prosperity and faith.[12]

This womanist theology of abundance is also distinct from Robert Orsi's influential theoretical category called "abundant events," in which people experience the divine or spirits as real and present and which is characterized by excess emotion and broken-down boundaries. These abundant events, such as Marian apparitions experienced by devout Catholics, spill over into other activities and experiences beyond the moment of divine presence. Souvenirs commemorating the event gain power, pilgrimages may begin, and devotees become accessible and vulnerable with one another as their religious imaginations become expansive and they commune over their shared faith and experience.[13] Abundant events also, according to Orsi, illuminate "the hopes, desires, and fears circulating among a group of people" and thus provide insight into a certain culture at a certain time.[14] In contrast, this Mormon womanist theology of abundance is not rooted in a moment of divine presence that spurs human activity and excess. Rather, it is a mindset that sees a metaphysical abundance of God's love and blessings for everyone, a personal abundance of human abilities and capacity, and a spiritual abundance of connections between this world and the next. This spiritual abundance has some overlap with Orsi's abundant events, as they both may involve interactions between the human and the spiritual realms, but Mormon women's experiences with the divine, often kept relatively private, do not generally lead to a flood of commemoration, community-gathering, and spin-off spiritual experiences.

American Women: Rejecting Scarcity, Embracing Abundance

The theological import of the concept of abundance was most clearly articulated by Nia, who took that concept in the most revolutionary direction of all the women with whom I spoke. Nia was a tall woman in her twenties with long black dreadlocks and a great sense of humor. The child of a white mother and Black father who divorced when she was young, Nia was raised in the Church of Jesus Christ of Latter-day Saints, often living with her white grandparents. She was typically the only Black person in her ward when she was growing up. Nia is the first person in her family to go to college, and she has been academically driven her whole life. During the course of her undergraduate and graduate work, Nia transitioned from politically conservative to liberal. She is now particularly attuned to microaggressions, structures of power, and patterns of behavior that diminish racial minorities and women. For instance, people often tell her she is articulate, but she now understands, she said "what the undercurrent there is when that's said—I'm an exception, you didn't expect for this Black woman to be articulate. I'd say those are daily things [I deal with]."[15] Within the church she has become adept at sifting out comments and ideas that she finds problematic: "I am constantly having to parse things out. If I sit in church, where is the actual gospel of Jesus Christ? Where's the truth? Because what I just heard was sexist, homophobic, racist, and anti-intellectual. And so I have to say to myself, 'Ok, is there a kernel of goodness?' I have to constantly sift and find what there is to hold onto."[16]

Despite the problems she hears in Mormon rhetoric and teachings, Nia has worked hard to maintain a place for herself within the church. Mormonism is her spiritual home, or as she said, "Mormonism is how spirituality has been packaged for me, how religion has been delivered, how Christ was delivered."[17] Yet in order to be spiritually fed and find applicability and significance in Mormon teachings, she has had to develop and embrace readings of scripture that promote justice and affirm the full humanity of all people.

Particularly striking to me were Nia's reflections on the importance of operating from a place of abundance rather than a place of scarcity. When asked about her favorite scriptural figure, she pointed to Jesus and to the stories of him miraculously feeding thousands with only a few loaves and fish. In both versions (five thousand in Matthew 14 and four thousand in

Matthew 15), his apostles, according to Nia, were "so concerned with him not being able to feed everybody. And yet he does it, and there's an abundance and more than enough."[18] Nia went on to reflect more on what this story conveys to her theologically:

> [This story conveys] this idea that we all struggle with this idea of scarcity. There's not enough. There's not enough salvation, there's not enough blessings, there's not enough. But there's always enough. There's always enough. Always more than enough. And I love that because I think that story exemplifies that.[19]

In Nia's reading of this story, the apostles are working within a context of scarcity, worried about not having enough to satisfy the hunger of the multitudes and reluctant to try. Even after Jesus performed the first miracle of feeding the five thousand, the apostles still did not let go of the scarcity mindset; they worried about feeding the next multitude. Yet as Nia states, Jesus is working in an entirely different framework, a framework of abundance, in which God's blessings and compassion pour out over multitudes. Instead of holding back sustenance in case there wouldn't be enough, Jesus gave what there was and it proved to be more than sufficient. In Nia's reading, life on Earth is not a zero-sum game. All can take part in the metaphysical bounty that God offers. What God and Jesus offer cannot be exhausted, so there is no need to hold back blessings, privileges, and opportunities from certain segments of the population.

Nia's thoughts about focusing on abundance rather than scarcity were sparked by an address she heard in 2015 by Fatimah Salleh, a liberation theologian with a Mormon background.[20] In this address, Salleh, a woman of African American, Malaysian, and Puerto Rican descent, passionately preached about the dangers of using religion and scripture to exclude certain people. "If we are always looking at texts and theology from [the perspective of] who is in and who is out, that's bad theology," she said. "We should not be engaged with questions of who is in and who is out. We should be engaged in who is not here, who is not at the table."[21] Good theology, for Salleh, is theology that identifies the marginalized and works to include them. The stories of Jesus feeding the multitudes, in Salleh's theologizing, emphasize Jesus's desire to pour out goodness, salvation, and blessings on all humanity, in the face of another worldview (embodied by the disciples), namely, that there is simply not enough for all:

> We think there's a scarcity of salvation, when there is none. You perceive in your mind there can only be so much. There can't be more than this. God

can't encompass more than this. We can't bring in more than this. It's the scarcity that scares the disciples. They are counting. They are like, "Jesus, you can't do this. We don't have a lot." The power in Jesus is that there is always enough. In fact, there's leftovers.

I want to challenge us not to see God in a scarce manner—that there is not enough of God's love, not enough of God's embrace, not enough for xyz people. Don't come to God and say, "We only have this much to give." You come to God and say, "Multiply." You come to God as the brother of Jared did and say, "Touch it." You don't come telling God what the situation is. He knows. He knows there is five [loaves] and two [fishes].

We think in a way that is scarce. We think in a way that [says] there is not enough. But the miracle in loving Christ is that there is always enough and there is more than enough. Change your theology to fit the fact that you believe in a God who has more than enough love to encompass us all, there is enough ordination for us all, there's more than enough liberty and freedom and love for us all. We don't have to be divided by . . . phenotypical, biological [factors]. . . . You are breaking things down out of scarcity. You think it's scarce. It isn't. In fact, it's overflowing. In fact, the miracle is there's an abundance.[22]

Notable in Salleh's commentary on this topic is her vision of what God's abundance consists of. Unlike prosperity preachers, who focus on God wanting to shower humans with wealth, God's abundance, for Salleh, is centered on less tangible blessings.[23] She points to an abundance of divine love, ordination, liberty, and freedom for everyone. She feels that a focus on moving away from a scarcity mindset and toward a mindset of metaphysical abundance would change practices and priorities in the contemporary Church of Jesus Christ of Latter-day Saints. The church's historical and contemporary policies of extending priesthood to only certain groups of people on the basis of their biological makeup is a very noticeable subtext in her sermon. In Salleh's theological worldview, God and Christ are ready and willing to fully include and bless every human. It is the disciples who must shake off their fears of scarcity, their tendencies to exclude, categorize, divide, and locate power among an elite few. Like many liberationist theologians, Salleh envisions a God standing in solidarity with the marginalized, willing the privileged to break out of narrow thinking and embrace the expansiveness of God's vision for all.[24] Connectedness and community, not division or exclusion, are hallmarks of her theological thought, as is a firm rejection of oppressive forces.

Nia sees certain implications for moving toward a framework of abundance within the Church of Jesus Christ of Latter-day Saints. In her mind, such a framework would mean that current church power structures and systems would "need to be completely deconstructed so that the corporation or the organization reflects the people. Right now it doesn't."[25] What would such a deconstruction look like? What would implementing an abundance framework within the church look like?

> That would look like ordaining everybody because there's enough ordination to go around. That would look like allowing culture to come through so that I maybe am not getting the same [church] lesson [in every country in the world]. It's very comforting for people (and troubling) that "I can go to any ward in the world and get the same exact lesson in Sunday School." I think that's harmful. I'm glad that comforts you, tourist in Peru, because you're on holiday. How lovely for you! But is it what the Peruvians need? Is it what they need in Mongolia or Kenya? No. The answer is no.[26]

According to Nia's worldview, there is no need to create an artificial system of division and scarcity regarding ordination because priesthood is in fact limitless and infinitely available. In the metaphysical bounty that God wants to extend to all, priesthood would not run out if it were extended to women as well as men. There is a limitless supply of it. An abundance framework would also fight against the homogenizing influences of the institutional church, which develops lessons and manuals in Salt Lake City and exports them to be used in every corner of the world. An abundance mentality would honor and promote the many cultures, customs, and wisdoms that Latter-day Saints the world over embrace. Opening up more lessons to local differentiation—to address specific needs and specific communities—would resonate with a theology of abundance, which sees ability, power, and godly insight as located broadly in humanity, not only in the institutionally powerful men in Utah. Concomitantly, a framework of abundance would also encompass a radical inclusion of men and women from all over the world in decision-making positions and a deconstruction of centralized Latter-day Saint power structures.

Ultimately, for Nia, a framework of abundance is intimately connected to concepts of justice and healthy connectedness. The top-down hierarchical structure of the centralized church, which locates most power and decision making in the hands of elite men and which controls much of people's experience in the worldwide church, is an affront to marginalized populations. For Nia, justice demands a dismantling of current power systems in the church. In her vision of the abundance of God's blessings and the abundance of capabilities in all humans, those that are most marginalized in the current system would be invited to the table and take part in all decision making. It is often "the least of these" people—those who are marginalized because of gender, nationality, race, and economic status—who have untold depths of vision, wisdom, and spiritual power to contribute to their communities. When Latter-day Saint leaders "seek to understand as opposed to teach," as Nia said, they will begin to embark on the path of embracing the abundance God is truly offering to all.[27] Nia's moral paradigm of non-oppressive connectedness, which undergirds many of her thoughts about abundance, takes on a distinct social justice edge because she believes that justice for the marginalized is a necessary precursor to authentic connection and true fellowship among Saints.

Jessica, a mother of five young children, also articulated a framework of abundance when we spoke. Unlike Nia, however, who used the concept of abundance to argue for widespread systemic change and inclusion of marginalized people, Jessica used the concept of abundance to speak of its internal, personal implications. Jessica is a devout Latter-day Saint who treasures her Native American heritage. Though she is genetically more European than Native American, she is tightly connected to her Inuit roots, having lived with her Inuit grandfather for a space of years. Her grandfather grew up in a tribal community and converted to Mormonism as a young man. Jessica reflected on how those two important parts of her identity come together. She primarily finds Mormonism to be a helpful, empowering influence in the Inuit context. Because so many of her non–Latter-day Saint Inuit cousins have been plagued by alcoholism and have even been killed in alcohol-related deaths, she values Mormonism for its emphasis on sobriety and provident living. She and her grandfather also treasure Book of Mormon teachings that promise that the land will return to the Lamanites after the Gentiles turn away from God. The fact that this promise is not conditional on Lamanite righteousness gives her grandfather hope that Native Americans will rise again and prosper.[28]

Her perspectives on issues of concern to Native Americans took up a good portion of our interview, but Jessica also spent time reflecting on her current life as she raises young children while her husband is in graduate school. It was in this context that she mentioned an abundance mentality:

[You fear] you don't have your own autonomy and your own identity, but I think that really with communion with God or with your communion with your spouse, your identity is actually expanded and empowered and made into something more real and fuller. . . . We grow up with a lot of these things about how motherhood can destroy your personal identity and your personal autonomy. But when I come back to it, I feel like these experiences are ultimately expanding, and not limiting, not erasing. I feel that way.

The more we serve ourselves into communion the more of ourselves we become. The more of ourselves there is to be. If you want to get New Age-y about it, it's the abundance mentality. The opposite of the abundance mentality is that you try to take all that you can for yourself, because there's a scarcity and you need to feed yourself. But the abundance mentality is that the more that you give, the more that there will be to give. And the more there is to go around. The more you give of yourself, the more of yourself exists![29]

Like Nia, Jessica sees danger in scarcity mindsets that lead individuals to protect their interests at the expense of others. Yet her focus on abundance is geared toward personal choices about how to spend one's time and energy rather than large-scale systems of power. She is compelled by the idea of communion and the idea that aligning oneself fully with God and one's spouse does not dissipate one's identity. Rather, it is a partnership with God and one's spouse that she envisions, a partnership that ultimately ennobles, enlivens, and builds the self, rather that dissolves it. The very term *communion*, comprised of two Latin words that mean "build together," reflects her perspective on the productive and vitality-bringing nature of partnering fully and devotedly with the divine and with one's spouse. In her paradigm of non-oppressive connectedness, serving and communing with God and others do not deplete her identity and autonomy; rather, they spark an abundance of self, as she grows into her true self and becomes herself more fully. In her thinking, the worldviews of abundance and non-oppressive connectedness come together, combining the emphases on healthy relationships and on the personal abundance of self that results from that moral focus.

The "New Age-y" ideas about abundance to which Jessica referred may stem from Latter-day Saint business leadership author Stephen Covey, who discusses the "Abundance Mentality." He writes, "Most people are deeply scripted in what I call the Scarcity Mentality. They see life as having only so much, as though there were only one pie out there. . . . The Abundance Mentality, on the other hand, flows out of a deep inner sense of personal worth and security. It is a paradigm that there is plenty out there and enough to spare for everybody. It results in sharing of prestige, of recognition, of profits, of decision making. It opens possibilities, options, alternatives, and creativity."[30] Jessica takes this idea of abundance out of a hierarchical business management setting and layers it onto a religious context of communion and personal progression. Her particular layering is centered in her current Mormon woman's world of nurturing, service, and connection with others. She does not, however, restrict herself and her abundance ideology to only her family and church community. Jessica is highly active in a resettlement organization as a cultural companion to recently arrived refugees from the Middle East. Meeting frequently with these traumatized families, Jessica helps them navigate their new lives in the United States. She is also a strong advocate of opening the country's borders to refugees fleeing from persecution and brutality. Jessica's religious ideas about abundance and communion, rooted in personal reflections on identity constitution and service, ultimately lead her to an outward orientation focused on helping the marginalized. In contrast to Nia's ideas about abundance, Jessica's abundance ideology is not a catalyst for her turning her critical gaze on the institutional church, nor does it lead to a questioning of contemporary Mormon gender roles. In rooting abundance firmly in the individual and in her personal decisions to serve others and thus become herself more fully, Jessica finds abundance ideology compatible with Latter-day Saint systems and structures.

There is an interesting confluence between Jessica's reflections on autonomy, identity, and the enhancement of self and the ethicist Sarah Hoagland's rejection of paradigms of self-sacrifice and self-abnegation. Hoagland developed her feminist ethical framework specifically for the lesbian community, in which she saw many women devote themselves to the community and to social causes, only to ultimately burn out and give up on such work and sometimes the community itself. Rather than categorizing one's choices to engage and serve as self-sacrifice or an action that helps others but hurts the self, she advocates what is in effect an abundance mindset. She states, "We can regard our choosing to interact as part of how we engage in this living. Such choices are matters of focus, not sacrifice. That I attend certain things and not others, that I focus here and not there, is part of how I create value. Far from sacrificing myself, or part of myself, I am creating."[31] Like Jessica, Hoagland does not see a depletion of the self resulting from one's choices to engage in the world and with others. Rather, she sees abundance, or as she says, creation, resulting from such choices. It might seem surprising that such confluences can be found in the devout Mormon worldview of Jessica and that of the lesbian ethicist Sarah Hoagland, but it does make sense on one level. Both women are concerned with female identity depletion and female autonomy. They both, therefore, advocate a reconfiguring of perspective when thinking about their worlds. Their decisions to engage and connect—though the substance of engagement and connection may differ in these different communities—result in creation and abundance, not a dissipation of the self.

Nia and Jessica represent different poles of Mormon orthodoxy, yet both have found ideologies of abundance spiritually enlivening. As they reflect on abundance, they both lay out promising directions that a Mormon theology of abundance might take. Nia's spiritual reflections on abundance, reflections which reject the idea that certain spiritual blessings and privileges are inherently scarce and thus carefully rationed out to only some people, point to the shattering of power structures and the inclusion of the racially, sexually, and otherwise marginalized populations in all decision-making bodies. Her theologizing is born of her experiences as a Black Latter-day Saint woman navigating systemic racism in the church and in American society. Jessica likewise rejects scarcity thinking, but her gaze is trained on the individual, particularly the individual woman who might be tempted to believe that she is losing herself in her gendered Mormon roles. Her theology of abundance and communion affirms the lives and choices of many Latter-day Saint women who devote themselves to service, caretaking, and relationship building. In such devotion, she argues, she engages in a process of coming into herself and developing herself that only expands her identity and well-being.

Southern African Women: Sufficiency and Abundance Within

Just as Nia's and Jessica's theological reflections on abundance emerge from their experiences in the United States, Samantha's and Warona's ideas likewise arise from their experiences in southern Africa. As such, their ideas about abundant living and selfhood have a slightly different theological flavor and focus than those of their American counterparts. Instead of envisioning Nia's endless metaphysical bounty and Jessica's self that abounds and increases as she serves herself into communion, Samantha and Warona both alluded to the concept of abundance in their discussion of being enough. They never used the word *abundance*, but their emphasis on the importance of knowing that they are "plenty" in themselves, complete as they are, and not deficient, ties into ideas of both sufficiency and abundance. This sense of being "plenty" in themselves is not exactly the increasing and growing self to which Jessica referred, but it is a sense that women are born abounding in ability and capacity. Forces in society, and even forces in the church at times, as Samantha mentioned, tear women down and make them think they are unworthy or lacking. But knowing that women are not only enough in themselves but actually teeming with ability and resources is a theological vision of human nature that lifts women up and sustains them as they face life's inevitable challenges.

Mormonism is unique among Christian faiths in its embrace of the Fall of Adam and Eve as a fortunate, divinely desired event. In conjunction with this, Mormonism rejects traditional Christian notions of original sin. The rejection is canonized in the second Article of Faith, which states, "Men will be punished for their own sins and not for Adam's transgression." The general sense of theological anthropology within Mormonism is that humans are not inherently sinful or broken but are instead filled with divine potential and vast capability.

Samantha enlarged on this Mormon sense of optimism about humanity's inherent nature as she articulated this sense that women—and particularly African Latter-day Saint women—need to know that they are enough and more than enough as they are:

> One thing that I've thought a lot in recent years is that if there's anything that I would like to stay focused on in my own life and hopefully teach my children to keep in the forefront of their minds is that understanding that you as a person are enough. You are plenty. You have everything that you need. You are imperfect, but you are complete in the sense that you have everything that you need to be ok. You have it already. There is nothing that someone else has that you need in order to be yourself, in order to be completely and wholly yourself. . . . It's something that I hope my children will know, especially [my daughter]. I hope she will know that she is enough. She doesn't have to be more than anybody else. She can change and she can be changed. She can have her heart changed. She can have things about her nature changed if that's what she wants, if that's what's going to bring her happiness. We can change things about ourselves, that's not to be more like anybody else, but to be more like ourselves. I hope that they will know that. I feel like I'm in a place where I care more about being the most authentic me I possibly can be. In this gospel I feel like it gives me that space. I honestly do. There are things that I don't know the answers to, there are things that I sometimes question, but I still feel I am still able to be completely myself. And if I feel like someone has tried to put me into a little box, it's always . . . been that person doing it, not God. I just hope my children know that being yourself is enough. You don't have to be anybody else.[32]

Here Samantha expresses an emphatic vision of humans being born complete, sufficient, and full of possibility. In her theological vision of human nature, change is possible and positive if it leads to happiness, but only if it is a change toward "be[ing] more like ourselves" and not toward conforming to the hopes or expectations of others. Even God rejects conformity, in her estimation, because in her experience, God has never been the one to constrain her choices or put her in a box. A profound sense of autonomy, self-sufficiency, and flexibility runs through her theologizing about human nature. Samantha speaks of "enough" and "plenty"—sufficiency and abundance—to express her conviction that each human is born with a wholeness and a profusion of abilities and internal resources. Using those abilities and resources, an individual can work to rise more fully into her true, authentic, and unique self.

Samantha's repeated refrain of the importance of knowing that you are enough in yourself implies that she has encountered forces in her life that tell her and others that they are lacking, deficient, and not enough. As a woman of color who dealt with systemic racism and poverty in South Africa, she has certainly experienced situations in which she and members of her Cape Coloured community were not seen as fully human. Scholars have attested to the toll that colonization and Apartheid have taken on these communities of mixed-race people, who were systematically segregated and relegated to their own "group area."[33] Patriarchal ideology was also a part of her Cape Coloured world, as it is in virtually every community around the globe.[34]

Mormonism has empowered her in many ways and given her important resources for formulating her convictions about people's inherent wholeness, but Samantha has also seen it contribute to messages which imply that African Black and Coloured women are not enough and complete in themselves. Samantha recounted this as she talked about being a leader in the Latter-day Saint Young Women organization in South Africa:

> I look at these pictures in the *Ensign*, and I see these articles and I see these Mormon videos with these smiling beautiful blonde white girls with perfect teeth and how they are just so happy to defer to their parents and their husbands and their brothers in everything they are, and they are so happy. It makes me feel sick. I look at them, and I say to the young women, "You are not those people. You are an African child. You have a different upbringing. You have different perspectives, and it's okay. It's okay to speak. It's okay to ask questions. It's okay. You don't have to be a white person to be a Mormon." That's my point. You are still very much who you are. It's okay to be who you are. Or you don't have to be an American to be a Mormon. You don't have to speak like them. You don't have to pray like them. You don't have to dress like the sister missionaries you see in the *Ensign*. There are other ways to be modest too. You can find who you are and that's perfectly acceptable to the Lord.[35]

For Samantha, messages from the institutional church that present a narrow vision of ideal appearance and behavior are damaging to young African women. She is aware of the power of Latter-day Saint media and its ability to promote messages of inclusion or exclusion, depending on who is represented. In contrast to what she often sees in church media, Samantha envisions an abundance of ways to live, look, and be Mormon. Gospel principles are important to her, but embracing diverse ways to live out those principles is essential if people of all nationalities, races, and cultures are to be uplifted. In her experience, specific (and Utah-based) prescriptions for conformity undermine Africans' sense of wholeness and being "plenty" in themselves. In her theological vision of abounding human nature as well as in her moral paradigm of a non-oppressive connectedness that yearns for wider representation in church contexts, Samantha articulates her vision of people everywhere finding space in Latter-day Saint communities to become the strong and unique individuals God has created them to be.

Warona, from Botswana, similarly held up the importance of embracing one's unique self in her final reflections on lessons she has learned in life. It is intriguing that she also mentioned the importance of moving away from a mindset of competition and scarcity:

> My Heavenly Father is going to use me with my weaknesses, with how loud I am, with how easy it is for me to smile, and how sensitive I am. He's going to use you just the way you are. I've also learned that when you get promoted at work, they're not taking a star from somebody else's shoulder to give it to you, so it doesn't have to be a competition. Even in the spiritual things. When Heavenly Father gives you a blessing, He's not taking from another person's pot of gold.[36]

Warona shares Samantha's conviction that God values people in their individuality and that they, as individuals, are infinitely precious to God. For Warona, as for Samantha, there is an abundance of ways to live out a worthy Mormon life. Worthiness is not contingent on homogeneity. This insight has no doubt helped her as she has made choices to further her career as Botswana's first female military officer. These choices have meant leaving her baby for months at a time to complete the required military service, thus putting her outside Mormon expectations about gender roles. Nevertheless, Warona is a devoted Latter-day Saint and has served in the highest leadership positions available to women at the ward and stake levels. Her experience with God has indeed taught her that God needs her as she is, with all her unique talents, questions, vision, and ambition, to help elevate and contribute to her community.

Her subsequent insight about moving away from a scarcity framework—that God's ability to pour forth blessings is not finite—echoes Nia's beliefs about God's metaphysical abundance. The subtext of Warona's thinking could very well be her experience with losing her newborn son. This son survived for only a few days, and for a period of time she found it painful to see other women and their healthy babies. In Botswana, which has one of the highest HIV rates in the world and which has an infant mortality rate higher than those of most Western countries, death is an ever-present part of life.[37] Warona's realization that blessings are not a zero-sum game and that one person's blessings do not entail loss for another person has helped bring her peace as she has navigated her career and motherhood. Warona, in the space of just a few sentences, thus brings together both the theme of metaphysical abundance and the theme of internal abundance, as God affirms and appreciates women in all their uniqueness.

Samantha's and Warona's reflections point to fruitful directions for constructing a theology of abundance. Arising from their own lives and experiences, the wisdom they have gained about embracing and accepting oneself, about not trying to compare and measure up to certain norms formulated in other communities, and about the infinite wholeness of one's unique self comprises religious insights that can undergird a Mormon theology of abundance. These women from southern Africa therefore add a self-focused dimension to the theme of non-oppressive connectedness which has undergirded many Latter-day Saint women's thinking and priorities. Developing a healthy, generous, and affirming relationship with one's unique and authentic self is a hallmark of their thoughts about sufficiency and abundance.

Mexican Women: An Abundance of Revelation

Southern African women described an abundance of internal resources and strength inherent in every woman. Mexican Latter-day Saint women, on the other hand, described the abundance of spiritual power available to them. This sense of spiritual power emerged as they discussed the revelatory experiences that connect them to the postmortal and divine realms. Dreams were an important element of their spirituality, and through dreams these women described a depth and breadth of spiritual connection that was striking. Dreams strengthened connections and relationships not only to divine parents but also to earthly parents and grandparents who had passed away.

Ana gives us a glimpse of how such revelatory dreams often function in these women's lives. She mentioned dreaming that her father accepted the Latter-day Saint proxy temple rituals that were performed for him following his death: "The week we came back from Mexico [City]—that's where we were sealed—I dreamed. I had such a special dream that when I woke up I felt so energized. I went to my mom's room and told her about my dream. When I'd described the dream, my mom hugged me and said, 'Dad chose you to tell us that he has accepted the gospel."[38] Both Ana and her mother unreservedly accepted this dream as revelation. As Ana later mentioned, dreams are an important spiritual conduit for Mexicans:

> We are a dreaming people. We're a dreaming people, so I dream many things. Everything has a meaning. My mother has died, my father has died, all of my brothers who I loved so much died, and we have this help, that they can come to us in dreams to guide us and help us. . . . If we are good, we can understand many of the things they tell us, what they foretell, because we admired them when they were here on earth. . . . I have a lot of experiences with this.[39]

Appropriate to both her identity as a Mexican Latter-day Saint and to her worldview of non-oppressive connectedness, Ana's dreams and the dreams of other Latter-day Saint women often served to strengthen connections between ancestors and the living. Given Mormonism's emphasis on redeeming the dead and turning the hearts of children to their fathers, it is understandable that these women's spirituality so often emphasized the bonds between the generations, living and dead.

Dreams and visions have been important characteristics of female religiosity and piety in Mexico for hundreds of years. In discussing the power of visionary and prophetic women's narratives and practices in Mexican history, Edward Wright-Rios traces this aspect of their piety to Catholicism. "The tight braiding of female piety and mysticism became a prominent feature of Catholicism in the Middle Ages, and it remained profoundly influential afterward. Visions became the centerpiece of most claims of sanctity for women."[40] He describes how the idea of the devout visionary Mexican Catholic woman—in particular, one Madre Matiana, who, according to legend, described the catastrophes coming to the nation in the face of liberalism and secularism—took the country by storm and became intertwined with nationalism and Catholic revivalism in the nineteenth century.

Mexico's female visionary culture, combined with Mormonism's own visionary history, has opened space for Mexican Latter-day Saint women to experience and claim this powerful spiritual phenomenon. Many of Mormonism's foundational stories center on Joseph Smith's visions of God and angels.[41] Other early church leaders had dreams or visions that they considered revelatory and that helped shape the direction of the church.[42] Nineteenth-century Latter-day Saint women likewise experienced revelatory dreams and visions. Lydia Knight's dream of Joseph Smith's approaching visit was considered by Smith to be revelation from God, and Prescindia Huntington saw angels on top of the Kirtland temple.[43] Such stories may be less common now in standard American Mormon rhetoric than they used to be, but Mormonism continues to affirm dreams and visions as legitimate vehicles for personal revelation.[44]

Like Ana's dream, Pilar's visionary experiences also incorporate and affirm unique Mormon elements and beliefs. At one point in her life Pilar became extremely ill, and while she was at the hospital, she had a dream that gave her comfort and religious insight. She said, "While I slept I had a dream about my [late] grandmother; I saw her going around me in the air in circles with several sisters dressed in white. I looked at my grandmother and she was smiling at me."[45] This dream became particularly meaningful for her later when she went to the temple for the first time and saw women dressed in the same clothing those in her dream had worn. When she saw the temple clothing, she started to cry and explained her dream to the temple worker. It is noteworthy that the temple—and the religious rituals performed there that bind family members together for eternity—played a role in both Ana and Pilar's most moving and meaningful dreams.

Perhaps the most striking dream I heard about as I interviewed Latter-day Saint women in Mexico was one that featured Heavenly Mother. The existence of an embodied divine woman, the consort of God the Father and mother of human spirits, is a belief treasured by many Mormons. Yet Heavenly Mother is rarely spoken of in Latter-day Saint meetings. Church leaders model male God language, consistently calling God "Heavenly Father," and President Gordon B. Hinckley explicitly instructed Latter-day Saints in the 1990s not to pray to Heavenly Mother. Folk doctrines that justify Latter-day Saints' silence about Heavenly Mother have arisen over the years, most notably one which claims that Heavenly Father wants Heavenly Mother to remain hidden since he is protecting Her from the taunts that humans often level at deity.[46]

Because of this "sacred silence" that has arisen around Heavenly Mother, Liliana's dream about Heavenly Mother speaking to her and telling her to disseminate a message of love to other women is remarkable. Liliana considers this dream to be revelatory:

One day I had a dream about Heavenly Mother. She spoke to me. I was in the town where I was born, and I was under an avocado tree. And suddenly I heard this voice. She began, "I love all my daughters." It was a beautiful voice. "I love all of them, and I want all of them to come back to me." I started to look up in heaven. It was a sweet voice. Not like my voice. It was a voice I never heard in my life. That voice filled my heart. "I love my daughters, and I want them to come to me. I know how much they suffer. I know how difficult it is to be there. I know that when they leave here, I cry because when they go there I know how difficult it is, but I want them to know that I love them and that they are not alone because I want all of them to come back to me." Then I found out where the voice came from—it came from earth! There were two little dry sticks and a mist coming between them, and that was her voice. I was always taught that Sacrament meeting was the most important meeting, but she said to go to all your meetings. Relief Society, Sacrament meeting, conferences, all types of meetings, and if it is about spiritual things, it will bring you close to me. "Attend it. Go to it. I love all my daughters. I want all of them to come to me. I know how difficult the world is for them. You may come to me. I'm waiting for you." That was the voice. She said, "Tell my daughters. Tell them."

I shared this dream with my sister who was having problems. I felt this dream was for her. I told her we don't just have Heavenly Father but also Heavenly Mother. Not just Heavenly Father and Jesus Christ, also our Heavenly Mother is with us. I shared with [my daughter] and everyone I could. But there was a time in Relief Society in our ward when I went to Relief Society, and the teacher had all these visual aids. I felt a warm air come to me, and I felt that I had to bear my testimony that day. I said, I have to bear my testimony? The class was on Heavenly Mother. And I said, "This is a very special dream, and I don't share this with many people except those that I feel the Spirit telling me I should tell, but the Spirit is telling me I should talk about it." And on that day, we were talking about Heavenly Mother so I had to give my testimony. There was a sister who was crying. Tears ran down and down, and she made me cry too. She was sobbing. I thought, why is she crying so much? When Relief Society was over, she said, "Thank you for your testimony—it's an answer to my prayer. I've been fasting the entire week and asking Heavenly Father if Heavenly Mother is true. And today he answered my prayer through you. I think I'm going to write this down." That was a testimony to me that the dream was real because it was an answer to a prayer, and it was from Heavenly Mother.[47]

Liliana's dream about a loving, empathetic God the Mother is striking in its combination of distinctly Mormon elements (encouraging her to go to her church meetings) and elements atypical of Mormon conceptions of embodied deity (a voice emerging as mist between two dry sticks, coming from inside the Earth). The dream is also striking in the way it explicitly authorized Liliana to prophetically speak with some sense of authority about God the Mother to other Latter-day Saint women: "Tell my daughters. Tell them." That Liliana and other women in this class found the courage to talk about Heavenly Mother, given Latter-day Saints' typical reluctance to mention Her, is itself unusual, and the courage it must have taken for Liliana to disseminate this message in a church setting cannot be underestimated. As Elizabeth Alvilda Petroff writes of female visionaries in previous centuries,

Liliana's dream gave her "a voice and a belief in herself as chosen to speak," and thus empowered her to assert herself as having a role to play in carrying God's message to others.[48] Liliana's spiritual gift of receiving revelation through dreams allowed her to commune directly with deity. Even more revolutionary, it compelled her to act as a messenger for Heavenly Mother to the women in her ward, who, as Liliana relates, were likewise hungry to know more about Her.

The Mexican women I interviewed did not directly theologize about the concept of abundance, but their experience of God opening the heavens and pouring down on them knowledge of the divine and postmortal realms can inform a womanist theology of abundance. In their worldview and experience, God has abundantly endowed these women with spiritual gifts and abilities to part the veil and to strengthen connections to deity and previous generations of family members. Thus Mexican women cultivated an abundance of relational ties to departed parents and grandparents, who appeared to them in dreams and communicated important insights or comfort to the women. Mormonism's affirmation of personal revelation from God—through dreams, visions, feelings, sudden insights, voices, and more—is ultimately an important counterweight to Mormonism's emphasis on church hierarchy and authority. It is also an element of piety that these women found inspiring, expanding, and ennobling, as they used their spiritual gifts to experience vistas and realms outside their mundane everyday lives. These women's experiences with God reaching through the veil to personally enlighten them serve as a powerful example of one way in which an abundance theology can manifest itself in women's lives.

Developing a Mormon Womanist Theology of Abundance

Embracing the Wisdom of Women Who Have Come Before

As feminist and womanist theologians have argued, the experiences of women are an essential source of theological insight when constructing theology.[49] The stories, insights, and scriptural reflections of everyday Latter-day Saint women such as Ana, Nia, Warona, Samantha, Pilar, Jessica, and Liliana are therefore important sources for developing a Mormon theology of abundance. Womanists have also argued that authoritative sources for ethics and theology can be found in a variety of formats and places. Womanists consider authoritative folk wisdom, the stories of their grandmothers, autobiographies and literature written by Black women and other women of color, and the scholarship of Black women and other women of color.[50] Uncovering and lifting up the words and wisdom of women of color is an essential project for womanists. Inspired by this methodology, which gives the weight of authority to a variety of women's stories, thoughts, and writings, I turn to the theological reflections of Chieko Okazaki, former General Relief Society presidency member, as another potentially fruitful source of authority in constructing a Mormon womanist theology of abundance. Many of her reflections echo or expand on the visions and religious imaginations of the women discussed above.

A native of Hawaii of Japanese descent and a convert from Buddhism, Okazaki stands as one of Mormonism's most prolific female theologians, having produced nine books of religious thought and reflection. Okazaki recognized in Latter-day Saint women a sense of insufficiency, of unwholeness, of worry that they were not good enough and were falling short. As a woman of color, she was more aware than many about the pitfalls of the inevitable exportation of culture along with gospel. In her famous sermon "Baskets and Bottles" she discusses this balance of finding and accepting new ways to live out the gospel and pushing gently against the conformity that Samantha and Nia decry:

> The doctrines of the gospel are indispensable. They are essential, but the packaging is optional. Let me share a simple example to show the difference between the doctrines of the church and the cultural packaging. Here is a bottle of Utah peaches, prepared by a Utah homemaker to feed her family during a snowy season. Hawaiian homemakers don't bottle fruit. They pick enough fruit for a few days and store it in baskets like this for their families. . . . The basket and the bottle are different containers, but the content is the same: fruit for a family. Is the bottle right and the basket wrong? No, they are both right. They are containers appropriate to the culture and the needs of the people. And they are both appropriate for the content they carry, which is the fruit.[51]

Okazaki goes on to explain that the fruit that sustains is the fruit of the Spirit: love, joy, peace, longsuffering, gentleness, goodness, faith, meekness, and temperance. How these ideals are packaged in various cultures matters not at all, so long as the basic principles are the same. With teachings like this, Okazaki strongly affirms individual and cultural diversity within a Mormon context. In so doing she emphasizes a Mormonism that is expansive in its scope and robust and flexible enough to work alongside global members' cultural loyalties and diverse worldviews. Implicit in her metaphor is a rejection of tendencies to judge others and insist on conformity regarding various practices. She understood that a stronger faith tradition, and a stronger sense of connectedness and respect among Saints, emerge when global members have the freedom to package Mormon principles in practices appropriate to their unique cultural contexts.

In addition to being particularly sensitive to the loyalties and cultural tensions of global Latter-day Saints, Okazaki also had an expansive vision of women's spiritual capacities and gifts. Much like the Mexican women I spoke with, Okazaki envisioned a world in which angels might interact with women and give them direct divine guidance for their lives:

> We say that we believe that God "will yet reveal many great and important things pertaining to the Kingdom of God." (Article of Faith 9.) Revelation to the Church will come through the prophet, but doesn't that article of faith make you ask questions? What are those great and important things? And who will he reveal them to? Could you be one of those who is struggling to "understand the matter, and consider the vision"? If you are, then you're one of those worthy to receive an angelic visitor. Furthermore, the promise of Joseph Smith to the Nauvoo Relief Society on 28 April 1844 was this: "Angels cannot be restrained from being your associates". . . . Has this promise come true for you? Both Joseph Smith and Alma promise the ministrations of angels to women. . . . Is it possible that we're asking the wrong questions and limiting the operation of the Holy Ghost, cutting off the spiritual gifts that the Father wants to bestow upon us, and feeling fear rather than faith?[52]

While Okazaki affirms the male hierarchy's role in obtaining revelation for the church, she simultaneously emphasizes that women should look to themselves for revelation pertaining to the kingdom of God. In her religious imagination, women are entitled to spectacular spiritual manifestations and revelation. It is women's fear and the limited vision of their own capacities that prevent more women from experiencing an abundance of spiritual gifts and manifestations. Okazaki, along with the women in Mexico, believed in the importance of women developing, honoring, and trusting in their spiritual capacity to receive revelation from the divine.

Okazaki also echoes Samantha's reflection on the importance of women knowing that they are not only enough, they are plenty. One of Okazaki's books, actually titled *Being Enough*, similarly emphasizes that what women in their individuality can bring to God and the kingdom is infinitely acceptable to the divine. She writes, "Who you are is enough. What you have to give is enough. Your best is sufficient. Your light shines enough to be a standard."[53] Okazaki ties together the concept of sufficiency with the concept of abundance in her reading of the story of the widow's mite: "I see in Jesus' praise of this poor widow a joyous acceptance, even a celebration of her gift. He attested that her offering was not only enough, but was incredibly generous, unbelievably abundant. What she had to give was enough and more than enough. . . . Jesus was probably the only person in all of Jerusalem who looked at this woman and saw that she had given with abundance."[54] Others might have seen scarcity in the widow's life and offering, but in Okazaki's reading, Jesus saw abundance. What she had, what she was, was eminently acceptable to and appreciated by Jesus. To Okazaki, there is a wholeness to each of us, and what we have to offer the world in our uniqueness is not meager. On the contrary, it is abundant.

When Samantha described her hopes that her children would know that they are enough as they are, I suspected that she had read Okazaki's book. But when I asked her, Samantha said she had never heard of Okazaki. Samantha's lack of knowledge of one of Mormonism's most prolific female general leaders points to one of the difficulties Latter-day Saint women have in embracing and holding up other women as spiritual authorities. Within Mormonism there is little institutional memory of women's theological insights. This stands in contrast to the insights of male general leaders, whose words are often repeated in lessons, talks, and teaching manuals. Because female general leaders now only occupy their positions of leadership in the Relief Society, Primary, and Young Women organizations for five years or so, there is also little chance for them to make a significant impact through large-scale projects. Thus, an integral part of a Mormon womanist theology of abundance is to recover, emphasize, and treat as authoritative the wisdom and insights of Mormonism's theologians of color whose reflections are in danger of being forgotten or lost. Okazaki is a prime source for authoritative insight in constructing such a theology, given both the sheer volume of her writing and her inclusive, sensitive theological reflections, which so often evince a commitment to the wholeness and inclusion of the faith's more vulnerable members.

Drawing on Women in the Scriptures

Highlighting scriptural archetypes to whom women can relate and from whom they can draw insight has been an important methodological device for womanist theologians. For instance, Delores Williams, a founding mother of womanist theology, grounded her theology in the scriptural figure of Hagar, to whom, Williams wrote, generations of Black women have looked for wisdom and inspiration. Like Black women in American history, Hagar

experienced slavery, oppression from men and women, poverty, homeless-
ness, and exploitation of her body. However, Williams recounts, Hagar also
encountered a God who spoke to her and helped her "make a way out of no
way."[55] This God might not have led her to liberation, but God did help her
survive her oppression and time in the wilderness.

This methodological device of highlighting women in scripture whose
challenges in life and experiences of God resonate with certain groups of
women is another promising direction for the construction of a Mormon
womanist theology of abundance. Eve may seem the obvious choice as an
important archetype for Latter-day Saint women. Not only do they assume
the place of Eve in sacred temple ceremonies, but Mormons also have a
unique take on Earth's first woman. Unlike the many Christian faiths that
traditionally conflate Eve with sin for eating the apple and causing the Fall,
modern Mormonism reconceptualizes Eve as enlightened, courageous, and
inspired. In choosing to eat the fruit, she led the way in propelling humankind
on its cosmic journey to obtain bodies, gain experience and wisdom, and
progress toward eventual divinity. In making that choice, Eve had to navigate
ambiguity and conflicting commandments. She had to make a painful and
courageous decision to move humanity forward, though it would eventually
cost her her life and result (paradoxically) in her subordination to Adam. In
this framework, Eve becomes something akin to a Jesus figure.[56]

When I asked Latter-day Saint women from southern Africa, Mexico, and
the United States who their favorite scriptural figure was, I fully expected Eve
to be repeatedly named. But she never was. Rather, a wide variety of responses
emerged. Job was mentioned several times in Mexico and Botswana. Nephi
was mentioned in all locations. Esther, Ruth, Jesus, and many more were
named. But it was a small handful of women's reflections on Mary, Mother
of Jesus, which caught my attention.

Mary, Mother of Jesus: Encapsulating Abundance and Mapping a Way Forward

Mary of Nazareth, mother of Jesus, may be a surprising choice as a scriptural model who might map a path forward for Latter-day Saint women on
the margins. But as a woman navigating her path in a system of colonization
and oppression, as a woman who prophetically proclaims what will become
a large part of her son's societal vision and mission, and as a person who
courageously says yes to God's call despite the real danger to her life, she
has distinct potential for that role. Her story can be particularly resonant

for Latter-day Saint women of color and offers a model of strength, vision, and power amid wider systems of oppression.

Many religious thinkers over the centuries have used Mary to represent ideal (passive) femininity.[57] This has led some feminists to reject her as an empowering figure for women.[58] Indeed, Mariology in Catholicism has, according to Mary Jo Weaver, "generally been used to preserve pure femininity, support complementarity, and justify male dominion. As a symbol of perfect motherhood and spotless virginity, Mary embodies an impossible combination of attributes."[59] Mary is not emphasized in Mormonism, but the few teachings Latter-day Saints have about Mary do not describe her as immaculately conceived and perpetually a virgin.[60] Church teachings instead tend to focus on her as an obedient woman and loving mother.[61] The women I interviewed who spoke of Mary had a more expansive vision of Mary, however, that did not reduce her to feminine passivity or a model of obedience. Rather, they saw in her story aspects of their own, both in the challenges she endured and in her courage, strength, and spiritual power. When read in this light, Mary embodies a theological conception of abundance as well as a commitment to non-oppressive connectedness, and her story offers empowering insights and confluences for Latter-day Saint women outside the privileged center.

Mary's power for marginal Latter-day Saint women is located in her social location in ancient Israel. Like many of the women with whom I spoke, she has to navigate a world shaped by poverty and systemic inequities. In Mary's time Israel was occupied by the Romans, and it is because of a decree by the Roman emperor Augustus that she and Joseph return to his hometown of Bethlehem to register for a Roman census. She is a girl of a colonized people, dealing with the strains of that oppression. Poverty, burdens, and the navigation of a system in which she and her people are at the mercy of an imperial power are backdrops to her story.

Samantha, the Cape Coloured native of South Africa who had experienced her fair share of structural inequities, was particularly sensitive to Mary's status as a vulnerable unwed pregnant girl in a harsh political and social environment. She pointed to the internal strength Mary had to have in order to succeed in her mission to bear and raise Jesus amid such oppression:

She [Mary] is the poster woman for unplanned pregnancy. She literally has an unplanned pregnancy. And she has to navigate a social system and class that I can't even begin to fathom. And she does it with such grace. . . . I'm sure she encountered people who just weren't nice to her and made things difficult for her. So I look at her and I go, "She did a very hard thing, and she didn't ask for any of this, and she was a woman and she had so little power, socially or politically, even within her own family. And yet she had such power because she was chosen." So she must have had such power that I don't even know if they could have even appreciated who she was and what she must have had in her own self. The kind of strength that she must have had. So her story is pretty inspiring to me.[62]

Samantha sees in Mary a marginal figure, oppressed politically, socially, and economically, who nevertheless draws on her inherent strengths and fulfills her difficult and dangerous mission. For Samantha, Mary embodies a type of internal abundance. Though marginalized in virtually every category, Mary has strengths and reserves abounding within that she is able to call forth. Samantha's Mary embodies unbounded resilience.

Despite this context of political and social oppression that might have made her powerless, Mary is powerful in her response to the challenges life laid out before her. In the face of the angel Gabriel's pronouncement that Mary would bear God's son, she courageously assents. This assent, often known as Mary's fiat, is read by some feminist theologians as an enthusiastic yes to God that springs from her own free will. Rosemary Radford Ruether sees in Mary's assent a model for the new redemptive community of Jesus, a community based on voluntary association and mutual choice.[63] Mary's "free act of faith"—she doesn't consult with Joseph or anyone else before agreeing—suggests to Ruether a co-creatorship between God and humanity.[64] Other liberative interpretations of the story suggest a Mary full of vision and power, as well as a God who sees and embraces the lowly and sets them on divine missions. God's choice of a poor, vulnerable girl for this role indicates to Weaver God's preference for the poor, and Mary thus "represents those classes of the subjugated who will be lifted up and filled with good things when the Messiah comes."[65] Indeed, Mary's story signifies the abundance of abilities and courage residing in "the least of these." Mary—poor, young, female, and colonized subject—believes she is capable of seeing this mission through. She believes that she can withstand the shame and threat to her life that an out-of-wedlock pregnancy would visit upon her. Though she has every reason to shrink from this mission, she embraces it with an abundance of courage and hope that she will be strong enough to bear God into the world. Mary's response in Luke 1:38, "Behold the handmaid of the Lord; be it unto me according to thy word," is sometimes read as feminine self-effacement and passive obedience. I, however, see this assent as a courageous step into the unknown, as she becomes a partner to God in bringing about the salvation of humanity.

While this openness to partnering with God to save humanity involves motherhood in Mary's case, my reading of Mary resists a reduction of her importance to her role as mother. Jesus himself forcefully refutes a reduction of women to their reproductive functions. When a woman in a crowd calls out to him, "Blessed is the womb that bore you and the paps that gave thee suck" Jesus replies to her, "Rather, blessed are those who hear the word of God and keep it."[66] Indeed, as Jesus indicates, Mary should not be reduced to her role as mother. Motherhood is a key factor in her story, but Mary symbolizes far more than this one role. She is a model of active, purposeful agency and discipleship as she sets out to accomplish the mission God has given her. Her femaleness is not defined by motherhood.

Mary emerges as a symbolically rich figure for women on the margins in two stories following the Annunciation. First is the story of Mary's meeting with her cousin Elizabeth. After Elizabeth, filled with the Spirit, prophesies that Mary's child will be the Lord, Mary, in a passage known as the Magnificat, in turn prophesies the "revolutionary transformation of an unjust social order."[67] With this advent of the Messiah into the world, Mary says, God has defeated the oppressors and has "scattered the proud in the imagination of their hearts. / He hath put down the mighty from their seats, and exalted them of low degree. / He hath filled the hungry with good things; and the rich he hath sent empty away."[68] In this prophetic song of praise, Mary sets out the framework of what will become much of Jesus's social mission of lifting up the poor and the marginal. Like her son, Mary is no meek supporter of the status quo. She too seeks justice for the oppressed. In this passage, Mary emerges as a prophetic figure abounding with spiritual power, speaking aloud her vision of breaking down the social barriers that push some people down and raise others up. Mary envisions an abundance of justice for those who have been marginalized and oppressed.

Mary again emerges as a figure of insight and vision in John 2 at the wedding feast at Cana where Jesus performs his first miracle. She is the initiator, the catalyst, the motivating force in the story. The passage reads, "And when they wanted wine, the mother of Jesus saith unto him, They have no wine. Jesus saith unto her, Woman, what wilt thou have me to do for thee? That will I do; for mine hour is not yet come. His mother saith unto the servants, Whatsoever he saith unto you, do it."[69] Mary knows her son is capable of miraculous deeds, and it is she who sets the stage for him to turn the water into wine. Not only does she first prompt him by pointing out the problem, she then prepares the way for the miracle by having the servants stand ready to give Jesus anything he might need. Though Jesus is reluctant to act, saying, "mine hour is not yet come," Mary understands that this is the time and place for him to begin his ministry and mission. Twice she goads him to take this step forward, to show the people who he is. Her wise judgment, her decisiveness, her confidence, and her vision of Jesus's potential bring about this first startling, miraculous event in Jesus' ministry. It is appropriate that this story, connected with themes of bounteous generosity and concern as well as themes of God meeting us in our individual crises, is driven by Mary, who knows that her son has come to offer a new vision of divine abundance.

In short, the biblical Mary of Nazareth stands as a potentially powerful model of insight and strength for Latter-day Saint women of color who similarly say yes to God, step into the unknown, confront systemic oppression, exercise agentive proactivity, and display spiritual power and insight. The theme of abundance runs throughout Mary's story as it runs throughout the reflections of various Latter-day Saint women of color. Like Nia and Salleh, Mary envisions an external abundance of justice and opportunities for the marginalized of the world. She also exhibits an internal abundance of courage, spiritual gifts, vision, and ability—all qualities that Liliana, Jessica, Samantha, and other Latter-day Saint women reference in their oral histories—as she agrees to partner with God and urges Jesus to embark on his divine mission. Like Mary, marginal Latter-day Saint women also have hidden depths of strength and insight. Their oral histories recount how God has abundantly gifted them with capabilities, and Mary's story likewise demonstrates that the most marginal contain quantities of wisdom and ability that are often overlooked by the elite. Mary's story entails sacrifice, but it is an agentive giving of self that begins her journey of, as Jessica might say, rising into herself and becoming herself. In Mary's story, we can see her vision and proactivity, her confidence and assertiveness, as she partners with God and Jesus to offer the world a new vision of life abundant.

Abundance, Non-Oppressive Connectedness, and Womanist Theology

In the wide variety of theological reflections and focuses that emerged in the dozens of oral histories of women from the United States, Mexico, and southern Africa, the theme of metaphysical, personal, and spiritual abundance stands out. These reflections take on different nuances in different locations: American women rejected notions of metaphysical and internal scarcity in favor of an abundance mindset, southern African women described an abundance of internal resources, and Mexican women described their spiritual lives as overflowing with vibrant dreams and visions. These focuses are distinct, but they share an expansive vision of human capacity and of God's concern and desire for our wholeness and well-being. They also share an emphasis on connection, community, and affirming relationships with God, others, and self.

Non-oppressive connectedness therefore emerges as an important theme in their reflections on abundance, albeit with distinct variances. Some American women's understandings of the abundance of God's blessings lead them to advocate for non-oppressive and inclusive church structures that could enable stronger, more authentic relationships between center and margins, whereas others' abundance thinking leads to wholehearted service and relationship building that only expand the self. The southern African women see in themselves an abundance of capabilities as they affirm that they are enough and more than enough, despite messages they might receive to the contrary. Thus, embracing a sense of themselves as complete and overflowing with possibility leads to a healthy and positive connection with themselves. For the Mexican women, with their sense of abundant spiritual and visionary power, fostering non-oppressive and soul-satisfying connections with the divine and postmortal realms is often a focus of their powerful dreams and visions. A commitment to non-oppressive connectedness therefore grounds these women's thinking about abundance.

As womanist theologians argue, the reflections, stories, and religious imaginations of everyday women of color are vital sources for constructing theologies. They also suggest that additional richness and power for such theologies can be found in the lives and stories of women in the community, past and present. Thus, recording the words of living women and searching through archives to find and highlight the reflections and wisdom of women of color who have died are important womanist projects. Chieko Okazaki, for example, is a rich source of such wisdom for the development of a Mormon theology of abundance and other yet-to-be articulated Mormon womanist and feminist theologies. Additional richness and depth for such theologies can be found in the stories of scriptural women whose experiences of life and God resonate with those of Latter-day Saint women. I suggest that Mary, mother of Jesus, is a rich symbol in such theological constructions, and others such as Abish, Deborah, Rebecca, Eve, and the daughters of Zelophehad could be useful in further Mormon womanist and intersectional feminist theological work.

This theme of abundance that manifests itself in different Latter-day Saint women's reflections on God, spirituality, and human nature is powerful in its flexibility. An abundance mindset can lead some to imagine liberative, radical restructurings of Latter-day Saint church hierarchy and governance. It can also be applied on an individual level in ways that leave current structures untouched as women see in themselves the potential for expansive spiritual power and personal strength. Whether abundance mindsets contribute to radical new imaginings of the church or retain current systems, a unifying drive and direction in abundance thinking is its expansive sense of women's capacities to be agents for God, to discern God's will, to form just and affirming communities, and to develop personally into whole, healthy, unique individuals. Perhaps not surprisingly, there is thus a distinct confluence between this aspect of Latter-day Saint women's theological imaginations and that of Joseph Smith, who imagined human capacity as so vast that godhood is the ultimate destiny for each of the Mother and Father's daughters.

A womanist Mormon theology of abundance is only one of many possible theological articulations that might be constructed from the experiences of global women. When the foundations of Mormon theological constructions are expanded to include ethnography and lived religion, exciting new possibilities emerge. Women of color from around the world who have navigated complex lives without white privilege, who have found and created ennobling, vitalizing ways to connect to God and envision the expansiveness of the Mormon tradition, stand as important guides and voices of wisdom for the rest of the church. As the contemporary church contends with serious issues of retention in the United States as well as around the globe, listening to these women, who have, in effect, beaten the odds by retaining their Mormon identities and who have formulated inclusive, inspiring, and hopeful religious insights, is essential. A theology of abundance—and other theologies from the margins—invite new vision, hope, and possibilities for the tradition as a whole.

Conclusion

Crossroads are a potent symbol for women navigating their lives at the intersections of race, class, culture, and religion. The Latter-day Saint women featured in this book contend with multiple identities, loyalties and contexts. This intermingling of various identities and contexts is tense at times for some women, but it is often generative. Latter-day Saint women at the crossroads are adept at navigating complications, honoring their various loyalties, and adopting and adapting this faith tradition into their own contexts. As they shared with me stories from their lives, a dominant moral priority emerged: non-oppressive connectedness. These women's discussions of conversion, family life, church, community, experiences with God, and religious understandings reveal a worldview that places a great deal of importance on forming positive relationships with self, others, and the divine. For traditional Latter-day Saint women of color in Mexico, Botswana, and the United States, gender equality was not the primary lens through which they evaluated their experiences at church or in the home. This became clear to me as I noticed a disconnect between my interview questions about gender equality and the stories and reflections the women wanted to share with me. I came to realize a different interpretive paradigm was needed, one that better reflected their moral priorities and worldviews. The paradigm of vitalizing, non-oppressive connectedness centered their worlds and emerged as the most productive interpretive framework through which to analyze and understand these women's lives, choices, and agency. It also stands as an interpretive paradigm that might illuminate the lives of traditional religious women within other faith traditions.

This paradigm of non-oppressive connectedness contains within it elements of female empowerment and uplift, though it is often rooted in a gender complementarian framework which bounds women's actions. Global Latter-day Saint women frequently found spaces within Mormonism's patriarchal ecclesiastical and familial structure to achieve the spirituality, self-development, and uplifting relationships that they wanted to center their lives. Mormonism's injunctions to men to be devoted, proactive, and kind within the family and the church community gave many interviewed Latter-day Saint women means to create healthier marriages and more satisfying relationships. For these traditional religious women, gender roles and gender complementarity were not experienced as the main evils to be overcome. Rather, alienation, violence, and oppression were the evils they worked to eliminate. Mormonism was often a powerful tool in this quest to eliminate interpersonal oppression, but as oral histories gathered in Botswana, Mexico, and the United States attest, this did not mean that questions about church leaders' Americentric emphases and positions of privilege were disregarded when church injunctions clashed with certain local traditions, realities, or priorities. As Latter-day Saint women carefully navigated between their chosen faith and sometimes conflicting personal or cultural values, they enacted a complex, creative, and thoughtful agency.

Just as theological musings on abundance led some women at the crossroads to imagine radical restructurings of the church, so, too, did some women's commitments to non-oppressive connectedness lead them to imagine systemic change in Mormonism that might raise women and other marginalized Latter-day Saints to greater structural power within the church. Such adaptations in structure, these feminist Latter-day Saints indicated, may facilitate healthier, more authentic, and vitalizing community and connectedness. For this minority of Latter-day Saint women with whom I spoke, greater gender equality, decolonizing practices, and non-oppressive connectedness folded together into one dominant moral priority.

Throughout the composition of this book I strove to find a productive balance between emphasizing women's personal agency, spiritual power, opportunities, and relationships within Mormonism—themes that the women themselves often stressed—and acknowledging the sometimes less emphasized structural limitations and challenges that exist for women and other marginalized people within Mormon contexts. The two interpretive lenses, those of personal agency and structural power, are important elements of any balanced analysis. By exploring both the ways Mormonism enables personal connection, opportunity, and change while still recognizing how it constricts women's choices in various racial, national, and class contexts, I worked to incorporate both interpretive frameworks. While my own white Western feminist lens naturally veers toward examinations of gendered structural power, the voices of women outside the privileged center reveal new understandings of how and why women in diverse contexts embrace Mormonism. In particular, the broader paradigm and ethical imperative of non-oppressive connectedness most especially illuminates the choices and agentive actions of Latter-day Saint women of color. I have every hope that future scholars, perhaps especially ones arising within the communities studied, will elaborate on and nuance this framework, as well as uncover others that are equally significant.

Having studied and reflected on these women's oral histories for years, I close this book with a few final reflections about important themes and issues this project has raised. First, I am impressed by the power and depth of oral histories as primary sources for research. Luciana's furrowed brows and tentative response to my question about gender equality might have first alerted me that there was something off about my line of inquiry. But it was her life story, and the stories of many other women around the world, elicited from general questions about challenges, hopes, hard decisions, and childhood, that pointed me toward the paradigm of non-oppressive connectedness through which so many interviewed women were viewing the world. The method of oral history allowed the women the freedom to voice their priorities and concerns and tell the stories they wanted to tell, despite my handful of questions revolving around gender equality. As such, oral history stands as a decolonizing method, one that complements intersectional analysis by allowing diverse contexts and priorities to surface. I see great potential for oral history as a method that captures the stories that most matter to people in various locales and cultures. Its very breadth fights against the narrowing impulses of scholars who inevitably bring to the project their own lenses and priorities.

Although the focus of this book is the stories, visions, and priorities of Latter-day Saint women at the crossroads, some last thoughts on the implications of this work on the future of institutions might be in order. I am struck by the potential for stories and perspectives of global women and women of color to point to constructive ways forward for the church as a whole. These women have a depth of wisdom and insight that can only enrich and productively inform the privileged center. What might the church look like if the concerns of global women and women of color were centered and their wisdom honored? If church leaders make non-oppressive connectedness and abundance thinking priorities as they discuss policies and doctrinal emphases?

For one thing, the institutional church might emphasize the issue of domestic violence and devise stronger policies and programs to support survivors. Domestic and gender-based violence emerged as a powerful theme in these oral life history interviews. Whether in Mexico, Botswana, or the United States, several Latter-day Saint women told of sexual assault and domestic abuse. Church leaders have condemned gender-based violence in a few sermons and articles over the years, and oral histories attest that these condemnations and the general training of men to be benevolent in their relationships have been both appealing to women and often useful in helping some women fashion lives free of abuse. However, these oral histories and other accounts by Latter-day Saint women also suggest that this problem still exists in Mormon communities around the world, just as it exists in secular and other faith-based communities.

The issue of domestic violence within Mormonism was brought into public focus in early 2018 in the United States when two ex-wives of White House Staff Secretary Rob Porter, a Latter-day Saint, went public with the domestic violence they suffered at the hands of their husband.[1] In response to mounting criticism of Latter-day Saint bishops who encouraged women not to divorce abusive husbands, the church updated its guidelines for local church leaders, emphasizing that reports of abuse should be taken seriously and that women should not be encouraged to stay with abusive spouses.[2] These are important steps toward making Latter-day Saint victims of abuse safer. As one Latter-day Saint Pasifika woman writes, however, there is more that can be done to address this problem. Lani Wendt Young, the aforementioned Samoan writer, has seen the pervasiveness of domestic violence and sexual abuse in Samoa, including in Latter-day Saint homes. In a short but devastating anecdote, she writes of driving home from church one day and seeing a man dressed in church clothing on the side of the road beating his cowering wife with his scriptures as he dragged her by her hair.

Young suggests that the church could contribute funds toward providing trained counselors and treatment programs to help abusers and survivors in Samoa, an intervention that the country badly needs. She also recommends training for bishops, Relief Society presidents, and other ward leaders on how to respond to and help those in their congregations living in abusive families.[3] The issue of domestic violence, usually rarely and vaguely addressed in local Latter-day Saint church contexts (as Ana in Mexico attested), could be one that brings together traditional Latter-day Saint women, Mormon feminists, and church leaders of various backgrounds, locations, and worldviews to make meaningful progress on an issue all could agree is important. Encouraging and modeling benevolent male behavior can be powerful forces in helping to improve women's lives, as these oral histories strongly indicate. But more comprehensive programs in various locales, perhaps something akin to the Addiction Recovery Program and survivor support groups, might help change the lives of other women who have lived with domestic violence and sexual assault. The stories of women's experiences with gender-based violence in these oral histories stand out to me as having particularly important practical implications for Mormon communities. They highlight not only the success of different Mormon communities in creating cultures of benevolent masculinity that have been life-changing for many women but also the further work that could be done to help eradicate violent behavior, support survivors of abuse, and help women realize their hopes and dreams of abundant living.

Giving special consideration to the voices and experiences of Latter-day Saint global women and women of color might also entail the examination of church structures and systems that place so much institutional decision making in the privileged administrative center. Embedded in my memory are the words of Abril, a Mexican woman, who tearfully said to me at the end of our interview, "Tell them to bring the Benemérito back." The closing of this church-sponsored boarding school in Mexico City, a decision made in Salt Lake City with little input from the Mexicans affected by this decision, was the most painful episode of her life as a Latter-day Saint. It brought to the forefront questions about privilege, power, and the costs to global members when so much decision making resides in the United States. "We were not allowed to defend the Benemérito. They imposed [the closure] on us," Hortensia sadly said. A commitment to global partnership and connectedness—and stepping away from pervasive top-down management—might entail meetings, discussions, and brainstorming sessions with and among those affected before such decisions are made. In such meetings, invested local Saints could voice possibilities and solutions and speak directly to church leaders about matters that deeply affect them and their children. Self-determination by local Saints regarding decisions about, for instance, global church schools might be pie-in-the-sky thinking, given the church's centralized administrative structure. Nevertheless, the practice of deciding with global Saints regarding major changes, rather than deciding for global Saints, is a good one. Perhaps someday, decision-making bodies tasked with making such determinations will reflect the diversity of the church. With more female and global voices at the table, innovative solutions born of intimate knowledge of global concerns and contexts can be considered.

Deeply intertwined with the Mexican women's distress about the closing of the Benemérito was their great love and appreciation for the church school that did so much to help their youth. The women explained to me that local public schools were not safe or adequate, and being able to send their teenagers to a strong school that supported their Mormon values was profoundly meaningful for them. A renewed commitment to church-sponsored education outside the United States would therefore be one highly impactful way of nurturing global partnerships. The church currently operates more than a dozen primary, middle, and secondary schools outside the United States, most in the Pacific Islands. Church schools, as these Mexican women attested, do more than simply educate children. They enhance Latter-day Saint community and fellowship, increase possibilities for social mobility, and foster a type of connectedness that centers the needs of global members within a worldwide church network. The church appears to be on a trajectory of closing these schools, but they are a powerful means to maximize the good that can be done in local global communities.[4]

Privileging the voices and experiences of women of color and global women might also shift doctrinal and spiritual discourse that emerges from church headquarters. Melissa Wei-Tsing Inouye touches on this as she suggests that the charismatic experiences of Latter-day Saints in the global South be circulated through church headquarters to the church as a whole. Stories of charismatic experiences are a particularly valuable resource for members in the North who do not tend to experience the same kinds of miraculous stories and visions that some members in the South have, Inouye explains. She also sees the possibility of the Mormon North and the Mormon South engaging in a kind of symbiotic relationship in which the Mormon South supplies to the North "natural resources" such as the aforementioned miracle stories, convert baptisms, and faith-promoting stories for missionaries. The Mormon North, in turn, supplies "finished goods" to the South in the form of General Conference talks, lesson manuals, handbooks, and church Newsroom statements.[5] This is a productive vision of how global Saints' voices might nourish and impact church headquarters and the rest of the church. I suggest we expand on this vision and include the moral priority of non-oppressive connectedness and other wisdom of global women and women of color as natural resources that might nourish the privileged center. Including more such women in administrative positions engaged in the "finishing" of products would also, no doubt, lead to an enrichment of official church discourse. I note that church magazines have recently improved with regard to including the voices and perspectives of global Saints.[6] Perhaps these magazines are a harbinger of even more inclusion of global Saints' voices in other segments of the institutional church.[7] Ultimately, women of color from around the globe speaking and writing as Latter-day Saint spiritual authorities enhance global church partnership and push against pervasive white American male articulations of gospel living.

One specific area of religious discourse that might be enriched by a centering of global women's priorities, experiences, and commitment to connectedness is that of family and kinship theology. Mormonism's promise and potential for redeemed manhood, redeemed families, and whole and vibrant communities are profoundly compelling to Latter-day Saint women at the cultural crossroads, many of whom selected this faith tradition as a means of fulfilling their deepest hopes and needs. Amid a world of dislocation, family breakup, and the dissolution of other traditional structures—due in large part to colonial and globalizing forces—Mormonism often helps heal the breaches and pain that many of these women encounter in their daily lives. Just as the church serves as a new village for many women in Botswana, so it does for other Latter-day Saint women, who often find in it not only the community and relationships they desire in this life but also the promise of such relationships in the next. In their commitment to non-oppressive connectedness, Latter-day Saint women of color are in some senses embracing the early cosmological vision of Mormonism, which, as Jonathan Stapley writes, included visions of knitting the Mormon community together in a chain of eternal relationships.[8] A confluence therefore emerges between early Mormonism's vision of kinship and these women's commitment to vitalizing relationality, connection, and community. Today's Mormonism tends to downplay this early theological vision of expansive kinship through community, instead emphasizing and idealizing the middle-class nuclear family. Yet the stories of Latter-day Saint women of color around the world bring to the forefront the latent power of this kinship theology. Indeed, the voices of these women who understand the power of kinship and community may ultimately set the course to reclaim this powerful, expansive, and uniquely Mormon vision of connectedness.

On the local level, many women at the crossroads will continue to agentively, and often innovatively, navigate. Mormonism is particularly successful when it provides support, structure, connections, and principles but makes room for applications and interpretations that work in their particular contexts. Women in Mexico using Relief Society classes to teach one another marketable skills that they built into businesses is an unalloyed success for the church in that region. Women in Mexico and the United States finding and cultivating room in Mormonism for spiritually fulfilling charismatic visions and dreams is another story of success for the church. Women in southern Africa navigating cultural issues and finding ways to honor and understand both their chosen religion and traditional principles is a success for the church. I was particularly struck by an oral history from a Latter-day Saint woman in South Africa who embraced her identity as "*sangoma* [traditional African healer] of the church," since she saw a connection between the traditional duties of a *sangoma* (ritually connecting to dead ancestors) and her Mormon practice of family history and temple work.[9] There is strength and vitality in this woman's Mormon expression, as she upholds and values the intent of traditional practices but reshapes them into her Mormon context.

Many of these women will remain practicing, devoted members. I tended to interview highly committed women in Botswana and Mexico, and converts in those countries who maintain activity in the church will beat the odds, as studies show that the church generally retains about twenty-five percent of global converts.[10] These devout Saints will likely continue to find value and soul-sustaining connectedness in their church practice, even as they continue to negotiate multiple loyalties. Maria from Mexico remains committed and practicing, as do Musa and Warona from Botswana. Others, however, will slip away. Retaining single women is a particularly difficult prospect, as oral histories of Batswana women attest. Mormonism's focus on a functioning, loving nuclear family has strengthened many marriages, but single women will often struggle with a sociology and theology that puts great emphasis on a family structure they will, in many cases, never achieve. Retaining women who emphasize gender equality rather than gender complementarity will also be a challenge. Samantha from South Africa became increasingly distressed with the church's stance on gender and race since the time of our interview. She is no longer practicing. Nadine from the United States continues to cherish the Latter-day Saint community, but her disagreement with church leaders about LGBTQ issues, women's ordination, and their refusal to apologize for the priesthood-temple ban has led to her taking a step back from full church activity. When women determine that church policies and teachings contradict deeply held values and principles and when they lose hope that the church will someday adopt more inclusive practices, activity in the church becomes painful and burdensome. Nevertheless, their articulations of an expansive, sustaining Mormonism that enables human and divine connectedness and operates within a paradigm of abundance—as well as the articulations of women who have maintained their activity in the church—provide valuable insight into what women around the world find compelling, inspiring, and hopeful within the Mormon tradition.

This project to document and analyze the stories of Latter-day Saint women at the crossroads of race, religion, and culture is part of a greater shift in many academic and faith-based communities to lift up the voices of those on the margins of institutional power in order to alter the terms of analysis and meaningfully complicate the concerns and paradigms of the privileged center. The 2012 document by the World Council of Churches about the changing roles of churches and missions describes and justifies this paradigm shift well: "People on the margins have agency, and can often see what, from the centre, is out of view. People on the margins, living in vulnerable positions, often know what exclusionary forces are threatening their survival and can best discern the urgency of their struggles; people in positions of privilege have much to learn from the daily struggles of people living in marginal conditions."[11] Indeed, oral histories conducted with Latter-day Saint women of color around the globe offer important intersectional insights about the challenges, power, and potential of carving out a Mormon life. Their insights and stories offer not only fresh theological visions and pragmatic possibilities for improving the experiences of global Latter-day Saint women but also important nuances to contemporary academic conversations about women's agency. Ultimately, the ethical orientation toward which Latter-day Saint women often use their agency—non-oppressive connectedness—emerges as an important paradigm that illuminates women's choices to affiliate with this communally minded, family-centered, and patriarchal religious tradition.

Oral Life History Interview Questions for Women in Mexico

Parte 1. Historia Personal

- ¿Cómo llegó a ser miembro de la iglesia mormona (SUD)? Su proceso de conversión?
- Describa el origen de su familia y primeros años de vida. ¿Cuáles fueron sus retos y alegrías durante su infancia? Las experiencias religiosas? ¿Cuáles fueron las ocupaciones de sus padres?
- Si se casó, por favor dígame sobre su matrimonio, sus hijos y su vida familiar.
- ¿Ha trabajado usted? ¿Quién obtiene ingresos para su hogar?
- ¿Cuáles han sido sus principales retos en la vida? ¿Se ha enfrentado a la pobreza, la violencia, la guerra, o a la enfermedad en su vida? Si es así, ¿cómo ha enfrentado a esos desafíos?
- ¿Hay cosas importantes en su vida que ahora usted piensa que habría podido hacer de otra manera? ¿Su vida ha sido como la imaginaba?
- Hábleme de algún momento en que tuvo que tomar una desicion dificil. ¿Cómo lo hizo? ¿Alguna vez ha tomado una decisión que entraba en conflicto con la posición de la iglesia ?
- ¿Cuáles son sus esperanzas y aspiraciones para su vida?

Parte 2. Actitudes Sobre la Mujer SUD

- ¿Como se siente de ser una mujer mormona en México? Cuales son los aspectos más gratificantes? Las dificultades?
- Conoce usted "La Familia: Una proclamación para el mundo" ¿Su vida refleja los cometidos descritos en él? ¿Por qué o por qué no?
- ¿Cómo percibe el papel de las mujeres en el mormonismo? ¿Siente

que las mujeres son iguales a los hombres? ¿Tienen las mujeres suficientes oportunidades para el liderazgo en la iglesia? ¿Por qué o por qué no? ¿Cuál ha sido su experiencia con los hombres poseedores del sacerdocio y su papel en el liderazgo en el hogar y en la iglesia? ¿Cómo ha la autoridad masculina en el hogar y la iglesia ha afectado a su matrimonio y experiencias en la iglesia?

- ¿Qué papel cree que las mujeres deben desempeñar en la sociedad y en la comunidad? ¿Cree que las mujeres deberían ser líderes (políticos, empresariales, etc.)?
- ¿Qué opina de las enseñanzas de la iglesia sobre tener niños, la fertilidad y la reproducción? Experiencias? Reflexiones sobre control de la natalidad?
- ¿Cuales son las ensenanzas de la iglesia sobre las mujeres que trabajan? Las enseñanzas de la iglesia han influido en su decisión de trabajar o no trabajar por un salario? ¿Cree usted que las mujeres deben ser madres y amas de casa de tiempo completo? ¿Por qué o por qué no?
- ¿Cómo se siente en la organización de la Sociedad de Socorro? ¿Qué significa la hermandad para usted?
- Usted ha tenido alguna experiencia donde se haya sentido excluida por causa de clases sociales, raza, ideología o forma de vida?
- ¿Si su madre y/o hijas eran/son también miembros de la iglesia, cómo son sus actitudes y experiencias diferentes a la suya en términos del matrimonio, la maternidad, la educación, el trabajo?
- ¿Cree que las mujeres tienen dones espirituales especiales o intuición?
- ¿Cuál es su concepto de una Madre Celestial?
- ¿Qué es lo que más le gusta del mormonismo? ¿Qué es lo que menos le gusta? ¿Qué cambiaría de la iglesia si pudiera?

Parte 3. Experiencia en la Iglesia SUD

- ¿Qué historias y figuras de las escrituras son importantes para usted? Por qué?
- ¿Que significa Dios para usted?
- ¿Cuáles han sido sus patrones de devoción personal (oración, ayuno, estudio de las escrituras, otros rituales importantes)? ¿Como ha sido la influencia de Dios en su vida?
- ¿Qué papel juegan las creencias y prácticas tradicionales mexicanas o católicas en su vida religiosa? ¿Por ejemplo cómo celebra el dia de los muertos?
- ¿Que importancia tiene el templo en su vida? ¿El asistir al templo, ha hecho un cambio en su vida? ¿Ha tenido alguna experiencia de revelación personal que le gustaria compartir?
- ¿Siente que usted ejerce el libre albedrío en su vida diaria?

- Describa su relación con los mormones de otras culturas o países en su barrio (misioneros). ¿Cuales son las diferencias o similitudes entre miembros de la iglesia de su cultura con las de otras culturas? (USA)
- ¿Como es el trato de raza o clases sociales en su barrio? ¿Se hacen diferencias? ¿Qué papel desempeñan las cuestiones de raza y clases sociales en la iglesia en general?
- ¿Cómo se ha sido influenciada su familia debido a las enseñanzas de la iglesia?
- ¿Qué podría hacer la iglesia para mejorar la vida de los miembros de su barrio, y para ayudar mejor a las personas en su comunidad en general, ya sean mormones o no mormones?
- ¿Ha experimentado cambios en la iglesia y en las organizaciones a través de los años? ¿Qué piensa usted de esos cambios?
- ¿Cuáles son algunas lecciones que la vida le ha enseñado?

Oral Life History Interview Questions for Women in Botswana

Note that these interview questions differ slightly from interview questions for Latter-day Saint women in Mexico and the United States. This is because the interviews of the forty-eight Latter-day Saint women in Botswana were part of a larger research project that entailed interviewing women of various faiths.

Part 1. Personal History

- How do you define your religious identity and affiliation?
- How did you come to be a member of your faith community? What was your conversion process? What factors and experiences led to your decision to become a part of or remain within your current religious community?
- Describe your family of origin and early life. What were your challenges and joys during your childhood? Religious experiences?
- Which tribe do you belong to? How does this influence your traditions and life practices?
- If married, please tell me about your marriage, your children, and your family life.
- What has been your work experience? Who earns income for your household? What has been your experience working with the community (volunteering, political work, etc.)?
- What have been your main challenges in life? Have you faced poverty, violence, war, or disease in your life? If so, how did you cope with those challenges?
- Are there important things you would have done differently? Did your life go according to plan?

- What is your process for making decisions? Tell me about a time you had to make a difficult decision. How did you make it? Have you ever made a decision that was different than what your faith community or church recommended?
- What are your hopes and aspirations for your life?
- What are your top three priorities?
- What sort of things do you do as a family? How do these activities contribute to your life?

Part 2. Attitudes About Religious Women's Issues

- What is it like to be a(n) [African Independent/Catholic/LDS/Muslim/Pentecostal] woman in Botswana? Difficulties? Rewarding aspects?
- How do you perceive women's roles in your faith community/religious group? What sources or experiences inform your view? Do you feel women are valued similarly to men? Do women have opportunities for leadership in your faith community? [if yes] Do you think they should have more opportunities? [if no] Would you like women to have leadership opportunities? Why or why not?
- What has been your experience with male (priesthood, spiritual, clerical, etc.) authority and its role in home and religious leadership?
- What role do women play in the home? What role do men play in the home? [If applicable] How has male authority in the home affected your marriage and family life?
- When you and your spouse feel differently about a particular issue, how do you work it out? Who usually gets their way within the marriage, or who has the more "dominant" opinion?
- How has male authority within your faith community/church affected your religious life?
- What role do you think women should play in society and in the community? Do you think they should be leaders (political, business, etc.)?
- How do you view your religion's teachings on children, fertility, and reproduction? Experiences? Thoughts on birth control?
- What do you perceive to be your faith's teachings on mothers contributing to the family income? Working for pay? How do these teachings compare with Setswana culture in general? Have religious teachings influenced your decision to work or not work for pay? Do you feel that women should be devoted solely to motherhood? Why or why not?
- Have you had experiences with cliques and exclusion because of class, race, ideology, lifestyle, or tribe?

- If your mother and/or daughters were/are also members of your faith, how are their attitudes and experiences different than yours in terms of marriage, motherhood, education, work?
- What does "modesty" mean to you? Tell me your feelings about that idea/concept.
- Do you feel valued by your religious leaders? Why or why not? Do you feel that women's value has changed throughout time within your faith community/religion? If so, how has it changed?
- What led you to marry your spouse?
- Do you think women have special spiritual gifts or intuition?
- What do you like best about your faith? What do you like least? What would you change about it if you could?

Part 3. Experience in the Faith Community

- What scriptural stories and figures mean the most to you? Why?
- How do you envision God? Loving? Judgmental?
- What have been your patterns of personal devotion (prayer, fasting, scripture study, charismatic gifts such as speaking in tongues, other rituals)? How do you feel God in your life?
- What role do traditional African beliefs and practices play in your religious life?
- Do you feel that you are able to exercise independence and agency in your life? In your religious life?
- Describe your relationship with members of your faith from other cultures or countries in your ward. Do you notice any differences between Batswana and those who do not originate from Botswana? What are race relations like in your local faith community? What role do issues of race, class, and tribe play in your denomination at large?
- How have experiences within your religious institution affected various members of your family?
- Who are memorable male and female leaders of the faith? Why were they successful? What could the church do to better help members of your faith community and to better help people in your larger community, both inside and outside of your religious group?
- Have you experienced changes in religious organization and practice during your life? What did you think of those changes?
- What are some lessons life has taught you?

Specific Questions: LDS

- Are you familiar with "The Family: A Proclamation to the World?" Does your life reflect the roles described in it? Why or why not?

- What does it mean to have a "patriarch of the home" to you?
- How do you feel about the Relief Society? What does sisterhood mean to you? What is your concept of a Mother in Heaven?
- What role has the temple played in your religious life? Have your feelings evolved? Do you want to mention any personal revelation?
- Do you feel connected to American church leaders?
- How are American and Batswana Latter-day Saints similar and different?

Oral Life History Interview Questions for Women in the United States

Part 1. Personal History

- How did you come to be a member of the LDS Church? What was your conversion process?
- Describe your family of origin and early life. What were your challenges and joys during your childhood? Religious experiences?
- If married, please tell me about your marriage, your children, and your family life.
- What has been your work experience? Who earns income for your household? What has been your experience working with the community (volunteering, political work, etc.)?
- What have been your main challenges in life? Have you faced poverty, violence, war, or disease in your life? If so, how did you cope with those challenges?
- Are there important things you would have done differently? Did your life go according to plan?
- Tell me about a time you had to make a difficult decision. How did you make it? Have you ever made a decision that conflicted with the church's position?
- What are your hopes and aspirations for your life?

Part 2. Attitudes About LDS Women's Issues

- What is it like to be a Mormon woman in the U.S.? Difficulties? Rewarding aspects?
- Are you familiar with "The Family: A Proclamation to the World?" Does your life reflect the roles described in it? Why or why not?

- How do you perceive women's role in Mormonism? Do you feel women are equal to men? Do they have enough opportunities for leadership? Why or why not? What has been your experience with male priesthood authority and its role in home and church leadership? How has male authority in the home and church affected your marriage and church experiences?
- What role do you think women should play in society and in the community? Do you think they should be leaders (political, business, etc.)?
- How do you view the church's teachings on children, fertility, and reproduction? Experiences? Thoughts on birth control?
- What do you perceive to be the church's teachings on mothers working for pay? Have church teachings influenced your decision to work or not work for pay? Do you feel that women should be full-time mothers? Why or why not?
- How do you feel about the Relief Society? What does sisterhood mean to you?
- Do you have experiences with cliques and exclusion because of class, race, ideology, or lifestyle?
- If your mother and/or daughters were/are also members of the church, how are their attitudes and experiences different than yours in terms of marriage, motherhood, education, work?
- Do you think women have special spiritual gifts or intuition?
- What is your concept of a Mother in Heaven?
- What do you like best about Mormonism? What do you like least? What would you change about the church if you could?

Part 3. Experience in the LDS Church

- What scriptural stories and figures mean the most to you? Why?
- How do you envision God? Loving? Judgmental?
- What have been your patterns of personal devotion (prayer, fasting, scripture study, other rituals)? How do you feel God in your life?
- What role has the temple played in your religious life? Have your feelings evolved? Do you want to mention any personal revelation?
- Do you feel that you exercise independent (free) agency in your religious life?
- Describe your relationship with Mormons from other cultures or countries in your ward.
- What are race relations like in your ward? What role do issues of race and class play in the church at large?
- How have church experiences affected various members of your family?

- Who are memorable male and female leaders of the church? Why were they successful? Do you feel connected to General Authorities and other general church leaders?
- What could the church do to better help members of your ward and to better help people in your larger community, Mormon and non-Mormon?
- Have you experienced changes in church organization and practice during your life? What did you think of those changes?
- What lessons has life taught you?

Demographic Information

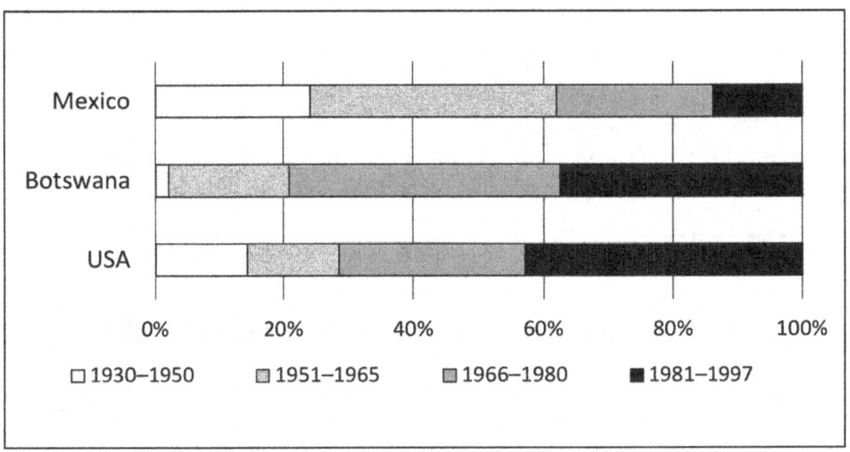

FIGURE 1. Birth Year of Interviewed LDS Women, by Country

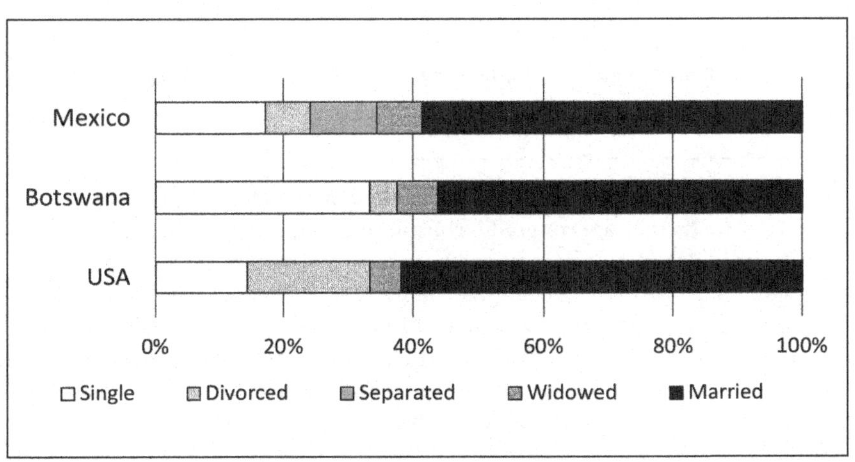

FIGURE 2. Marital Status Distribution of Interviewed LDS Women, by Country

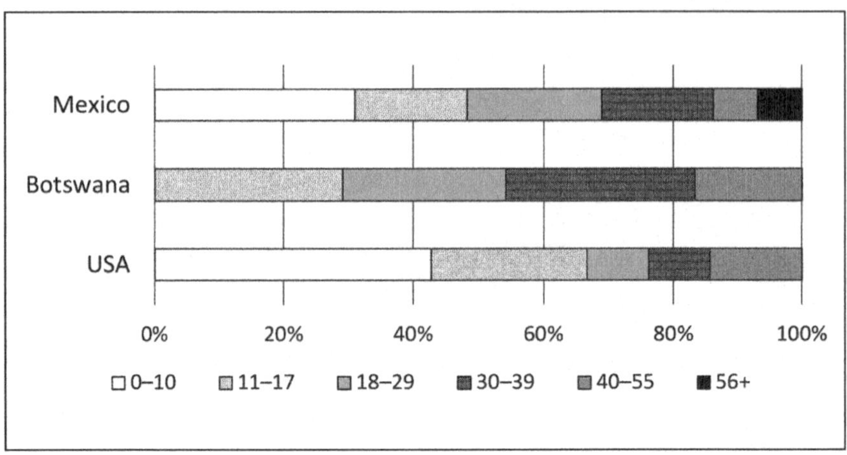

FIGURE 3. Age at LDS Conversion/Affiliation for Interviewed LDS Women, by Country. The 0–10 category represents children who were either born into Mormon affiliation or who began affiliating as young children. The other categories represent the age at which women were baptized into the LDS faith.

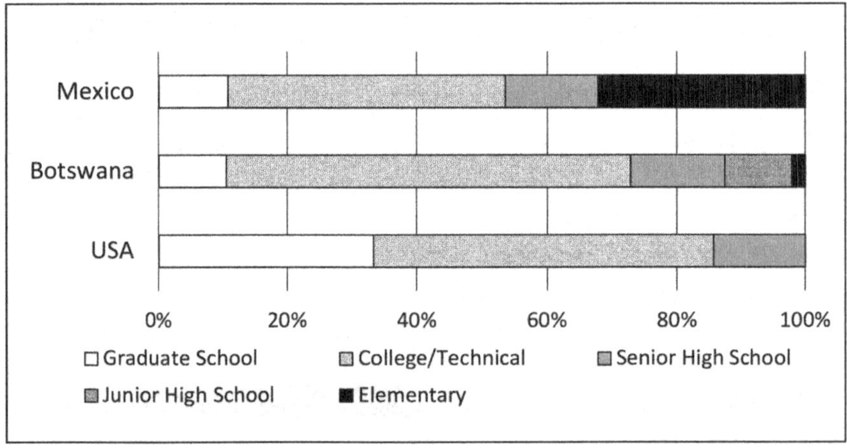

FIGURE 4. Highest Education Attained by Interviewed LDS Women, by Country. Note that the ages or grades constituting elementary school differ by country. In Botswana, elementary school goes up to the seventh year of instruction (equivalent to seventh grade in the United States), while in Mexico the highest grade is generally sixth grade. In the United States, the highest grade in elementary school is usually fifth or sixth grade. Secondary school also has a different structure in Botswana. Junior high school consists of grades 8 through 10, and senior high school consists of two additional years of instruction.

Notes

Introduction

1. I use the term *traditional religious women* to describe women who unapologetically embrace patriarchal religions and work to further these religions' goals. Amy Hoyt uses this term similarly. Amy Hoyt, "Agency, Subjectivity and Essentialism with Traditional Religious Cultures: An Ethnographic Study of an American Latter-day Saint Community" (PhD diss., Claremont Graduate University, 2007), 4.

2. Ibid., 1, 3; Saba Mahmood, *Politics of Piety: The Islamic Revival and the Feminist Subject* (Princeton: Princeton University Press, 2005), 1–39.

3. Kimberlé Crenshaw, "Demarginalizing the Intersection of Race and Sex: A Black Feminist Critique of Antidiscrimination Doctrine, Feminist Theory and Antiracist Politics," *University of Chicago Legal Forum* 1 (1989): 139–167. Patricia Hill Collins likewise discusses interlocking matrixes of oppression. Patricia Hill Collins, *Black Feminist Thought: Knowledge, Consciousness, and the Politics of Empowerment* (Boston: Unwin Hyman, 1990), 234.

4. Kimberlé Crenshaw, "Mapping the Margins: Intersectionality, Identity Politics, and Violence Against Women of Color." *Stanford Law Review* 43, no. 6 (1991): 1241–1299, https://doi.org/10.2307/1229039.

5. Grace ji-Sun Kim and Susan M. Shaw, *Intersectional Theology: An Introductory Guide* (Minneapolis: Fortress, 2018), 2.

6. Alice Walker, *In Search of Our Mothers' Gardens* (San Diego: Harcourt Brace Jovanovich, 1983), xi–xii.

7. Ibid., xi, emphasis in original.

8. Delores S. Williams, "Womanist Theology: Black Women's Voices," *Christianity and Crisis* 47, no. 3 (March 2, 1987): 68.

9. Mary Daly, *The Church and the Second Sex* (Boston: Beacon, 1968); Mary Daly, *Beyond God the Father: Toward a Philosophy of Women's Liberation* (Boston: Beacon,

1973); Rosemary Radford Ruether, *Sexism and God-Talk: Toward a Feminist Theology* (Boston: Beacon, 1983); Judith Plaskow, *Standing Again at Sinai: Judaism from a Feminist Perspective* (San Francisco: HarperSanFrancisco, 1990); Rita Gross and Nancy Falk, eds., *Unspoken Worlds: Women's Religious Lives* (New York: Harper & Row, 1980); Carol Christ and Judith Plaskow, eds., *Womanspirit Rising* (New York: Harper & Row, 1979); Elizabeth Schüssler Fiorenza, *In Memory of Her: A Feminist Theological Reconstruction of Christian Origins* (New York: Crossroad, 1983).

10. Darlene M. Juschka, "General Introduction," in *Feminism in the Study of Religion: A Reader*, ed. Darlene M. Juschka (New York: Continuum, 2001). Juschka discusses how feminist methods of analysis challenged the masculinist productions of knowledge that dominated the academy. Fiorenza, for example, developed a feminist hermeneutics of suspicion as a means to analyze androcentric texts.

11. Judith Plaskow, "We Are Also Your Sisters: The Development of Women's Studies in Religion," *Women's Studies Quarterly* 21, no. 1/2 (1993): 10.

12. Ibid., 11–12.

13. Fiorenza, *In Memory of Her*, xii–xxv. Fiorenza's introduction discusses the need to reconstruct and reclaim early Christian women's history. Plaskow mentions this point in her article "We Are Also Your Sisters," 13.

14. Delores Williams, *Sisters in the Wilderness: The Challenge of Womanist God-Talk* (Maryknoll, NY: Orbis, 1993); Mercy Amba Oduyoye, *African Women's Theology* (Cleveland, OH: Pilgrim 2001); Ada Maria Isasi-Díaz, *Mujerista Theology: A Theology for the Twenty-First Century* (Maryknoll, NY: Orbis, 1996); Kwok Pui-lan, *Introducing Asian Women's Theology* (Sheffield, UK: Sheffield Academic Press, 2000).

15. Robert A. Orsi, *Thank You, St. Jude: Women's Devotion to the Patron Saint of Lost Causes* (New Haven: Yale University Press, 1998).

16. R. Marie Griffith, *God's Daughters: Evangelical Women and the Power of Submission* (Berkeley: University of California Press, 1997), 175.

17. Ibid., 201–209.

18. Mahmood, *Politics of Piety*, 14.

19. Hoyt, "Agency, Subjectivity and Essentialism," 136.

20. Catharine Brekus, "Mormon Women and the Problem of Historical Agency," *Journal of Mormon History* 37, no. 2 (2011): 78–85.

21. Ibid., 86–87.

22. Mary Daly, "Be-friending: The Lust to Share Happiness," in *For Lesbians Only: A Separatist Anthology*, ed. S. Hoagland and J. Penelope (London: Onlywomen, 1988), 208; Andrea Dworkin, *Right-Wing Women* (New York: Putnam, 1983), 34. R. Marie Griffith discusses Dworkin's assessment of conservative women embracing fear and ignorance, noting how this viewpoint "exemplifies rigid victimization theory that continues to dominate most feminist analyses of nonfeminist women." Griffith, *God's Daughters*, 204.

23. Carol Gilligan, *In a Different Voice: Psychological Theory and Women's Development* (Cambridge, MA: Harvard University Press, 1982).

24. Hoyt, "Agency, Essentialism, and Subjectivity," 66.

25. For reliable overviews of Mormon history see Matthew Bowman, *The Mormon People: The Making of an American Faith* (New York: Random House, 2012); Daniel Walker Howe, "Emergent Mormonism in Context," in *The Oxford Handbook of Mormonism*, ed. Terryl Givens and Philip Barlow (Oxford: Oxford University Press, 2015); Thomas Alexander, *Mormonism in Transition: A History of the Latter-day Saints, 1890–1930* (Chicago: University of Illinois Press, 1996); Jan Shipps, *Mormonism: The Story of a New Religious Tradition* (Chicago: University of Illinois Press, 1985).

26. Armand Mauss, *All Abraham's Children: Changing Mormon Conceptions of Race and Lineage* (Chicago: University of Illinois Press, 2003), 237.

27. Bowman, *Mormon People*, 217.

28. Ibid., 220.

29. Terryl L. Givens, *People of Paradox: A History of Mormon Culture* (New York: Oxford University Press, 2007), 8.

30. Richard Lyman Bushman, *Rough Stone Rolling: A Cultural Biography of Mormonism's Founder* (New York: Knopf, 2005), 439–440. See also Todd Compton, *In Sacred Loneliness: The Plural Wives of Joseph Smith* (Salt Lake City: Signature, 1997).

31. Women's subordination in marriage was standard practice in nineteenth-century Christianity, so Mormonism was well within societal norms regarding patriarchal marriage. Plural marriage, however, was highly uncommon and roundly denounced by the larger American culture.

32. See Doctrine and Covenants 25:7 and Catherine Brekus, *Strangers and Pilgrims: Female Preaching in America, 1740–1845* (Chapel Hill: University of North Carolina Press, 1998), 128, 165.

33. Martha Sonntag Bradley, *Pedestals and Podiums: Utah Women, Religious Authority and Equal Rights* (Salt Lake City: Signature, 2005), 7–8.

34. Joanna Brooks, "Mormonism as Colonialism, Mormonism as Anti-Colonialism, Mormonism as Minor Transnationalism: Historical and Contemporary Perspectives," in *Decolonizing Mormonism: Approaching a Postcolonial Zion*, ed. Gina Colvin and Joanna Brooks (Salt Lake City: University of Utah Press, 2018), 166. The Book of Mormon verse that connects dark skin to a curse is 2 Nephi 5:21.

35. Ibid., 164–166. See also Hokulani K. Aikau, *A Chosen People, A Promised Land: Mormonism and Race in Hawai'i* (Minneapolis: University of Minnesota Press, 2012), 42–43, and Robert Parsons, "Hagoth and the Polynesians," in *The Book of Mormon: Alma, the Testimony of the World*, ed. Monte S. Nyman and Charles D. Tate Jr. (Provo, UT: Religious Studies Center, Brigham Young University, 1992).

36. 2 Nephi 26:33.

37. On March 31, 2018, an Asian American man and a Brazilian man became two of the Apostles in the Quorum of the Twelve Apostles. This day marked the moment when, for the first time its nearly two-hundred-year history, this crucial and powerful decision-making body in the Church of Jesus Christ of Latter-day Saints was not comprised entirely of white men.

38. Bowman, *Mormon People*, 220–221.

39. Russell M. Nelson, "The Correct Name of the Church," address given at the

Semiannual General Conference of the Church of Jesus Christ of Latter-day Saints, October 2018, https://www.churchofjesuschrist.org/study/general-conference/2018/10/the-correct-name-of-the-church?lang=eng.

40. See Jill Mulvay Derr, Janath Russell Cannon, and Maureen Ursenbach Beecher, *Women of Covenant: The Story of Relief Society* (Salt Lake City: Deseret Books, 1992); Bradley, *Pedestals and Podiums*, 7–8; Maureen Ursenbach Beecher and Lavina Fielding Anderson, eds., *Sisters in Spirit: Mormon Women in Historical and Cultural Perspective* (Chicago: University of Illinois Press, 1987); Claudia Bushman, ed., *Mormon Sisters: Women in Early Utah* (Logan, UT: Utah State University Press, 1997).

41. Dave Hall, "A Crossroads for Mormon Women: Amy Brown Lyman, J. Reuben Clark, and the Decline of Organized Women's Activism in the Relief Society," *Journal of Mormon History* 36, no. 2 (2010): 205–249; Marie Cornwall, "The Institutional Role of Mormon Women," in *Contemporary Mormonism: Social Science Perspectives*, ed. Marie Cornwall et al. (Chicago: University of Illinois Press, 1994); Laura Vance, "Evolution of Ideals for Women in Mormon Periodicals, 1897—1999," *Sociology of Religion* 63, no. 1 (2002): 104; Linda King Newell, "The Historical Relationship of Mormon Women and Priesthood," in *Women and Authority: Re-emerging Mormon Feminism*, ed. Maxine Hanks (Salt Lake City: Signature, 1992).

42. Margaret Toscano, "Is There a Place for Heavenly Mother in Mormon Theology? An Investigation into Discourses of Power," *Sunstone* 133 (2004): 14–22; Janice Allred, "Toward a Mormon Theology of God the Mother," in *God the Mother and Other Theological Essays* (Salt Lake City: Signature, 1997); Sonja Farnsworth, "Mormonism's Odd Couple: The Motherhood-Priesthood Connection," in *Women and Authority: Re-emerging Mormon Feminism*, ed. Maxine Hanks (Salt Lake City: Signature, 1992).

43. Jolene Edmunds Rockwood, "The Redemption of Eve," in Beecher and Anderson, *Sisters in Spirit*; Caroline Kline, "The Mormon Conception of Women's Nature and Role: A Feminist Analysis," *Feminist Theology* 22, no. 2 (2014): 186–202.

44. Michelle Meagher, "Patriarchy," in *The Concise Encyclopedia of Sociology*, ed. George Ritzer and J. Michael Ryan (Oxford: Wiley-Blackwell, 2011), 441.

45. B. Carmon Hardy, "Lords of Creation: Polygamy, the Abrahamic Household, and Mormon Patriarchy," *Journal of Mormon History* 20 (Spring 1994): 138–139.

46. In Mormon endowment ceremonies women embody the biblical figure of Eve, who functions as an archetype for every woman. In the pre-2019 ritual, women made covenants pertaining to Eve's experience before and after the Fall. One of those covenants pertained to the biblical injunction that Adam rule over Eve after she eats the fruit. Consequently, women ritually promised to hearken unto their husbands' counsel as their husbands hearken unto God. For a brief discussion of this covenant see David John Buerger, *The Mysteries of Godliness: A History of Mormon Temple Worship* (San Francisco: Smith Research Associates, 1994), 178. In January 2019 this ritual was changed so that women no longer covenant to hearken unto their husband's counsel. Now they, like men, make an obedience covenant to God. See Peggy Fletcher Stack and David Noyce, "LDS Church Changes Temple Ceremony; Faithful

Feminists Will See Revisions and Additions as a 'Leap Forward,'" *Salt Lake Tribune*, January 2, 2019, https://www.sltrib.com/religion/2019/01/02/lds-church-releases/.

47. See, e.g., Boyd K. Packer, "For Time and All Eternity," *Ensign*, November 1993, https://www.churchofjesuschrist.org/study/ensign/1993/11/for-time-and-all -eternity?lang=eng; Bruce C. Hafen, "Crossing Thresholds and Becoming Equal Partners," *Ensign*, August 2007, https://www.churchofjesuschrist.org/study/ensign/ 2007/08/crossing-thresholds-and-becoming-equal-partners?lang=eng. Much of Latter-day Saint church leaders' rhetoric concerning male benevolent headship mirrors that of conservative Protestants, who often encourage male "servant-leadership," which W. Bradford Wilcox describes as soft patriarchy in *Soft Patriarchs, New Men: How Christianity Shapes Fathers and Husbands* (Chicago: University of Chicago Press, 2004), 172.

48. For a Christian understanding of complementarianism see John Piper, "A Vision of Biblical Complementarity: Manhood and Womanhood Defined According to the Bible," in *Recovering Biblical Manhood and Womanhood: A Response to Evangelical Feminism*, ed. John Piper and Wayne Grudem (Wheaton, IL: Crossway, 2012).

49. "The Family: A Proclamation to the World," *Ensign*, November 1995, 102. For an overview of the evolving Latter-day Saint institutional rhetoric regarding decision-making power in marriages, see Caroline Kline, "Saying Goodbye to the Final Say: The Softening and Reimagining of Mormon Male Headship Ideologies," in *Out of Obscurity: Mormonism Since 1945*, ed. Patrick Mason and John Turner (New York: Oxford University Press, 2016).

50. Sheila Taylor, "The Problem of Female Salvation in LDS Theology," *Element* 5, no. 2 (2009): 5–6.

51. Colleen McDannell, *Sister Saints: Mormon Women Since the End of Polygamy* (New York: Oxford University Press, 2019), 153–166.

52. Carrie Miles, "LDS Family Ideals Versus the Equality of Women: Navigating the Changes Since 1957," in *Revisiting Thomas F. O'Dea's* The Mormons: *Contemporary Perspectives*, ed. Cardell Jacobson et al. (Salt Lake City: University of Utah Press, 2008); Laurence R. Iannaccone and Carrie A. Miles, "Dealing with Social Change: The Mormon Church's Response to Change in Women's Roles," *Social Forces* 68, no. 4 (1990): 1231–1250.

53. Lori G. Beaman, "Molly Mormons, Mormon Feminists and Moderates: Religious Diversity and the Latter-Day Saints Church," *Sociology of Religion* 62, no. 1 (2001): 65–86; Amy Hoyt, "Beyond the Victim/Empowerment Paradigm: The Gendered Cosmology of Mormon Women," *Feminist Theology* 16, no. 1 (2007): 89–100; Claudia Bushman and Caroline Kline, eds., *Mormon Women Have Their Say: Essays from the Claremont Oral History Collection* (Salt Lake City: Greg Kofford, 2013).

54. Joanna Brooks, Rachel Hunt Steenblik, and Hannah Wheelwright, eds. *Mormon Feminism: Essential Writings* (New York: Oxford University Press, 2015).

55. The Church of Jesus Christ of Latter-day Saints, "Facts and Statistics," Newsroom, accessed September 22, 2021, https://newsroom.churchofjesuschrist.org/facts -and-statistics/country/mexico.

56. For more on the mestizo race and identity, which was heavily promoted by Mexican post-revolutionary elites as positive and a source of national unity, see Christina A. Sue, *Land of the Cosmic Race: Race Mixture, Racism, and Blackness in Mexico* (New York: Oxford, 2013), 15–17.

57. F. LaMond Tullis, *Mormons in Mexico: The Dynamics of Faith and Culture* (Logan: Utah State University Press, 1987), 137–159.

58. The Church of Jesus Christ of Latter-day Saints, "Facts and Statistics," Newsroom, accessed September 22, 2021, https://newsroom.churchofjesuschrist.org/facts-and-statistics/country/botswana

59. Christian John Makgala, "A Survey of Race Relations in Botswana, 1800–1966," *Botswana Notes and Records* 36 (2004): 14.

60. World Atlas, "The Major Ethnic Groups of Botswana," accessed July 19, 2018, https://www.worldatlas.com/articles/the-major-ethnic-groups-of-botswana.html.

61. The term *Batswana* refers to the inhabitants (plural) of Botswana. The singular form of Batswana is Motswana. *Setswana* refers to both the language and culture of the Tswana people. While this language is commonly used in Botswana and was preferred by the women I interviewed, it is not without controversy, because it implies that all the inhabitants of Botswana are from the Tswana ethnic group. See Sitinga Kachipande, "Botswanan or Batswana? It's Complicated," *Voices of Africa* (blog), April 17, 2015, https://tinyurl.com/y2lwkpyj.

62. Sherna Berger Gluck and Daphne Patai, "Introduction," in *Women's Words: The Feminist Practice of Oral History*, ed. Sherna Berger Gluck and Daphne Patai (New York: Routledge, 1991), 2.

63. These oral history interviews with Mormon women in Botswana were part of a larger research project organized primarily by Deidre Green and Karen Jo Torjesen called "Gender, Narrative, and Religious Practice in Southern Africa." Approximately two dozen oral histories with women of other faith traditions were collected in Botswana as well.

64. Purposive sampling entails targeting different demographics, and snowball sampling entails finding interviewees based on the recommendation of interviewed women. For more on sampling techniques for oral historians see Mary A. Larson, "Research Design and Strategies," in *Handbook of Oral History*, ed. Thomas L. Charlton et al. (Lanham, MD: Altamira, 2006). Whereas some oral history researchers emphasize a variety of techniques to ensure some degree of representative coverage, other oral historians question whether doing so is necessary. See Donald Ritchie, *Doing Oral History* (Oxford: Oxford University Press, 2003), 121–122.

65. Steven L. Schensul, Jean J. Schensul, and Margaret D. LeCompte, *Essential Ethnographic Methods: Observations, Interviews, and Questionnaires* (Walnut Creek, CA: Altamira, 1999), 91.

66. Victor C. deMunck and Elisa J. Sobo, eds. *Using Methods in the Field: A Practical Introduction and Casebook* (Walnut Creek, CA: Altamira, 1998), 43.

67. Linda Tuhiwai Smith, *Decolonizing Methodologies: Research and Indigenous Peoples*, 2nd ed. (London: Zed Books, 2012), 9.

68. Ibid., 205.

69. Ibid., 143.

70. Ibid., 144–154.

71. Other scholars of women in the global South have written of the way Western researchers have often missed the mark when analyzing gender issues in such contexts. See Chilla Bulbeck, *Re-Orienting Western Feminisms: Women's Diversity in a Postcolonial World* (Cambridge: Cambridge University Press, 1998), and Achola Pala, "Definitions of Women and Development: An African Perspective," *Signs* 3, no. 1 (1977): 10. I tried to avoid such pitfalls (and I was somewhat successful, I believe) by making many of my interview questions so broad that subjects could take them in nearly any direction they wished. See appendixes A, B, and C for lists of questions from which I drew as I interviewed women.

72. Gluck and Patai, "Introduction," 3.

73. Ibid.

74. Joey Sprague and Mark Zimmerman, "Overcoming Dualism: A Feminist Agenda for Sociological Methodology," in *Theory on Gender/Feminism on Theory*, ed. Paula England (New York: Aldine DeGruyter, 1993), 266; Marjorie L. Devault, *Liberating Method: Feminism and Social Research* (Philadelphia: Temple University Press, 1999), 31.

75. Sharlene Nagy Hesse-Biber, Patricia Leavy, and Michelle L. Yaiser, "Feminist Approaches to Research as a Process: Reconceptualizing Epistemology, Methodology, and Method," in *Feminist Perspectives on Social Research*, ed. Sharlene Nagy Hesse-Biber et al. (Oxford: Oxford University Press, 2004), 14.

76. Ibid., 12, emphasis in original.

77. Ibid.

78. See Sandra Harding, "Introduction: Is There a Feminist Method?," in *Feminism and Methodology: Social Science Issues*, ed. Sandra Harding (Bloomington: Indiana University Press, 1988).

79. Some of these exceptions are Stacilee Ford, "Sister Acts: Relief Society and Flexible Citizenship in Hong Kong," in Colvin and Brooks, *Decolonizing Mormonism: Approaching a Postcolonial Zion*; Taunalyn Rutherford, "Conceptualizing Global Religions: An Investigation of Mormonism in India" (PhD diss., Claremont Graduate University, 2018); and Melissa Wei-Tsing Inouye, "Culture and Agency in Mormon Women's Lives," in *Women and Mormonism: Historical and Contemporary Perspectives*, ed. Kate Holbrook and Matthew Bowman (Salt Lake City: University of Utah Press, 2016). Colleen McDannell also offers some fascinating glimpses into the lives and navigations of a handful of global female converts in her chapter titled "A Church of Converts." McDannell, *Sister Saints*, 131–152.

80. Elizabeth V. Spelman, *Inessential Woman: Problems of Exclusion in Feminist Thought* (Boston: Beacon, 1988), 3.

Chapter 1. Mexican Women, Agency, and Liberation

1. Elements of Mexican Latter-day Saint women's spirituality are discussed in this chapter, but the majority of discussion of Mexican Latter-day Saint women's dreams, visions, and theological insight is in Chapter 4 of this book.

2. Spelman, *Inessential Woman*, 137.

3. See Crenshaw, "Mapping the Margins"; Crenshaw, "Demarginalizing the Intersection of Race and Sex"; Patricia Hill Collins, "Learning from the Outsider Within: The Sociological Significance of Black Feminist Thought," in *Beyond Methodology: Feminist Scholarship as Lived Research*, ed. Mary Margaret Fonow et al. (Bloomington: Indiana University Press, 1991), 41–43.

4. A classic example of this is the feminist call in the 1960s and 1970s to enter the workforce. Many white college-educated women felt liberated by this move, but this call did not resonate with working-class women and women of color, who were already in the workforce and not feeling particularly empowered by it. See Maxine Baca Zinn, Pierrette Hondagneu-Sotelo, and Michael A. Messner, "Introduction: Sex and Gender Through the Prism of Difference," in *Gender Through the Prism of Difference*, ed. Maxine Baca Zinn et al. (New York: Oxford University Press, 2011), 3.

5. Anonymous, interview by Caroline Kline and April Carlson, March 15, 2015, in Veracruz, Mexico, Claremont Mormon Women Oral History Collection, #170, transcript, p. 2, Special Collections, Claremont Colleges Library, Claremont, California (hereafter Claremont Mormon Women OHC). "Odiaba todo, tuvo hijos con diferentes hombres. Ella nunca quiso a nadie, y como yo no encajaba en su mundo siempre me llevaba la contraria. A mí me odiaba, yo siento. Creo que en la vida no tuve peor enemigo que me odiara tanto como mi madre."

6. Ibid., 3. "Los niños empiezan a tomar desde chiquitos, andan con mujeres desde los diez, once, doce años. Inclusive los padres acostumbran llevarlos desde muy niños con prostitutas para que 'se hagan hombres' dicen ellos. Pero desde que yo tuve uso de razón para mí eso no era correcto. Yo recuerdo que a los ocho ó nueve años, yo odiaba ese mundo."

7. See Elizabeth Stevens, "Marianismo: The Other Face of Machismo in Latin America," in *Female and Male in Latin America*, ed. A. Pescatello (Pittsburg: University of Pittsburg Press, 1973); Elizabeth Brusco, *The Reformation of Machismo: Evangelical Conversion and Gender in Colombia* (Austin: University of Texas Press, 1995). Stevens wrote that machismo is derived from sixteenth- and seventeenth-century Mediterranean concepts of shame and honor, imported from the Old World to the Americas via colonization. It is important to note that some scholars have challenged the concept of marianismo, stating that it is too simplistic, lacking in class analysis, and far too overarching, among other critiques. See Marysa Navarro, "Against Marianismo," in *Gender's Place: Feminist Anthropologies of Latin America*, ed. Rosario Montoya et al. (New York: Palgrave MacMillan, 2002).

8. Bron B. Ingoldsby, "The Latin American Family: Familialism Vs. Machismo,"

Journal of Comparative Family Studies 22, no. 1 (1991): 57–58. Recently, some scholars have critiqued the emphasis on machismo when discussing Latino masculinity and advocate a wider discussion about Latino masculinities, including that of gay men with feminist consciousnesses. See Aida Hurtado and Mrinal Sinha, *Beyond Machismo: Intersectional Latino Masculinities* (Austin: University of Texas Press, 2016), 11–15.

9. Bulbeck, *Re-Orienting Western Feminisms*, 145. See also Manuel Pena, "Class, Gender and Machismo: The 'Treacherous-Woman' Folklore of Mexican Male Workers," *Gender and Society* 5, no. 1 (1991): 31; Olivia Espin, "Cultural and Historical Influences on Sexuality in Hispanic/Latin Women," in *Race, Class, and Gender*, ed. Margaret L. Anderson and Patricia Hill Collins (Belmont, CA: Wadsworth, 1992), 144; Denise A. Segura and Jennifer L. Pierce, "Chicana/o Family Structure and Gender Personality: Chodorow, Familism, and Psychoanalytic Sociology Revisited," *Signs* 19, no. 1 (1993): 79.

10. Claremont Mormon Women OHC, #170 (2015), 1. "Había un poco de violencia pero lo que más había era desobligación. Él era mujeriego, lo ocultó por un tiempo y desatendía a la familia económicamente y moralmente."

11. Brusco, *Reformation of Machismo*, 82–83.

12. Stevens, "Marianismo," 94–95.

13. Claremont Mormon Women OHC, #170 (2015), 1. "Yo sentía que ellos eran cómplices de mi esposo, yo decía porque se entienden muy bien. Yo vivía en guardia contra los misioneros."

14. Ibid., 2. "Yo me sentía triste, anhelaba ir."

15. Ibid. "Nunca me gustó vivir en ese mundo; nunca lo entendí. Para mí nunca hubo cabida porque yo iba en contra de todo, en ese mundo nunca hubo un lugar para mí, siempre estuve sola. Me sentía pisoteada, triste, ofendida, y de pronto acá donde ahora estaba ahora sentía paz, me sentía bien."

16. Henri Gooren, "The Mormons of the World: The Meaning of LDS Membership in Central America," in *Revisiting Thomas O'Dea's* The Mormons: *Contemporary Perspectives*, ed. Cardell K. Jacobson, John P. Hoffman, and Tim B. Heaton (Salt Lake City: University of Utah Press, 2008), 374–375.

17. Wesley W. Craig Jr., "The Church in Latin America: Progress and Challenge," *Dialogue: A Journal of Mormon Thought* 5, no. 3 (1968): 69; F. LaMond Tullis, "Three Myths About Mormons in Latin America," *Dialogue* 7, no. 1 (1981): 79–87; Henri Gooren, "Latter-day Saints Under Siege: The Unique Experiences of Nicaraguan Mormons," *Dialogue* 40, no. 3 (2007): 150; David G. Stewart Jr., "Growth, Retention, and Internationalization," in Jacobson, Hoffman, and Heaton, eds., *Revisiting Thomas O'Dea's* The Mormons, 329; David Knowlton, "Thoughts on Mormonism in Latin America," *Dialogue* 25, no. 2 (1992): 50. The attraction to middle-class values and social mobility is a prime marker of difference between Mormon converts and Pentecostal converts in Latin America. Pentecostal converts are drawn mainly from the working class and tend to stay in the working class. Robert Williamson, *Latin America: Cultures in Conflict* (New York: Palgrave MacMillan, 2006), 187.

18. Claremont Mormon Women OHC, #170 (2015), 7–8. "Les he dicho que siempre

va [a] estar con nosotros. Pueden venir malos momentos . . . pero eso no quiere decir que ya estamos derrotados, porque el Padre nos va a dar, nos va [a] ayudar y eso se los repito cada que puedo. . . . Y como dicen las escrituras el infierno puede estar abriendo su boca sobre nosotros pero el Padre va [a] estar ahí y él nos va a levantar."

19. Ibid., 7. "Pero al leer las escrituras siento como si me transportara. Es algo que siento muy vivido, muy real cuando me pongo a leer las escrituras. Y puede pasar el tiempo y no quiero que nadie me hable. Como que el leer las escrituras me deja un buen sabor de boca, como que comprendo mejor el amor del Padre."

20. Maria Pilar Aquino, *Our Cry for Life: Feminist Theology from Latin America*, trans. Dinah Livingstone (Eugene, OR: Wipf and Stock, 1993), 53.

21. Brekus, "Mormon Women," 71–72.

22. Mahmood, *Politics of Piety*, 3–14.

23. Brekus, "Mormon Women," 78.

24. Claremont Mormon Women OHC, #170 (2015), 6. "Aquí yo puedo tener un problema grande con alguien porque los he tenido, y la mente racional me dice: 'vete.' Pero mi corazón, ese yo interno que tengo que no me explico, me mantiene aquí. Un día mis hijos se rieron mucho porque yo tomé una decisión y les dije, 'Yo no me voy a ir aunque nadie me quisiera, solo que mi obispo me dijera ya no vengas.' Yo no dejo el evangelio así como así, para mí es lo más grande que el Señor me dio. Y cuando estoy triste, deprimida, derrotada, yo sé que tengo un lugar en la casa de mi Padre."

25. Orsi, *Thank You, St. Jude*, 106.

26. Claremont Mormon Women OHC, #170 (2015), 3. "En las entrevistas para ir al templo me preguntaron de mis sentimientos y les dije que no quería a mi mamá, entonces el líder que me entrevistó me ayudó mucho. Tengo la bendición de que tengo mi carácter introvertido y es muy raro, muy difícil que me entiendan los demás. Pero tengo la bendición de entender que las palabras de mis líderes son ley para mí. Entonces para mí fue fácil cambiar mi relación o sentimientos con mi mamá. Se puede decir que mejoró porque la empecé a comprender, en especial porque comprendí que solo Dios tiene derecho a juzgarla. Comprendí que yo tengo el deber de perdonar a todos."

27. Ibid., 6. "Mis líderes han sido mi todo porque ellos me han ayudado a entender mi vida. Yo he tenido líderes excelentes. Si yo puedo hablar con ustedes es por ellos. Yo no hablaba con nadie."

28. The feminist theologian Nelle Morton first described the process of "hear[ing] one another to speech," and this has become an important concept among many feminists. Nelle Morton, *The Journey Is Home* (Boston: Beacon, 1985), 127–128.

29. Williams, *Sisters in the Wilderness*, 20–33.

30. Claremont Mormon Women OHC, #170 (2015), 5. "Porque solo él puede ayudarnos. El patrón es muy duro. Le pedimos al Señor que conmueva su corazón y le dé un poco de sed de justicia."

31. Anonymous, interview by April Carlson, March 22, 2015, Veracruz, Mexico, Claremont Mormon Women OHC, #173, transcript, p. 2. "Él ya tenía metas más

específicas y yo todavía no estaba lista para eso. Yo lo veía y él me daba miedo. Pero, pues, como [mi] mamá él decía 'Todo lo que yo diga es lo mejor para ti,' yo obedecí. Siempre fue la obediencia."

32. Ibid., 3. "[Y] pregunté al Padre, 'Lo debo de hacer? ¿Él es la persona correcta? . . .' Y no sentí una contestación."

33. Ibid. "[E]l Padre no me iba a decir. La decisión era mía. O sea, el libre albedrío, él no me lo va a quitar al decirme, 'Sí, ese es' o 'No, ese no es.' Eso es parte de la decisión que yo tenía que tomar."

34. Ibid., 4. "Fueron desafíos fuertes a los que no estaba yo acostumbrada a llevar. Y ni siquiera sabía si eran correctos o no eran correctos porque yo nunca había oído de una situación así. Entonces fueron unos desafíos muy fuertes. Luego me di cuenta de que la mayoría de las mujeres en México los pasan, nada más que todos callamos y nadie lo dice."

35. Ibid. "Sí. A todas lo pasa, pero nadie habla. Nadie lo dice porque . . . no sé, por temor."

36. Ibid., 5. "Tienes que aguantar esto, es lo normal."

37. Ibid. "Divórciate. Quédate, ya no regreses."

38. Ibid. "[Él] me dijo, '¿Qué es lo que quieres hacer? ¿Te quieres divorciar?' Y le dije, 'No. No, porque él es un buen hombre. Es un buen miembro de la iglesia, solamente que tiene este desafío. . . . Necesito ayudarlo a que desaparezca, pero no sé como. No tengo la habilidad para manejarlo, no sé como hacerlo.'"

39. Ibid. "'Aquí están los papeles de divorcio. Vamos a dárselos. Si él firma es porque quiere cambiar, y no volvera a suceder,' etc. 'Si no lo hace, quiere decir que no debes regresar porque no está él seguro de poder hacerlo.'"

40. Ibid., 6.

41. Ibid. "Cambió totalmente, [t]odo cambió. Fue como el comienzo de un nuevo matrimonio."

42. Ibid. "Entonces fue cuando yo me di cuenta de que nosotras somos las que tenemos las respuestas de decidir cómo cambiar a nuestros propios esposos. Nosotras vivimos más con ellos que sus propias madres, y nosotros los terminamos de educar. . . . Cuando las cosas no están siendo correctos, nada más es porque nos da miedo hacerlo. Como cualquier mamá que le da miedo castigar a su bebé porque no sabes si el bebé va a reaccionar bien o va a reaccionar mal, no lo hacemos. Y ese es el motivo por lo cual las cosas siguen igual—por miedo."

43. Ibid., 19. "Desde que escogió a José y ella sabía que es lo que quería. Aúnque sus padres no estaban de acuerdo, ella fue firme en lo que quiso. Y también fue firme en soportar todo lo que tenía que soportar."

44. Linda King Newell and Valeen Tippetts Avery discuss Emma Smith's resistance to polygamy—and occasional acquiescence to it—at length. They cite evidence that by the last several months of Emma Smith's marriage to Joseph Smith, she had taken a firm stance against the practice and was becoming increasingly outspoken about her opposition to it. Yet in spite of growing pressure from Emma, Joseph Smith continued to privately teach the practice and authorize plural marriages. Linda King Newell

and Valeen Tippets Avery, *Mormon Enigma: Emma Hale Smith* (Chicago: University of Illinois Press, 1994), 130–182.

45. Claremont Mormon Women OHC, #173 (2015), 8. "Necesitaba yo vivir una experiencia muy fuerte para también tener un carácter fuerte. Mi carácter era muy débil."

46. Ibid., 9. "Las mujeres tenemos una habilidad y una capacidad tremenda de conseguir las cosas que nosotras queremos sin que ellos se den cuenta. Les hacemos creer que son ellos que toman la decisión, pero en realidad están haciendo lo que nosotras pensamos que es lo mejor."

47. Ibid. "Todo el tiempo él escogía los muebles, él escogía el color de la casa, y nada de eso a mi me gustaba. . . . Y no tenía . . . mi poder de negocio para decir, 'Este color . . . y fíjate este mueble me gusta . . . ' Hasta que empezaba a buscar la forma de decirle que la cocina me gustaría que fuera blanca con azul, y dije, '¿Cómo se lo explico? ¿Cómo se lo digo? ¿Cómo escojo mis colores?'. . . . Un día fuimos a la casa de una amiga que estaba remodelando su cocina y a mí me gustó. ¿Cómo le decía yo que ese era el color que quería? En esa ocasión que fuimos, en ese tiempo esa familia eran muy amigos nuestros. Cuando regresamos de su casa, en el camino, le hice comentarios del buen gusto del esposo de ella había tenido a escoger esos colores. Entonces, después de que regresé de un tiempo para acá, estaban los mismos colores en mi cocina."

48. Sarah Hoagland, *Lesbian Ethics: Toward New Values* (Palo Alto, CA: Institute of Lesbian Studies, 1988), 53.

49. Griffith, *God's Daughters*, 181.

50. Ana could not remember the name of the woman, but it is a high probability that the woman she was referring to was the former model, image consultant, philanthropist, and motivational speaker Barbara Barrington Jones.

51. Claremont Mormon Women OHC, #173 (2015), 10. "Cuando ella habla y cuenta su historia que fue de demasiada violencia, todas como que 'Ahh! No soy la única!' Y cuando todas empiezan a escribir y empiezo a voltear a ver y vi que todos están escribiendo. Y nada más fuéramos quince de barrio, ¿y las demás? Es cuando me di cuenta de que no es aquí, no es allá, es en todos lados."

52. Ibid., 11–12. "Hicieron cambios de looks a las hermanas, nos enseñaron la tableta de colores, como maquillarnos, que colores nos quedan. Terminamos con la pasarela, modelando ropa, nuevos cortes, nuevos looks. Sales con una mentalidad diferente. . . . [Este fin de semana se trató de] Tu valor como mujer . . . Y sobre todo que no tienes que quedarte callado."

53. Ford, "Sister Acts," 222–223.

54. Claremont Mormon Women OHC, #173 (2015), 11. "Sí, y el sacerdocio lo sabe. Lo que a mi me da mucha pena es que no."

55. Ibid. "Yo creo que deben de haber clases más específicas, o talleres más específicos. Cosas más directas. Porque cuando se habla al aire, se deja la imaginación. . . . Tienen que ser personas capacitadas, miembros de la iglesia, que sean directas. Porque si no, puede ser contraproducente."

56. Admittedly, the stake president may not have had the financial resources to bring a prominent American speaker to Veracruz, even if he wanted to. He could, however, have organized local trainings, regardless of his budget.

57. Kline, "Saying Goodbye to the Final Say," 216–222.

58. See, e.g., Richard G. Scott, "To Heal the Shattering Consequences of Abuse," *Ensign*, May 2008, 40–43. Whether or not members in Mexico actually hear or read sermons from general church leaders is highly variable. Some women I interviewed were familiar with general church leaders and their sermons, while others were not. In general, though, members who attended more meetings would be more likely to hear messages like this one.

59. Kline, "Saying Goodbye to the Final Say," 220–221.

60. Claremont Mormon Women OHC, #173 (2015), 14. "En casa de él ellos no lavan platos, no lavan ropa, no barren, golpean. Él es machista. Y él no. Él siempre ayudó con niños, siempre lavó mamilas, siempre lavó pañales. Me ayuda con la comida, con las cosas. Y me permite trabajar. Permite que yo tenga mi dinero, que yo gaste mi dinero."

61. While Ana's husband's domestic labor reflects changing norms for Mormon men, they may also reflect changing norms for Mexican men. Matthew Gutmann's study of masculinity in Mexico City notes that younger men participate in more domestic chores than did men of the previous generation. Matthew Gutmann, *The Meanings of Macho: Being a Man in Mexico City*, 10th anniv. ed. (Berkeley: University of California Press, 2007), 151.

62. Anonymous, interview by April Carlson, March 16, 2015, Veracruz, Mexico, Claremont Mormon Women OHC, #174, transcript, p. 1. "Mi esposo tomaba mucho, me pegaba, recibí maltrato físico y yo encontré refugio en el evangelio."

63. Ibid. "A los nueve años me fui a entregar con una familia para que me dieran trabajo y yo tuviera para comer."

64. Ibid., 2. "Quería ser otra persona no quería ser la misma."

65. Ibid., 3. "Yo me di como adoptada en la Iglesia."

66. Ibid., 1. "Yo nunca fui a la escuela, nunca estudié. Yo aprendí a leer con el Libro de Mormón, con la Biblia, leyendo los libros, las escrituras, así empecé a escribir. No tomé clases. Ahora me doy cuenta que puedo levantarme a hablar, opinar de ciertas cosas, platicar e instruir cuando se requiere como líder dentro de la Sociedad de Socorro. Eso me ayudó mucho dentro y fuera dela iglesia he sido muy bendecida."

67. Craig, "Church in Latin America," 69.

68. Claremont Mormon Women OHC, #174 (2015), 4–5. "Esto me gusta transmitírselo a las mujeres que no son dela iglesia y comparto mi testimonio cuando las hermanas tienen un testimonio muy débil les hablo pero ellas me admiran mucho, tengo cartas muy bonitas . . . de las misionera, ellas le estuvieron dando las pláticas a mi hermano para que el salga de la obscuridad, una de ellas que es de Guatemala llorando me dijo, 'hermana cuando yo sea grande quiero ser como usted.'"

69. Ibid., 2. "He sido una mujer luchona . . . hago pay para vender. . . . Antes cuando era más joven trabajaba en las casas haciendo limpieza, pero dejaba a mis hijos

solos así que decidí hacer mis ventas y con eso he venido subsistiendo ayudando a mi esposo. Pero hace como trece años mi esposo se enfermó de diabetes, así que ya no trabaja, depende de mí y de mi hija. . . . Los pay los aprendí hacer en la Iglesia; la hermana [Teresa] nos enseñó."

70. These weekday classes, in which women would often learn to produce various products for home use or for vending, were called by different names by different women. One woman called them manual arts classes. Another called them self-sufficiency classes. Most just referred to them generically as classes taught to Relief Society women. From the women's descriptions, these classes sound equivalent to the "Homemaking" or "Enrichment" meetings of the Relief Society in the United States.

71. Anonymous, interview by Caroline Kline, March 18, 2015, Veracruz, Mexico, Claremont Mormon Women OHC, #171, transcript, p. 3 "Entonces un día yo dije, 'Yo no hago nada, tengo que ayudar a mi esposo.' Mis hijos estudiaban, años antes había tomado curso de soya por medio de la iglesia en México cuando fui a ver a mi hija. Me gustó mucho el curso. Todo lo he aprendido en la iglesia. Yo dije, 'Sé hacer leche de soya, pues la puedo vender y hacer productos.' Empecé a vender y sigo vendiendo. . . . Con este apoyo a mi esposo en la situación financiera, ya tengo clientes que me piden. También trabajo con el trigo y la gente del mundo como no conoce eso les gusta. Cuando me preguntan ¿dónde aprendió eso? les digo, 'En mi iglesia.'"

72. For an overview of the changing institutional church discourse on mothers working for pay, see Miles, "LDS Family Ideals," 109–120. Miles notes that this discourse, which was particularly negative about working mothers in the 1970s and 1980s, has become more accommodating of employed mothers over time.

73. These home-based businesses were most often discussed by women in their fifties, sixties, and seventies. Younger Mexican women did not mention turning skills learned in Relief Society into businesses.

74. Anonymous, interview by Caroline Kline, February 9, 2015, via video conferencing, Claremont Mormon Women OHC, #158, transcript, pp. 9–10. This woman spoke to me in English.

75. Although critiques of working motherhood by church authorities have diminished in recent years, some still do appear. See M. Russell Ballard, "That the Lost May Be Found," *Ensign*, May 2012, 100. He stated to the young women of the church, "No career can bring you as much fulfillment as rearing a family."

76. Anonymous, interview by Caroline Kline, March 14, 2015, in Veracruz, Mexico, Claremont Mormon Women OHC, #178, transcript, p. 6. This woman spoke to me in English.

77. Anonymous, interview by Caroline Kline and April Carlson, March 17, 2015, Veracruz, Mexico, Claremont Mormon Women OHC, #177, transcript, p. 7.

78. David Stoll, *Is Latin America Turning Protestant? The Politics of Evangelical Growth* (Berkeley: University of California Press, 1990), xvi.

79. Anonymous, interview by Caroline Kline and April Carlson, March 18, 2015, Veracruz, Mexico, Claremont Mormon Women OHC, #175, transcript, p. 3 "Empecé a realizar formularios de productos los cuales, de 1984 a la fecha, existen ciento di-

ecisiete técnicas. Al iniciar con la elaboración del formulario platiqué con mi presidente de estaca para pedir su consejo si podíamos enseñar en la organización a las hermanas. Su respuesta fue inmediata y afirmativa. Así se inició la capacitación a las hermanas de todos los barrios de la estaca. . . . Actualmente continuamos en diferentes estados capacitando a los barrios de las estacas."

80. Claremont Mormon Women OHC, #174 (2015), 1. "Mi esposo cambió no al 100% pero más o menos, aun siendo miembros dela iglesia tomaba. Le dio mucho trabajo cambiar."

81. Ibid., 3. "Los retos que he tenido son los de enfrentar a mi esposo con sus debilidades."

82. Ibid., 4. "Le digo 'tu testimonio es muy débil,' platico con él le leo las escrituras, le digo 'sino estamos a fines con el Señor todo nos produce miedo, si tú fortaleces tu testimonio en Jesucristo vas a tener valor para enfrentarte en todo así como yo me he enfrentado en tantas cosas.'"

83. Brusco, *Reformation of Machismo*, 6.

84. Sofia spoke of seeing a vision of Jesus Christ in the temple. She also spoke of how meaningful it was to her that temple ceremonies connected her for eternity to her children. Claremont Mormon Women Oral History Collection, #174 (2015), 8.

85. Anonymous, interview by April Carlson, March 22, 2015, Veracruz, Mexico, Claremont Mormon Women OHC, #176, transcript, p. 9. "A ese momento no lo comprendí a verdad, pero por eso fue difícil, porque yo tuve que bajarme al nivel, al rol, que me correspondía. A ser una hija de Dios, dispuesta a someterse, a ser buena madre, buena esposa, buena hija, buena hermana, buena vecina. . . . Entonces he ido bajando de todo de ese periodo, pero solamente a través del poder de dios."

86. For example, Debra Renee Kaufman, *Rachel's Daughters: Newly Orthodox Jewish Women* (New Brunswick: Rutgers University Press, 1991), 2–3.

87. Margaret Anderson, "Thinking About Women: A Quarter Century's View," *Gender & Society* 19, no. 4 (2005): 444.

88. Gina Colvin and Joanna Brooks discuss the way neocolonialism and Mormonism are intertwined. "Mormonism's rise in the nineteenth century and its global growth in the twentieth century also took place within the context of colonization and neo-colonization and drew from colonialist and neocolonialist ideas and attitudes." Gina Colvin and Joanna Brooks, "Introduction: Approaching a Postcolonial Zion," in *Decolonizing Mormonism: Approaching a Postcolonial Zion*, ed. Gina Colvin and Joanna Brooks (Salt Lake City: University of Utah Press, 2018), 7.

89. The *Liahona* is an official magazine of the Church of Jesus Christ of Latter-day Saints. Until 2021 its audience was international members, and the magazine was published in many languages. In 2021 the *Liahona* became the official magazine for all adult members, and it is available in many languages.

90. Donald Meyers, "New Mormon Missionary Training Center Building Plan Upsets Residents." *Salt Lake Tribune*, May 16, 2012, accessed January 15, 2021, http://archive .sltrib.com/story.php?ref=/sltrib/news/54118360–78/building-church-residents -heaton.html.csp.

91. Anonymous, interview by April Carlson, March 18, 2015, Veracruz, Mexico, Claremont Mormon Women OHC, #172, transcript, p. 11. "Nos sentimos tristes porque ese era un lugar para nuestros jóvenes y ya no hay un lugar. La decisión fue porque realmente necesitaban un CCM., pero también se que Estados Unidos no permitió que fuera allá, por eso lo hicieron en México, y eso fue una desilusión porque dijimos ellos si se defendieron y a nosotros no nos permitieron defender el Benemérito a nosotros no los impusieron, fue difícil y desilusión muy grande."

92. Colvin and Brooks, "Approaching a Postcolonial Zion," 10–11.

93. Brooks, "Mormonism as Colonialism," 184.

Chapter 2. African-Born Women Navigating an American-Born Church

1. As Ornulf Gulbrandsen explains, Tswana chiefs eventually accepted the offer of British "protection," but this "must be understood against a backdrop of other colonizing forces at work which was perceived by Northern Tswana as an indeed dangerous threat." Thus, becoming a British protectorate was seen as the most palatable of options, particularly since the British had promised that the chiefs would be left to govern their own tribes and that in tribal territories white settler communities would be firmly restricted. Ornulf Gulbrandsen, *The State and the Social: State Formation in Botswana and Its Precolonial and Colonial Genealogies* (New York: Berghahn, 2012), 47.

2. Makgala, "Survey of Race Relations in Botswana," 12.

3. Gulbrandsen, *The State and the Social*, 29. *Kgosi* can be translated to "Chief."

4. For more on Botswana's economic and political success see Daron Acemoglu, Simon Johnson, and James Robinson, "An African Success Story: Botswana," in *In Search of Prosperity: Analytic Narratives on Economic Growth*, ed. Dani Rodrik (Princeton: Princeton University Press, 2003).

5. Fidelis Nkomazana, "The Botswana Religious Landscape," in *The Faith Sector and HIV/AIDS in Botswana: Responses and Challenges*, ed. Lovemore Togarasei et al. (Cambridge: Cambridge Scholars Publishing, 2011), 11–12, 14.

6. For more basic statistics about Botswana, including information about religious groups in the country, see the Association of Religion Data Archives, http://www.thearda.com/internationalData/countries/Country_29_1.asp

7. The Church of Jesus Christ of Latter-day Saints, "Facts and Statistics," Newsroom, accessed September 22, 2021, https://newsroom.churchofjesuschrist.org/facts-and-statistics/country/botswana. See also E. Dale LeBaron, "Botswana," in *Encyclopedia of Latter-day Saint History*, ed. Arnold K. Garr et. al. (Salt Lake City: Deseret Books, 2000).

8. Dorothy L. Hodgson, *The Church of Women: Gendered Encounters Between Maasai and Missionaries* (Bloomington: Indiana University Press, 2005); Teresa M. Hinga, "Jesus Christ and the Liberation of Women in Africa," in *The Will to Arise:*

Women, Tradition, and the Church in Africa, ed. Mercy Amba Oduyoye et al. (Maryknoll, NY: Orbis, 1992), 187–190.

9. Jane E. Soothill, *Gender, Social Change and Spiritual Power: Charismatic Christianity in Ghana* (Boston: Brill Academic, 2007), 219.

10. When asked about why services in Botswana are in English, one interviewed Motswana wrote, "I feel as English is used there is nobody who feels a certain local language is preferred over the other." Although about 79 percent of Batswana have Setswana as their native language, there are some minority native languages as well. This woman saw English as a way to unite various church members in Botswana, no matter their tribe or native language, though she did acknowledge that "English can be a challenge for some members who don't speak it so well." Private email, February 16, 2016.

11. Walter E. A. van Beek, "Church Unity and the Challenge of Cultural Diversity: A View from Across the Sahara," in *Directions for Mormon Studies in the Twenty-First Century*, ed. Patrick Q. Mason (Salt Lake City: University of Utah Press, 2016), 72.

12. Brooks, "Mormonism as Colonialism," 163–185.

13. Ibid. See also Aikau, *Chosen People*.

14. Musa W. Dube, "Postcoloniality, Feminist Spaces, and Religion," in *Postcolonialism, Feminism, and Religious Discourse*, ed. Laura E. Donaldson and Kwok Pui-lan (New York: Routledge, 2002).

15. Chandra Talpade Mohanty, "Under Western Eyes: Feminist Scholarship and Colonial Discourse," in *Third World Women and the Politics of Feminism*, ed. Chandra Talpade Mohanty et al. (Bloomington: Indiana University Press, 1991), 51–80.

16. Gayatri Spivak, "Can the Subaltern Speak?," in *Marxism and the Interpretation of Culture*, ed. Cary Nelson and Lawrence Grossberg (London: Macmillan, 1988), 287.

17. John McLeod, *Beginning Postcolonialism* (Manchester, UK: Manchester University Press, 2000), 195.

18. Whereas my work focuses on the agency of religious women in the global South who convert to a Western religion, several other scholars have explored the question of global women's agency, most often outside the context of religion or in the context of indigenous religions. Lyn Parker helpfully introduces the concept of agency in social science literature, focusing on the perennial debate about the relationship between individual agency and societal structures. Several other essays in her edited volume examine how agency is enacted for women in various Asian contexts. *The Agency of Women in Asia*, ed. Lyn Parker (Singapore: Marshall Cavendish Academic), 2005. Jenny Sharpe seeks to complicate notions of slave women's agency beyond the idea of resistance, noting the negotiated practices and semi-autonomous actions they engaged in in order to survive. Jenny Sharpe, *Ghosts of Slavery: A Literary Archaeology of Black Women's Lives*, Minneapolis: University of Minnesota Press, 2003), xvi–xvix. Marjorie Keniston McIntosh explores the ways in which Yoruba women in Nigeria "enjoyed considerable agency," despite some indigenous and co-

lonial patriarchal structures, during the nineteenth and early twentieth centuries. They at times held political and religious power, directed domestic tasks, acted as female chiefs, carved out spaces for themselves in the public economy, and utilized the labor of dependents. Marjorie Keniston McIntosh, *Yoruba Women, Work, and Social Change* (Bloomington: Indiana University Press, 2009), 239–246. With a more theoretical focus, Kalpana Ram challenges Spivak's assertion of the silenced subaltern and claims that though third-world women have been oppressed, they have not been entirely deprived of agency or silenced. Kalpana Ram, "Too 'Traditional' Once Again: Some Poststructuralists on the Aspirations of the Immigrant/Third World Female Subject," *Australian Feminist Studies* 8, no. 17 (1993): 5–28. Contributors to *Women, Religion and Space* analyze how women in colonial contexts negotiated access to and prohibition from various religious spaces. *Women, Religion and Space: Global Perspectives on Gender and Faith,* ed. Karin M. Morin and Jeanne Kay Guelke (Syracuse: Syracuse University Press, 2007).

19. McDannell, *Sister Saints,* 150.

20. Anonymous, interview by Caroline Kline, June 1, 2015, in Botswana, # 26, transcript, p. 5, Gender, Narrative, and Religious Practice in Southern Africa Oral History Collection, Special Collections, Claremont Colleges Library, Claremont, California (hereafter Gender, Narrative, and Religious Practice in Southern Africa). Relief Society president is a significant calling (church assignment), typically considered to be the most burdensome and respected calling among women in a Latter-day Saint congregation.

21. Gordon B. Hinckley, "Reverence and Morality," *Ensign,* May 1987, 46–47. Hinckley stated, "We should reach out with kindness and comfort to the [HIV-]afflicted, ministering to their needs and assisting them with their problems. We repeat, however, that the way of safety and the road to happiness lie in abstinence before marriage and fidelity following marriage."

22. Gender, Narrative, and Religious Practice in Southern Africa, #26 (2015), 5.

23. Rebecca Upton, "'Women Have No Tribe': Connecting Carework, Gender, and Migration in an Era of HIV/AIDS in Botswana," in *Global Dimensions of Gender and Carework,* ed. Mary K. Zimmerman et al. (Stanford, CA: Stanford Social Sciences, 2006), 278.

24. David N. Suggs, *A Bagful of Locusts and the Baboon Woman: Constructions of Gender, Change, and Continuity in Botswana* (Fort Worth, TX: Harcourt, 2002), 46–47.

25. Wendy Izzard, "The Impact of Migration on the Roles of Women in Botswana: Patterns, Causes, and Consequences," *Final Report: National Migration Study* (Gaborone, Botswana: Central Statistics Office, 1982), 3: 664–665.

26. Suggs, *Bagful of Locusts,* 30.

27. Ibid.

28. I do not have statistics that attest to the gender imbalance in the church in Botswana, but I do have anecdotal comments from women I interviewed about there being fewer Latter-day Saint men than woman. One Motswana woman I interviewed

later wrote: "Yes there are more women than men in my ward. I think it starts right from the beginning when missionaries find people to teach, more women are usually receptive listening to missionaries messages than men, and these usually results in more women getting baptized than men." Private email, November 1, 2016.

29. Dominique Meekers and Ghyasuddin Ahmed, "Adolescent Sexuality in Southern Africa: Cultural Norms and Contemporary Behavior," paper presented at the International Union for the Scientific Study of Population General Conference, Beijing, China, October 1997, pp. 4–7, https://www.psi.org/wp-content/uploads/1997/10/WP02.pdf.

30. Gender, Narrative, and Religious Practice in Southern Africa, #26 (2015), 9.

31. See Tim B. Heaton, Kristen L. Goodman, and Thomas B. Holman, "In Search of a Peculiar People: Are Mormon Families Really Different?," in *Contemporary Mormonism: Social Science Perspectives*, ed. Marie Cornwall et al. (Urbana: University of Illinois Press, 1994), 102. The authors write, "Mormon leaders stress a division of labor for husbands and wives. Men are to be breadwinners, while women are to be homemakers. . . . Both are to be involved with raising their children, but the mother bears the primary responsibility for child care." See also Beaman, "Molly Mormons," and Kline, "Mormon Conception of Women's Nature."

32. "The Family: A Proclamation to the World," *Ensign*, November 1995, 102. This document is commonly known as "The Proclamation" among Latter-day Saints. It states, "By divine design, fathers are to preside over their families in love and righteousness and are responsible to provide the necessities of life and protection for their families. Mothers are primarily responsible for the nurture of children."

33. Sheri Dew, "Are We Not All Mothers?" *Ensign*, November 2001, https://www.churchofjesuschrist.org/study/ensign/2001/11/are-we-not-all-mothers?lang=eng.

34. John A. Widtsoe, *Priesthood and Church Government*, rev. ed. (Salt Lake City: Deseret Books, 1954), 39. Sonja Farnsworth, in her seminal essay on this correlation of priesthood with motherhood, notes that this quotation from Widtsoe is the first time the connection was made in official Latter-day Saint discourse. Farnsworth, "Mormonism's Odd Couple," 300–301. A recent article attests, however, that this framework was laid out in 1933 by Leah Dunford Widtsoe. Kathryn H. Shirts, "The Role of Susa Young Gates and Leah Dunford Widtsoe in the Historical Development of the Priesthood/Motherhood Model," *Journal of Mormon History* 44, no. 2 (April 2018): 127–128. Farnsworth critiques this parallel, noting that because of it "the word mother has become a kind of sacred title, like elder or bishop. . . . Through application of the title 'mother' Mormon women are named out of the priesthood" ("Mormonism's Odd Couple," 301). In this way, Farnsworth argued, the equation serves as a distraction from the real situation—that women are excluded from leadership structures in the church.

35. Allison Keeney and Susan Woster, "Motherhood," in *Mormon Women Have Their Say: Essays from the Claremont Oral History Collection*, ed. Claudia Bushman and Caroline Kline (Salt Lake City: Greg Kofford, 2013).

36. Gender, Narrative, and Religious Practice in Southern Africa, #26 (2015), 9.

37. Judith Van Allen, "Radical Citizenship: Powerful Mothers and Equal Rights," in *Power, Gender, and Social Change in Africa,* ed. Muna Ndulo and Margaret Grieco (Cambridge: Cambridge Scholars Publishing, 2009), 65.

38. Ibid.

39. Ibid., 71.

40. Ibid., 73.

41. Ezra T. Benson, "To the Mothers in Zion," fireside address, February 22, 1987, https://www.churchofjesuschrist.org/study/manual/eternal-marriage-student-manual/womens-divine-roles-and-responsibilities/to-the-mothers-in-zion?lang=eng.

42. Iannaccone, "Dealing with Social Change," 1231–1250. Benson's "To the Mothers in Zion" was a notable outlier to that more accommodative shift. Lavina Fielding Anderson writes about the anger and hurt that many women felt in the wake of this talk, given that many felt that it ignored the economic realities of the 1980s, which often necessitated two incomes. Lavina Fielding Anderson, "A Voice from the Past: The Benson Instructions for Parents," *Dialogue* 21, no. 4 (1988): 105.

43. Miles, "LDS Family Ideals," 118.

44. Heaton, "In Search of a Peculiar People," 101.

45. Suggs, *Bagful of Locusts,* 49.

46. In Mormonism, husbandhood should also precede fatherhood, so no double standard exists here.

47. Gender, Narrative, and Religious Practice in Southern Africa, #26 (2015), 14–15.

48. Ibid., 5–6.

49. Anonymous, interview by Caroline Kline, June 6, 2015, Botswana, #38, transcript, p. 4, Gender, Narrative, and Religious Practice in Southern Africa. The "law of wisdom" she is referring to is the Latter-day Saint scriptural passage in the Doctrine and Covenants known as the Word of Wisdom, which is a health code for Latter-day Saints.

50. Anonymous, interview by Caroline Kline, June 3, 2015, Botswana, #30, transcript, p. 18, Gender, Narrative, and Religious Practice in Southern Africa. In this oral history, the narrator said that a marriage carried out without family participation or traditional cultural elements such as lobola "destroys families."

51. Jennifer Finlayson-Fife, "Female Sexual Agency in Patriarchal Culture: The Case of Mormon Women," (PhD diss., Boston College, 2002), 234.

52. Anonymous, interview by Caroline Kline, June 3, 2015, Botswana, unarchived interview, #1B, p. 5. Musa said, "Even in the church, there is pressure coming from members. Some would say, 'Yeah, you can have just one child.' Women would say to you, 'Your biological clock is ticking; come on, you can repent later.' . . . It's even more painful and harder to be a single sister who doesn't have children. It's really, really, really hard." I do not have a sense of how widespread this attitude (get pregnant now, repent later) is, but these were significant moments for Musa, who saw this attitude as evidence of just how much pressure there was for women in Botswana to become mothers.

53. See Munyaradzi Felix Murove, ed., *African Ethics: An Anthology of Comparative and Applied Ethics* (Scottsville, South Africa: University of KwaZulu-Natal Press, 2009). Many essays in this book touch on the concept of Ubuntu.

54. John Mbiti, *African Religions and Philosophies* (Oxford: Heinemann, 1969), 108.

55. Kipton E. Jensen, "The Politics of Faith-Based HIV Prevention Policies and Programs in Botswana," in Togarasei et al., *Faith Sector and HIV/AIDS in Botswana*, 62.

56. Mbiti, *African Religions*, 108.

57. Fainos Mangena, "The Search for an African Feminist Ethic: A Zimbabwean Perspective," *Journal of International Women's Studies* 11, no. 2 (September 2009): 24.

58. Visiting teaching was a program for Latter-day Saint women which entailed most practicing sisters visiting and delivering brief spiritual messages to a handful of women assigned to them. This program was discontinued in 2018 and replaced by a similar, though less formal, system called ministering.

59. Gender, Narrative, and Religious Practice in Southern Africa, #26 (2015), 11.

60. Ibid.

61. Ibid., 10.

62. Andrea Cornwall, "Introduction: Perspectives on Gender in Africa," in *Readings in Gender in Africa*, ed. Andrea Cornwall (Oxford: James Currey, 2005), 1.

63. Anonymous, interview by Heather Sundahl, June 7, 2015, #57, transcript, p. 7, Gender, Narrative, and Religious Practice in Southern Africa.

64. Anonymous, unarchived interview, #1B (2015), 11.

65. "Cohabiting Opposite-Sex Couples Can Now Be Baptized," *Nearing Kolob* (blog), July 2, 2015, accessed July 14, 2016, http://www.nearingkolob.com/cohabiting-opposite-sex-couples-can-now-baptized/. The author of the blog, a missionary in the Philippines, writes, "We have had more success in our work and our numbers are improving. The area presidency recently released a new rule that as long as two people have been living together for 5 years or more, they are allowed to be baptized, just because it is really hard for people here to get married or to get a divorce. Which means that one of our investigators who has really been wanting to be baptized is now able to. It also means that we will probably be having about 5 baptisms this month."

66. Ibid. In addition, Spencer W. Kimball's 1977 biography discusses how Kimball helped devise a new policy that allowed common-law couples to be baptized, given the difficulties of obtaining a divorce in some South American countries: "Elder Kimball helped to establish as Church policy that such couples could be baptized if they showed that they had done what they could to legalize their relationship, had been faithful to one another, had met responsibility to their previous family, and had conformed to the expectations of custom." Edward L. Kimball and Andrew E. Kimball Jr., *Spencer W. Kimball: Twelfth President of the Church of Jesus Christ of Latter-day Saints* (Salt Lake City: Bookcraft, 1977), 316.

67. RJH, "Common-Law Marriages," *By Common Consent* (blog), January 17, 2006, https://bycommonconsent.com/2006/01/17/common-law-marriage/. See comments by Karl and Eric Russell, among others.

68. Ifeanyi A. Menkiti, "Person and Community in African Traditional Thought," in *African Philosophy: An Introduction*, ed. Richard Wright (Lanham, MD: University Press of America, 1984), 171.

69. Anonymous, unarchived interview, #1B (2015), 12.

70. LDS Family Services, "Adoption and the Unwed Mother," *Ensign*, February 2002, https://www.churchofjesuschrist.org/study/ensign/2002/02/adoption-and-the-unwed-mother?lang=eng.

71. Anonymous, unarchived interview, #1B (2015), 12.

72. Rita Abrahamsen, "African Studies and the Postcolonial Challenge," *African Affairs* 102, no. 407 (April 2003): 206.

73. "Unwed Pregnancy," the Church of Jesus Christ of Latter-day Saints, accessed January 3, 2020, https://www.churchofjesuschrist.org/study/manual/gospel-topics/unwed-pregnancy?lang=eng.

74. It is interesting that the church also abandoned its full-service adoption agency in 2014, in part because increasing numbers of unwed mothers chose to keep their babies. See Ryan Morgenegg, "LDS Family Services No Longer Operating as Adoption Agency," *Church News*, July 1, 2014, https://www.churchofjesuschrist.org/church/news/lds-family-services-no-longer-operating-as-adoption-agency?lang=eng.

75. Anonymous, unarchived interview, #1B (2015), 12.

76. Amy Hoyt, "Reconceptualizing Agency," *Element* 5, no. 2 (Fall 2009): 75.

77. Mbiti, *African Religions and Philosophies*, 108.

78. Chandra Talpade Mohanty, *Feminism Without Borders: Decolonizing Theory, Practicing Solidarity* (Durham, NC: Duke University Press, 2004), 80.

79. Gloria Anzaldua refers to this as a "mestiza consciousness." Gloria Anzaldua, *Borderlands/La Frontera: The New Mestiza* (San Francisco: Spinsters, 1987), 79–80. Alarcon calls it a "plurality of self." Norma Alarcon, "The Theoretical Subject(s) of *This Bridge Called My Back* and Anglo-American Feminism," in *The Postmodern Turn: New Perspectives on Social Theory*, ed. Steven Seidman (Cambridge: Cambridge University Press, 1994), 152.

80. In the Church of Jesus Christ of Latter-day Saints, an Institute of Religion is a local organization that teaches religious classes to young adults.

81. Anonymous, unarchived interview, #1B (2015), 8.

82. Ibid.

83. Gender, Narrative, and Religious Practice in Southern Africa, #30 (2015), 14–15.

84. Ibid. Punctuation has been changed for clarity.

85. Ibid., 16.

86. An area authority is a leader appointed by church headquarters in Salt Lake City to have regional responsibilities over a part of the world.

87. Dallin H. Oaks, "The Gospel Culture," *Ensign*, March 2012, https://www.churchofjesuschrist.org/study/ensign/2012/03/the-gospel-culture?lang=eng.

88. Ibid.

89. Gender, Narrative, and Religious Practice in Southern Africa, #57 (2015), 11.

90. Van Beek, "Church Unity," 78.

91. Ibid., 84.

92. Aleah Ingram, "Church Leaders Speak About Dowry in Africa," *LDS Daily*, January 25, 2016, http://www.ldsdaily.com/church-lds/church-leaders-speak-about -dowry-in-african-culture/.

93. Caroline White, "'Close to Home' in Johannesburg: Gender Oppression in Township Households," *Women's Studies International Forum* 16, no. 2 (1993): 160.

94. Nogget Matope, Nyevero Marunzani, Efirtha Chauraya, and Beatrice Bondai, "Lobola and Gender Based Violence: Perceptions of Married Adults in Gweru Urban, Zimbabwe," *Journal of Education Research and Behavioral Sciences* 2, no. 11 (November 2013): 192–200.

95. Godisang Mookodi, "Male Violence Against Women in Botswana: A Discussion of Gendered Uncertainties in a Rapidly Changing Environment," *African Sociological Review* 8, no. 1 (2004): 122.

96. Spivak, "Can the Subaltern Speak?," 296–297.

97. Miriam Cooke, "Saving Brown Women," *Signs* 28, no. 1 (2002): 468–470.

98. Spivak is pessimistic about the prospect that the perspectives of women in the developing world can actually be recovered, given the power of colonization and patriarchy. But other scholars, such as Benita Parry, believe that the native woman's voice can indeed be heard at times. Benita Parry, "Problems in Current Theories of Colonial Discourse," *Oxford Literary Review* 9, nos. 1/2 (1987): 39.

99. Marnia Lazreg, "Decolonizing Feminism," in *African Gender Studies: A Reader*, ed. Oyeronke Oyewumi (New York: Palgrave Macmillan, 2005), 75.

100. White, "Close to Home," 149–150. White writes that three central concerns of white feminists are marriage and family, lack of work opportunities for women, and sexism. She then describes why these topics do not necessarily resonate with Black women: Marriage is sought after because racism and colonization historically have prevented Black people from forming families; work is drudgery, not liberation, for Black women; and men are not oppressors but brothers in the struggle against oppression.

101. Gender, Narrative, and Religious Practice in Southern Africa, #30 (2015), 17. Punctuation has been changed for clarity.

102. Van Beek, "Church Unity," 84. Van Beek writes, "Western feminism has had its problems with the custom [lobola], but was confronted with a massive African female response that Western values should not be imposed and that African women were perfectly capable of deciding on their own what was important in their culture and what was not" (84).

103. McDannell, *Sister Saints*, 147.

104. Gender, Narrative, and Religious Practice in Southern Africa, #30 (2015), 17.

105. Ibid.

106. Ibid., 19.

107. See Dallin H. Oaks, "Gospel Culture."

108. Van Beek, "Church Unity," 95–96.

109. Philip Jenkins, "Letting Go: Understanding Mormon Growth in Africa," *Journal of Mormon History* 35 (Spring 2009): 1–25; Jehu Hanciles, "'Would That All God's People Were Prophets': Mormonism and the New Shape of Global Christianity," *Journal of Mormon History* 41 (April 2015): 35–68.

110. Gina Colvin, "There's No Such Thing as a Gospel Culture," *Dialogue* 50, no. 4 (2017): 58.

111. Gina Colvin, comment on Feminist Mormon Housewives Society Facebook group, January 25, 2016. https://www.facebook.com/groups/fmhsociety/search/?query =dowry.

112. Gina Colvin, "The Future of Global Mormonism: Decolonization and Inclusivity," *Exponent II* 34, nos. 2/3 (Fall 2014/Winter 2015): 40.

113. Ibid.

114. Ryan Dunch, "Beyond Cultural Imperialism: Cultural Theory, Christian Missions, and Global Modernity," *History and Theory* 41, no. 3 (2002): 307.

115. Mercy Amba Oduyoye, *African Women's Theology* (Cleveland, OH: Pilgrim, 2001), 12.

116. Ibid., 13–14.

117. Ibid., 14.

118. Sibonile Edith Ellece, "'Be a Fool Like Me': Gender Construction in the Marriage Advice Ceremony in Botswana—A Critical Discourse Analysis," *Agenda* 25, no. 1 (2011): 47.

119. Ibid., 50.

120. Ibid., 44.

121. "The Family: A Proclamation to the World," 102.

122. Buerger, *Mysteries of* Godliness, 170, 178.

123. Kline, "Saying Goodbye to the Final Say."

124. Stack and Noyce, "LDS Church Changes Temple Ceremony." The article describes the changes to the covenant in this way: "Men and women make all the same covenants, or promises, to God, rather than separate ones. Women also no longer covenant to hearken to their husbands."

125. Spencer W. Kimball, *The Teachings of Spencer W. Kimball* (Salt Lake City: Deseret Books, 1982), 248. See also "An Apostle Speaks About Marriage to John and Mary," *Improvement Era*, February 1949, 76; "John and Mary, Beginning Life Together," *New Era*, June 1975, 7—8.

126. Lynn G. Robbins, "Agency and Love in Marriage," *Ensign,* October 2000, https://www.churchofjesuschrist.org/study/ensign/2000/10/agency-and-love-in -marriage?lang=eng; Rachel Sterzer, "BYU Professor Teaches How to Take the Fear out of Dating," *Deseret News*, September 10, 2015, http://www.deseretnews.com/ article/865636457/Taking-the-fear-out-of-dating.html?pg=all.

127. Anonymous, interview by Caroline Kline, June 3, 2015, Botswana, #34, transcript, p. 4, Gender, Narrative, and Religious Practice in Southern Africa.

128. Ibid., 3.

129. Ibid., 7.

130. Ibid.

131. Ibid., 8.

132. Ibid.

133. Sasha might also have been thinking of the covenant of consecration, which she described as leading to unity and "not just for us out there at church. It starts in families and in marriages."

134. Gender, Narrative, and Religious Practice in Southern Africa, #34 (2015), 8.

135. Ibid., 11. Punctuation has been changed for clarity.

136. Anonymous, interview by Jennifer Platt, June 7, 2015, Botswana, #22, transcript, p. 2, Gender, Narrative, and Religious Practice in Southern Africa.

137. Mookodi, "Male Violence," 122.

138. Anonymous, interview by Caroline Kline, June 14, 2015, Botswana, #32, transcript, pp. 10–11, Gender, Narrative, and Religious Practice in Southern Africa.

139. Ibid., 10.

140. Anonymous, interview by Jennifer Platt, June 2, 2015, Botswana, #23, transcript, p. 4, Gender, Narrative, and Religious Practice in Southern Africa.

141. For more on the ways colonialism has disempowered men in sub-Saharan Africa, see Margarethe Silberschmidt, "Poverty, Male Disempowerment, and Male Sexuality: Rethinking Men and Masculinities in Rural and Urban East Africa," in *African Masculinities*, ed. Lahoucine Ouzgane and Robert Morrell (New York: Palgrave Macmillan, 2005).

142. Gooren, "Mormons of the World," 363; Taunalyn Rutherford, "Conceptualizing Global Religions: An Investigation of Mormonism in India" (PhD diss., Claremont Graduate School, 2017), 277–284.

143. Anonymous, interview by Caroline Kline, June 6, 2015, Botswana, #27, transcript, p. 6, Gender, Narrative, and Religious Practice in Southern Africa.

144. American church authorities have rejected notions of mothers deferring to priesthood-holding sons and have asserted mothers' role of presiding over sons and daughters in the family when their husbands are absent, but this idea has received little attention compared to the repeated emphasis on husbands and wives functioning as equal partners. See Dallin H. Oaks, "Priesthood Authority in the Family and the Church," General Conference of the Church of Jesus Christ of Latter-day Saints, Salt Lake City, October 2005.

145. Jana Riess discusses millennial Latter-day Saints in the United States who embrace marriages and gender dynamics that downplay female subordination. Jana Riess, *The Next Mormons: How Millennials Are Changing the LDS Church* (New York: Oxford, 2019), 58.

146. Robert Morell and Lahoucine Ouzgane, "African Masculinities: An Introduction," in *African Masculinities*, ed. Lahoucine Ouzgane and Robert Morrell (New York: Palgrave Macmillan, 2005), 5.

147. See Givens, *People of Paradox*. His first chapter, "The Iron Rod and the Liahona: Authority and Radical Freedom," elaborates on this paradoxical Mormon pairing of authority and agency.

148. Anonymous, interview by Heather Sundahl, June 7, 2015, Botswana, #59, transcript, p. 5, Gender, Narrative, and Religious Practice in Southern Africa.

149. Gender, Narrative, and Religious Practice in Southern Africa, #27 (2015), 9.

150. Ibid., 6.

151. McDannell, *Sister Saints*, 152.

152. Anonymous, interview by Caroline Kline, June 1, 2015, Botswana, #24, transcript, p. 8, Gender, Narrative, and Religious Practice in Southern Africa.

153. Ibid., 5.

154. Laurel Thatcher Ulrich, "Stirring up LDS History," lecture sponsored by Sunstone and Friends of the Marriott Library, University of Utah, Salt Lake City, December 11, 2011, https://stream.lib.utah.edu/index.php?c=details&id=8263.

155. Marie Cornwall, "The Institutional Role of Mormon Women," in *Contemporary Mormonism: Social Science Perspectives*, ed. Marie Cornwall et al. (Chicago: University of Illinois Press, 1994), 250.

156. Gender, Narrative, and Religious Practice in Southern Africa, #22 (2015), 3.

Chapter 3. Privilege, Complexity, and Women of Color in the United States

1. On March 31, 2018, an Asian American man and a Brazilian man became two members of the Quorum of the Twelve Apostles, thereby adding some racial and ethnic diversity that the body had previously been lacking. At the time of my interviews (2015–2017) with Latter-day Saint women of color, these most powerful positions were held only by white men.

2. Peggy Fletcher Stack, "Feeling Excluded, Black Mormon Women Ask: 'Do They See Me?'" *Salt Lake Tribune*, October 9, 2015, http://www.sltrib.com/home/3048039 -155/feeling-excluded-black-mormon-women-ask. Graham-Russell discusses the invisibility of Black Latter-day Saint women—as well as their hypervisibility given rampant stereotypes of Black women as Mammys and Jezebels—and how these two forces combine to silence them. Janan Graham-Russell, "On Black Bodies in White Spaces: Conversations of Women's Ordination and Women of African Descent in the Church of Jesus Christ of Latter-day Saints," in *Mormon Feminism: Essential Writings*, ed. Joanna Brooks et al. (Oxford: Oxford University Press, 2015), 268–270.

3. See Lester Bush Jr., "Mormonism's Negro Doctrine: An Historical Overview," *Dialogue* 8, no. 1 (Spring 1973): 11–68. Max Perry Mueller discusses the effect of this practice on Mormonism's most famous nineteenth-century Black female convert, Jane Manning James, who sought but was denied access to the temple endowment. Max Perry Mueller, *Race and the Making of the Mormon People* (Chapel Hill: University of North Carolina Press, 2017), 119–152. W. Paul Reeve discusses Joseph Smith's and other early church leaders' thoughts and actions regarding people of African descent, finding that distaste for miscegenation was an important driver of Brigham Young's ultimate decision to exclude Black men from ordination and Black women and men from certain temple ceremonies. W. Paul Reeve, *Religion of a Different Color: Race*

and the Mormon Struggle for Whiteness (New York: Oxford University Press, 2015), 106–139.

4. Bush, "Mormonism's Negro Doctrine"; Mueller, *Race and the Making of the Mormon People*; Reeve, *Religion of a Different Color*. See also Armand Mauss's chapter, "The Curse of African Lineage in Mormon History," in Mauss, *All Abraham's Children*.

5. Newell Bringhurst, *Saints, Slaves, and Blacks: The Changing Place of Black People Within Mormonism* (Westport, CT: Greenwood, 1981), 171. Bringhurst writes that in the early twentieth century Joseph Fielding Smith "further developed and gave prominent publicity to the preexistence hypothesis, that is, the concept that the black man's inability to hold the priesthood was a consequence of his behavior during a premortal existence." Bringhurst notes that Joseph Fielding Smith in *The Way to Perfection* said that Blacks "did not stand valiantly" and "sympathized with Lucifer" in the premortal war between God and Satan. Joseph Fielding Smith, *The Way to Perfection* (Salt Lake City: Deseret News Press, 1931), 43–44, 97–111.

6. "Church of Jesus Christ of Latter-day Saints, Race and the Priesthood," accessed January 3, 2020, https://www.churchofjesuschrist.org/study/manual/gospel-topics -essays/race-and-the-priesthood?lang=eng.

7. Bruce R. McConkie, *Mormon Doctrine*, 2nd ed. (Salt Lake City: Bookcraft, 1966), 527–528.

8. Graham-Russell, "On Black Bodies," 268–270.

9. Kiskilili, "Renaming the 'Priesthood Ban,'" *Zelophehad's Daughters* (blog), June 8, 2008, http://zelophehadsdaughters.com/2008/06/08/renaming-the-priesthood -ban/.

10. 2 Nephi 5:21 in the Book of Mormon.

11. Doctrine and Covenants 49:24.

12. See Aikau, *Chosen People*, 185–186.

13. 2 Nephi 26:33; Moses 7:18. One American woman of color I interviewed named the Mormon concept of Zion as the most compelling and inspiring idea in Mormonism.

14. This chapter focuses on the lives and thoughts of women in the United States, as opposed to American women. A significant minority of the women I interviewed for this chapter have lived in the United States for years but are citizens of other countries.

15. bell hooks, *Feminist Theory: From Margin to Center* (New York: Routledge, 2015), xiii.

16. Collins, *Black Feminist Thought*, 18.

17. Anonymous, interview by Caroline Kline, November 30, 2016, in Connecticut, #155, transcript, p. 2, Claremont Mormon Women Oral History Collection, Special Collections, Claremont Colleges Library, Claremont, California (hereafter Claremont Mormon Women OHC).

18. Ibid., 5.

19. Ibid.

20. Ibid., 7.

21. Ibid.

22. Ibid., 7–8.

23. Ibid., 8. For information about Apartheid policies that fractured Black families in South Africa, see Keith U. C. Appolis, *From Fragmentation to Wholeness: The Black South African Family Under Siege* (New York: University Press of America, 1996).

24. Brusco, *The Reformation of Machismo*, 123.

25. Claremont Mormon Women OHC, #155 (2016), 14.

26. Ibid., 15.

27. Ibid., 14.

28. Ibid., 14–15.

29. Ibid., 14.

30. Anonymous, interview by Caroline Kline, November 13, 2016, Massachusetts, #204, transcript, p. 2, Claremont Mormon Women OHC.

31. Ibid., 2–3.

32. Ibid., 3.

33. Ibid., 4.

34. Ibid., 9.

35. Ibid.

36. Ibid., 16.

37. Ibid., 4.

38. Anonymous, interview by Caroline Kline, December 4, 2016, Connecticut, #152, transcript, pp. 3–4, Claremont Mormon Women OHC.

39. Ibid., 5.

40. Ibid., 4.

41. Ibid., 2.

42. Ibid., 5.

43. Ibid., 9.

44. Walker, *In Search of Our Mothers' Gardens*, xi.

45. Ibid.

46. Williams, *Sisters in the Wilderness*, xiv.

47. Katie Cannon, *Katie's Canon: Womanism and the Soul of the Black Community* (New York: Continuum, 1995), 24.

48. Peggy Fletcher Stack, "For Many Black Mormons, Racism Is a Bigger Issue Than Sexism," *Salt Lake Tribune*, September 4, 2014, accessed June 21, 2017, http://archive .sltrib.com/story.php?ref=/sltrib/news/58361569–78/women-says-black-church.html. cspT.

49. Ibid.

50. Janan Graham-Russell supports this point, writing that white Latter-day Saint women have had access to the temple and therefore priesthood for far longer than Black women (and men). Thus, comparisons between the experiences of the two groups fall somewhat flat for her as well. Graham-Russell, "On Black Bodies," 269.

51. Paulette Payne, "Hallelujah and Amen: The African-American Religious Aes-

thetic and Black Women in the Church of Jesus Christ of Latter-day Saints in Southwest Atlanta, Georgia" (Master's thesis, Clark Atlanta University, 2009), 81–82.

52. Paulette Payne, panel participant at the Black, White and Mormon Conference in Salt Lake City, October 9, 2015, http://thc.utah.edu/lectures-programs/bwm-conference/raceandmormonwomen.php. In this panel Payne explicitly mentions the lack of attention to contemporary issues of social justice in Mormonism. It is important to point out, however, that within the faith there are religious narratives that promote social justice. As Grant Hardy writes, the Book of Mormon features several passages about what constitutes a just society. In it, pride, costly apparel, and inequality are concerns that religious leaders express repeatedly. Grant Hardy, "The Book of Mormon and Social Justice," *Meridian*, March 20, 2011, https://ldsmag.com/article-1-7677/. Moreover, apostle Dallin Oaks recently denounced racism and said that Black lives matter, affirming that that statement should be a "universally acceptable message." Oaks did not, however, affirm the Black Lives Matter movement. He also implied that the church's priesthood and temple ban was authored by God. Peggy Fletcher Stack, "Black Lives Matter, LDS Leader Dallin Oaks Tells BYU Audience, and Is a Cause All Should Support," Salt Lake Tribune, October 27, 2020, https://www.sltrib.com/religion/2020/10/27/black-lives-matter-lds/.

53. The Maori womanist Gina Colvin calls attention to this danger of focusing on patriarchy and ignoring the other inequities present in the church, such as those based on race, class, and Americentricism. Gina Colvin, "I'll Be at the Ordain Women Event, But . . ." *KiwiMormon* (blog), April 2, 2014, http://www.patheos.com/blogs/kiwimormon/2014/04/ill-be-at-the-ordain-women-event-but/.

54. Peggy McIntosh, "White Privilege: Unpacking the Invisible Knapsack," in *Race, Class and Gender: An Anthology*, 9th ed., ed. Margaret Andersen and Patricia Hill Collins (Boston: Wadsworth, 2015), 74.

55. W. E. B. Du Bois, *Black Reconstruction in America: An Essay Toward a History of the Part Which Black Folk Played in the Attempt to Reconstruct Democracy in America, 1860—1880* (New York: Free Press, 1965), 700.

56. Joe Kincheloe, *Critical Pedagogy Primer* (New York: Peter Lang International, 2008), 62. For an extended treatment of White privilege, see David Roediger, *The Wages of Whiteness: Race and the Making of the American Working Class* (New York: Verso, 1999).

57. Allen G. Johnson, *Privilege, Power, and Difference* (New York: McGraw Hill, 2018), 31–32.

58. Abigail Brooks, "Feminist Standpoint Epistemology: Building Knowledge and Empowerment Through Women's Lived Experience," in *Feminist Research Practice: A Primer*, ed. Sharlene Nagy Hesse-Biber and Patricia Lina Leavy (Thousand Oaks, CA: Sage, 2006), 56.

59. Anonymous, interview by Caroline Kline, November 13, 2016, Massachusetts, unarchived interview, #2C, transcript, p. 3.

60. Ibid., 4.

61. Ibid., 3–4.

62. Ibid., 4.

63. McDannell, *Sister Saints*, 165–166. McDannell sees the Proclamation on the Family as enabling the expansion of women's roles, given its lack of specificity about what constitutes female nurturing. She therefore sees the Proclamation as offering a "theology of silence" regarding women's activities apart from nurturing. In the face of this silence, she argues, women can overlook earlier injunctions to avoid wage labor.

64. Anonymous, unarchived interview, #2C (2016), 4–5.

65. Ada Maria Isasi-Diaz, *En la Lucha: Elaborating a Mujerista Theology* (Minneapolis: Fortress, 2004), 43.

66. Anonymous, unarchived interview, #2C (2016), 5.

67. Dorothy Smith, *The Conceptual Practices of Power: A Feminist Sociology of Knowledge* (Boston: Northeastern University Press, 1990), 19.

68. A. Brooks, "Feminist Standpoint Epistemology," 63.

69. Ibid., 64.

70. Alison Jagger, "Feminist Politics and Epistemology: The Standpoint of Women," in *The Feminist Standpoint Theory Reader: Intellectual and Political Controversies*, ed. Sandra Harding (New York: Routledge, 2004), 60.

71. Gordon B. Hinckley, "Women of the Church," *Ensign*, November 1996, https://www.churchofjesuschrist.org/study/ensign/1996/11/women-of-the-church?lang=eng. Hinckley states, "I recognize . . . that there are some women . . . who have to work to provide for the needs of their families. To you I say, do the very best you can. I hope that if you are employed full-time you are doing it to ensure that basic needs are met and not simply to indulge a taste for an elaborate home, fancy cars, and other luxuries."

72. Brigham Young, "The Persecutions of the Saints—Their Loyalty to the Constitution—The Mormon Battalion—The Laws of God Relative to the African Race," *Journal of Discourses* 10 (1863): 110, http://contentdm.lib.byu.edu/cdm/ref/collection/JournalOfDiscourses3/id/4266. Joseph Smith Jr. stated on January 2, 1843, "Had I anything to do with the negro, I would confine them [sic] to their own species." D. Michael Quinn, *Mormon Hierarchy: Origins of Power* (Salt Lake City: Signature, 1994), 636. For more on Brigham Young's opinions of interracial marriage with those of African descent see Reeve, *Religion of a Different Color*, 128–139. Reeve shows that early Mormon leaders like Young had a far different reaction to the idea of interracial marriage with those of Native American descent; Young actively encouraged those marriages. Ibid., 77–87.

73. McConkie, *Mormon Doctrine*, 114.

74. In 1977 Boyd K. Packer said, "We've always counseled in the Church for our Mexican members to marry Mexicans, our Japanese members to marry Japanese, our Caucasians to marry Caucasians, our Polynesian members to marry Polynesians. . . . The counsel has been wise." Boyd K. Packer, "Follow the Rule," BYU Devotional, January 14, 1977, https://speeches.byu.edu/talks/boyd-k-packer_follow-rule/. A 1995 Aaronic Priesthood lesson manual for adolescent boys features a quote

that discourages interracial marriage. See https://www.churchofjesuschrist.org/bc/
content/shared/content/english/pdf/34822_AaronicPriesthood3/ap3–31-choosing
-an-eternal-companion_34.pdf. In 2020 the *Come Follow Me* Sunday School manual
featured commentary that described the dark skin of the Lamanites as the sign of
a "curse" and inferred a discouragement of interracial marriage. The inclusion of
this commentary was later declared an "error" by a church spokesperson, and the
online version of the manual removed the troubling statement. Peggy Fletcher Stack,
"Error in Printed LDS Church Manual Could Revive Racial Criticisms," *Salt Lake
Tribune*, January 18, 2020, https://www.sltrib.com/religion/2020/01/18/error-printed
-lds-church/.

75. Anonymous, interview by Caroline Kline, August 4, 2015, Utah, #160, transcript,
pp. 4–5, Claremont Mormon Women OHC. Punctuation has been changed for clarity.

76. Church of Jesus Christ of Latter-day Saints, "Race and the Priesthood." Although the Gospel Topics essay addresses and disavows racist church teachings of
the past, contemporary church leaders continue to condemn racism more generally.
In the wake of the 2017 Charlottesville, Virginia, white nationalist rally, the church
issued a statement condemning racism, saying, "White supremacist attitudes are
morally wrong and sinful, and we condemn them. Church members who promote
or pursue a 'white culture' or white supremacy agenda are not in harmony with the
teachings of the Church." See Church of Jesus Christ of Latter-day Saints, "Church Releases Statement Condemning White Supremist Attitudes," *Church News*, August 15,
2017, https://www.churchofjesuschrist.org/church/news/church-releases-statement
-condemning-white-supremacist-attitudes?lang=eng. Church president Russell M.
Nelson also clearly condemned racism in the months after the 2020 killing of George
Floyd, saying, "I grieve that our Black brothers and sisters the world over are enduring
the pains of racism and prejudice. Today, I call upon our members everywhere to
lead out in abandoning attitudes and actions of prejudice." Russell M. Nelson, "Let
God Prevail," address given at the Semiannual General Conference of the Church of
Jesus Christ of Latter-day Saints, October 4, 2020, https://www.churchofjesuschrist
.org/study/general-conference/2020/10/46nelson?lang=eng.

77. Tad Walch, "Essays on Mormon History, Doctrine Find New Visibility
in Official App, Sunday School," *Deseret News*, December 26, 2016, https://www
.deseretnews.com/article/865669945/Essays-on-Mormon-history-doctrine-find
-new-visibility-in-official-app-Sunday-School.html.

78. Peggy Fletcher Stack, "Landmark 'Mormon Doctrine' Goes out of Print," *Salt
Lake Tribune*, May 21, 2010, http://archive.sltrib.com/story.php?ref=/ci_15137409.

79. Note President Gordon B. Hinckley's 1996 response to Mike Wallace when
asked about past Mormon teachings about Black people having the cursed mark of
Cain: "It's behind us. Look, that's behind us. Don't worry about those little flicks of
history," he said. "Former President of Mormon Church, Gordon B. Hinckley, Gives
First Ever Interview," *World Religion News*, accessed June 22, 2017, http://www.world
religionnews.com/religion-news/former-president-of-mormon-church-gordon-b
-hinckley-gives-first-ever-interview.

80. Terryl Givens, *Wrestling the Angel: The Foundations of Mormon Thought; Cosmos, God, Humanity* (New York: Oxford University Press, 2015), 45.

81. Terryl Givens, "Christ, Atonement and Human Possibilities in Mormon Thought," in *The Oxford Handbook of Mormonism*, ed. Terryl Givens and Philip Barlow (New York: Oxford University Press, 2015), 265.

82. Claremont Mormon Women OHC, #155 (2016), 5.

83. Gina Colvin, "#110: Mormonism, Liberation Theology and Womanism: A Conversation with Fatimah Salleh and Janan Graham," *A Thoughtful Faith*, podcast, August 24, 2015, http://www.athoughtfulfaith.org/mormonism-liberation-theology-and-womanism-a-conversation-with-fatimah-salleh-and-janan-graham/.

84. Anonymous, interview by Caroline Kline, August 4, 2015, Utah, #166, transcript, p. 2, Claremont Mormon Women OHC.

85. Ibid.

86. Givens, *People of Paradox*, 3–19.

87. Claremont Mormon Women OHC, #166 (2015), 9.

88. Anonymous, interview by Caroline Kline, February 2, 2017, California, #157, transcript, p. 9, Claremont Mormon Women OHC.

89. Anonymous, email message to Caroline Kline, May 22, 2015.

90. Claremont Mormon Women OHC, #157 (2017), 7.

91. Ibid., 14.

92. Buerger, *Mysteries of Godliness,* 178.

93. Claremont Mormon Women OHC, #157 (2017), 7.

94. Mary Bednarowski, *The Religious Imagination of American Women* (Bloomington: Indiana University Press, 1990), 19.

95. Ibid., 20.

96. Claremont Mormon Women OHC, #157 (2017), 7–8.

97. Melvin R. Brooks, *LDS Reference Encyclopedia* (Salt Lake City: Bookcraft, 1960), 309—310.

98. Claremont Mormon Women OHC, #157 (2017), 7.

99. Ibid., 10.

100. Ibid., 8.

101. Ibid.

102. Ibid.

103. See Petroff's discussion of female Catholic visionaries, whose spiritual experiences authorized women to speak. Elizabeth Alvilda Petroff, "Introduction: The Visionary Tradition in Women's Writing; Dialogue and Autobiography," in *Medieval Women's Visionary Literature*, ed. Elizabeth Alvilda Petroff (New York: Oxford University Press, 1986), 6. For female American preachers' self-authorization, see Catherine Brekus, *Strangers and Pilgrims: Female Preaching in America, 1740–1845* (Chapel Hill: University of North Carolina Press, 1998).

104. William Andrews, "Introduction," in *Sisters of the Spirit: Three Black Women's*

Autobiographies of the Nineteenth Century, ed. William Andrews (Bloomington: Indiana University Press, 1986).

105. Maxine Hanks, Margaret Toscano, Janice Allred, and Kate Kelly are Mormon feminists who were excommunicated for their writings and speeches about gender issues in Mormonism. See Philip Lindholm, *Latter-Day Dissent: At the Crossroads of Intellectual Inquiry and Ecclesiastical Authority* (Salt Lake City: Greg Kofford, 2010).

Chapter 4. Toward a Mormon Womanist Theology of Abundance

1. Jennifer Reader and Kate Holbrook's edited volume featuring the religious discourses of Latter-day Saint women is one recent attempt to recover and promote women's theologizing, which might otherwise fade into the mists of time. *At the Pulpit: 185 Years of Discourses by Latter-day Saint Women*, ed. Jennifer Reader and Kate Holbrook (Salt Lake City: Church Historian's Press, 2017).

2. Toscano, "Is There a Place for Heavenly Mother?," 14–15.

3. Eliza R. Snow originally called this poem "My Father in Heaven" when it was published in *Times and Seasons* on November 15, 1845, but she later renamed it "Invocation, or the Eternal Father in Mother" when she published *Poems: Religious, Historical, and Political* (1856). This poem is now the text for the LDS hymn "O My Father." Jill Mulvay Derr, "The Significance of 'O My Father' in the Personal Journey of Eliza R. Snow," *BYU Studies Quarterly* 36, no. 1 (1996): 85–126. Linda P. Wilcox also discusses its origins in "The Mormon Concept of a Mother in Heaven," in *Sisters in Spirit: Mormon Women in Historical and Cultural Perspective*, ed. Maureen Ursenbach Beecher and Lavina Fielding Anderson (Urbana: University of Illinois Press, 1992), 65. See also David L. Paulsen and Martin Pulido, "'A Mother There': A Survey of Historical Teachings About Mother in Heaven." *BYU Studies Quarterly* 50, no. 1 (2011): 71.

4. See Martha Sonntag Bradley, *Pedestals and Podiums: Utah Women, Religious Authority and Equal Rights* (Salt Lake City: Signature, 2005), 12–13; Maxine Hanks, "Historic Mormon Feminist Discourse—Excerpts," in *Women and Authority: Re-emerging Mormon Feminism*, ed. Maxine Hanks (Salt Lake City: Signature, 1992), 69–86.

5. Peggy Fletcher Stack, "A Mormon Mystery Returns: Who Is Heavenly Mother?" *Salt Lake Tribune*, May 16, 2013, http://archive.sltrib.com/story.php?ref=/sltrib/news/56282764-78/eternal-female-god-heaven.html.csp; Janice Allred, "Toward a Mormon Theology of God the Mother," in *God the Mother and Other Theological Essays* (Salt Lake City: Signature, 1997); Margaret Toscano and Paul Toscano, "The Divine Mother," in *Strangers in Paradox: Explorations in Mormon Theology* (Salt Lake City: Signature, 1990); Toscano, "Is There a Place for Heavenly Mother?"

6. *At the Pulpit* is one exception, because it includes a small handful of religious discourses by women of color. Reader and Holbrook, *At the Pulpit*. Other notable

exceptions are the women of color in recent General Relief Society presidencies (Silvia Allred [2007–2012] and Reyna Aburto [2017-]). These women have therefore had the opportunity to deliver a few sermons during General Conference and other meetings during their tenures. Another important exception is a recent social justice commentary on the Book of Mormon. Fatimah Salleh and Margaret Olsen Hemming, *The Book of Mormon for the Least of These*, vol. 1, *1 Nephi—Words of Mormon* (Salt Lake City: By Common Consent, 2020).

7. See Stephanie Y. Mitchem, *Introducing Womanist Theology* (Maryknoll, NY: Orbis, 2002), ix, 5. In setting out a framework for a womanist theology of abundance, I recognize that I am treading a fine line. As a white woman, I am not a womanist because it is a term reserved for women of color working to end multiple oppressions. However, I greatly admire womanist thought, and I recognize that the term *womanist* is appropriate for this theological framework because it arises from the lives and thoughts of women of color.

8. Kate Bowler, *Blessed: A History of the American Prosperity Gospel* (New York: Oxford University Press, 2013), 7.

9. Ibid., 11.

10. Tom Gjelton, "With His Choice of Inauguration Prayer Leaders, Trump Shows His Values," *National Public Radio*, January 13, 2017, http://www.npr.org/2017/01/13/509558608/with-his-choice-of-inauguration-prayer-leaders-trump-shows-his-values.

11. See 2 Nephi 1:20 in the Book of Mormon.

12. Such equations did not appear to be a dominant message at church or in these women's informal Mormon networks.

13. Robert Orsi, "Abundant History: Marian Apparitions as Alternative Modernity," *Historically Speaking* 9, no. 7 (September/October 2008): 12–16.

14. Ibid., 15.

15. Anonymous, interview by Caroline Kline, August 4, 2015, Utah, #164, transcript, p. 6, Claremont Mormon Women OHC.

16. Ibid.

17. Ibid.

18. Ibid., 9.

19. Ibid.

20. Fatimah Salleh, "God of the Gentiles, Theology from the Margins," paper presented at Sunstone's Theology from the Margins Conference, Salt Lake City, UT, March 2015, https://www.sunstonemagazine.com/2015-theology-from-the-margins-conference-keynote-speech-by-fatimah-salleh/.

21. Ibid.

22. Ibid.

23. Salleh's ideas about mindsets of scarcity and abundance may stem from progressive biblical scholars. Walter Brueggemann clearly articulated this distinction, though his focus is the Hebrew Bible. Walter Brueggemann, "The Liturgy of Abundance, the Myth of Scarcity," *Christian Century* 116, no. 10 (1999): 342–347.

24. Particularly powerful is Salleh's reading of the story of the Canaanite woman who approaches Jesus and asks for her daughter to be healed in Matthew 15:21–28. Jesus initially ignores her, and his apostles tell him to send her away. Jesus then rebuffs her by telling her that he has been sent to the Israelites and then compares helping her to taking food away from children and casting it to the dogs. She persists, however, and he does eventually bless her. Salleh's reading of this story indicates that Jesus, like contemporary church leadership, can learn and grow when listening to the voices of the marginalized. She compares this marginal woman's faith to the faith of Black women in the Church of Jesus Christ of Latter-day Saints, who have historically been turned away, denied, rejected, and told they are not worthy. Just as this woman persisted in the face of rejection, so have Black Latter-day Saint women persisted and sought their miracles amidst contexts of overt racism.

25. Claremont Mormon Women OHC, #164 (2015), 12.

26. Ibid.

27. Ibid., 13.

28. Anonymous, interview by Caroline Kline, December 10, 2016, Connecticut, #151, transcript, pp. 4–5.

29. Ibid., 14.

30. Stephen R. Covey, *The 7 Habits of Highly Effective People: Restoring the Character Ethic* (New York: Fireside, 1990), 219–220.

31. Hoagland, *Lesbian Ethics*, 91.

32. Anonymous, interview by Caroline Kline, November 30, 2016, in Connecticut, #155, transcript, p. 21, Claremont Mormon Women OHC.

33. Elaine Salo, "Social Construction of Masculinity on the Racial and Gendered Margins of Cape Town," in *From Boys to Men: Social Constructions of Masculinity in Contemporary Society*, ed. T. Shefer, K. Ratele, N. Shabalala, and R. Buikema (Cape Town: University of Cape Town Press, 2007), 162.

34. "South Africa—Family Life in Colored Families," *Marriage and Family Encyclopedia*, accessed May 1, 2018, http://family.jrank.org/pages/1615/South-Africa -Family-Life-in-Colored-Families.html.

35. Claremont Mormon Women OHC, #155 (2016), 10–11.

36. Gender, Narrative, and Religious Practice in Southern Africa, #30 (2015), 20.

37. In 2019 Botswana had an infant mortality rate of 32 deaths per 1,000 live births. The United States had a rate of 6. Sweden had a rate of 2, and Afghanistan had a rate of 47. See http://data.worldbank.org/indicator/SP.DYN.IMRT.IN.

38. Claremont Mormon Women OHC, #173 (2015), 17. "A la semana que regresamos de México—porque allí fue donde nos sellamos—soñé. Tuve un sueño tan especial que cuando desperté me desperté muy acelerada. Me fui al cuarto de mi mamá y le platiqué mi sueño. Cuando le platiqué mi sueño, mi mamá me abrazó y me dijo, 'Papá te ha escogido a ti para decirnos que él ha aceptado el evangelio.'"

39. Ibid. "Somos un pueblo de soñadores, entonces yo sueño muchas cosas, y todas cosas tienen un significado. Mi mamá y falleció, mi papá ya falleció, todos de mis hermanos de los que quería yo mucho fallecieron, y tenemos esa ayuda, que

ellos pueden venir a nosotros a través de los sueños y guiarnos y ayudarnos. . . . Si nosotros estamos bien, podemos entender muchos de tales cosas que ellos nos dicen, nos previenen, precisamente porque los admiramos cuando estuvieron aquí en la tierra. Sabemos que fueron buenas personas, entonces. Yo tengo muchas experiencias con eso."

40. Edward Wright-Rios, *Searching for Madre Matiana: Prophecy and Popular Culture in Modern Mexico* (Santa Fe: University of New Mexico Press, 2014), 29.

41. See D. Michael Quinn, "Visions and the Coming Forth of the Book of Mormon," in *Early Mormonism and the Magic Worldview* (Salt Lake City: Signature, 1998).

42. For instance, Hokulani K. Aikau writes that George Q. Cannon "had a vision in 1851 that traced Polynesian lineage to The Book of Mormon and to Israel. This articulation expanded the racial and religious boundaries of the Church of Jesus Christ of Latter-day Saints." Aikau, *Chosen People*, 1.

43. Carol Lynn Pearson, *Daughters of Light* (Salt Lake City: Bookcraft, 1982), 29, 42.

44. Richard G. Scott, "How to Obtain Revelation and Inspiration for Your Personal Life," *Ensign*, May 2012, https://www.churchofjesuschrist.org/study/ensign/2012/05/saturday-afternoon-session/how-to-obtain-revelation-and-inspiration-for-your-personal-life.html?lang=eng#title1.

45. Anonymous, interview by Caroline Kline, March 22, 2015 in Veracruz, Mexico, unarchived, #1A. My interpreter directly translated the interview into English.

46. M. R. Brooks, *LDS Reference Encyclopedia*, 309—310.

47. Anonymous, interview by Caroline Kline, March 21, 2015, Veracruz, Mexico, unarchived, #4A, transcript, pp. 17–18.

48. Petroff, "Visionary Tradition," 6.

49. Williams, "Womanist Theology," 67.

50. Ibid. Although most womanist thought, theory, and theology is articulated by Black women and focuses on the experiences of Black women, many womanists also draw insights from the lives of non-Black women of color. Layli Phillips, for example, describes womanism as "a social change perspective rooted in Black women's and other women of color's everyday experiences and everyday methods of problem solving." Layli Phillips, "Womanism: On Its Own," in *The Womanist Reader*, ed. Layli Phillips (New York: Routledge, 2006), xx.

51. Chieko Okazaki, "Baskets and Bottles," address given at the Church of Jesus Christ of Latter-day Saints Annual General Conference, Salt Lake City, UT, April 1996, https://www.churchofjesuschrist.org/study/general-conference/1996/04/baskets-and-bottles?lang=eng.

52. Chieko Okazaki, *Aloha* (Salt Lake City: Deseret Books, 1995), 177–178.

53. Chieko Okazaki, *Being Enough* (Salt Lake City: Bookcraft, 2002), 1.

54. Ibid., 3–5.

55. Delores Williams writes that the phrase "God helped them make a way out of no way" has been used by many Black women to describe their experiences with God amid various challenges. Williams, *Sisters in the Wilderness*, 6.

56. Kline, "Mormon Conception of Women's Nature," 191–192.

57. Mary Jo Weaver, *New Catholic Women: A Contemporary Challenge to Traditional Religious Authority* (Bloomington: Indiana University Press, 1995), 201.

58. Kari Borresen, "Mary in Catholic Theology," in *Mary in the Churches*, ed. Hans Kung and Jurgen Moltmann (New York: Seabury, 1983), 48–56.

59. Weaver, *New Catholic Women*, 201.

60. Mary is not emphasized in Mormonism, but she is one of only six named women in the Book of Mormon, where she is associated with the Tree of Life in Nephi's vision. This evocative and potentially empowering association has not been highlighted in Latter-day Saint teachings.

61. See, e.g., Susan Easton Black, "Mary, His Mother," *Ensign*, January 1991.

62. Claremont Mormon Women OHC, #155 (2016), 20.

63. Ruether, *Sexism and God-Talk*, 154.

64. Ibid.

65. Weaver, *New Catholic Women*, 204.

66. Luke 11:27–28.

67. Ruether, *Sexism and God-Talk*, 153.

68. Luke 1:51–53.

69. John 2:3–5, Joseph Smith Translation. The original King James version reads: "And when they wanted wine, the mother of Jesus saith unto him, They have no wine. Jesus saith unto her, Woman, what have I to do with thee? Mine hour is not yet come. His mother saith unto the servants, Whatsoever he saith unto you, do it."

Conclusion

1. Daniel Burke and M. J. Lee, "Rob Porter, and Mormonism's #MeToo Moment," *CNN Politics*, February 11, 2018, https://www.cnn.com/2018/02/09/politics/rob-porter -mormonism-metoo/index.html.

2. "Church Provides Updated Guidelines for Preventing and Responding to Abuse," *Church News*, March 26, 2018, https://www.churchofjesuschrist.org/church/ news/church-provides-updated-guidelines-for-preventing-and-responding-to -abuse?lang=eng&_r=1.

3. Lani Wendt Young, "Rejoice in the Diversity of Our Sisterhood: A Samoan Mormon Feminist Voice on Ordain Women (2014)" in *Mormon Feminism: Essential Writings*, ed. Joanna Brooks et al. (New York: Oxford University Press, 2016).

4. In addition to the 2013 closure of the Benemérito, Church College of New Zealand closed in 2009. Peggy Fletcher Stack, "LDS Closing School in New Zealand," *Salt Lake Tribune*, July 17, 2006, https://archive.sltrib.com/story.php?ref=/ utah/ci_4060944.

5. Melissa Wei-Tsing Inouye, "The Oak and the Banyan: The 'Glocalization' of Mormon Studies," *Mormon Studies Review* 1, no. 1 (2014): 74.

6. In January 2021 the church replaced its four magazines (three of which were in English) with three global magazines available in numerous languages. The January 2021 issue of *Liahona* features several articles and perspectives from global members.

7. General Conference, in particular, needs diversifying. The vast majority of General Conference speakers continue to be white men, and the talks given there serve as lesson materials in Relief Society and Elders Quorum classes throughout the world.

8. Jonathan Stapley, *The Power of Godliness: Mormon Liturgy and Cosmology* (New York: Oxford, 2018), 1–9.

9. Anonymous, interview by Elizabeth Layton Johnson, June 6, 2016, Johannesburg, South Africa, #226, transcript, p. 3, Claremont Mormon Women OHC.

10. Claudia Bushman summarizes a number of studies that discuss convert retention around the globe. Claudia L. Bushman, *Contemporary Mormonism: Latter-day Saints in Modern America* (Lanham, MD: Rowman & Littlefield, 2008), 72.

11. World Council of Churches, "Together Towards Life: Mission and Evangelism in Changing Landscapes," March 9, 2012, http://archived.oikoumene.org/en/resources/documents/wcc-commissions/mission-and-evangelism/together-towards-life-mission-and-evangelism-in-changing-landscapes.html.

Bibliography

Abrahamsen, Rita. "African Studies and the Postcolonial Challenge." *African Affairs* 102, no. 407 (April 2003): 189–210.

Acemoglu, Daron, Simon Johnson, and James Robinson. "An African Success Story: Botswana." In *In Search of Prosperity: Analytic Narratives on Economic Growth*, edited by Dani Rodrik, 80–120. Princeton: Princeton University Press, 2003.

Aikau, Hokulani K. *A Chosen People, A Promised Land: Mormonism and Race in Hawai'i*. Minneapolis: University of Minnesota Press, 2012.

Alarcon, Norma. "The Theoretical Subject(s) of *This Bridge Called My Back* and Anglo-American Feminism." In *The Postmodern Turn: New Perspectives on Social Theory*, edited by Steven Seidman, 140–152. Cambridge: Cambridge University Press, 1994.

Alexander, Thomas. *Mormonism in Transition: A History of the Latter-day Saints, 1890–1930*. Chicago: University of Illinois Press, 1996.

Allred, Janice. "Toward a Mormon Theology of God the Mother." In *God the Mother and Other Theological Essays*, 42–68. Salt Lake City: Signature, 1997.

"An Apostle Speaks About Marriage to John and Mary." *Improvement Era*, February 1949.

Anderson, Lavina Fielding. "A Voice from the Past: The Benson Instructions for Parents." *Dialogue* 21, no. 4 (1988): 103–113.

Anderson, Margaret. "Thinking About Women: A Quarter Century's View." *Gender and Society* 19, no. 4 (2005): 37–55.

Andrews, William. "Introduction." In *Sisters of the Spirit: Three Black Women's Autobiographies of the Nineteenth Century*, edited by William Andrews, 1–22. Bloomington: Indiana University Press, 1986.

Anzaldua, Gloria. *Borderlands/La Frontera: The New Mestiza*. San Francisco: Spinsters, 1987.

Appolis, Keith U. C. *From Fragmentation to Wholeness: The Black South African Family Under Siege*. New York: University Press of America, 1996.

Aquino, Maria Pilar. *Our Cry for Life: Feminist Theology from Latin America*. Translated by Dinah Livingstone. Eugene, OR: Wipf and Stock, 1993.

Ballard, M. Russell. "That the Lost May Be Found." *Ensign*, May 2012, 97–100.

Beaman, Lori G. "Molly Mormons, Mormon Feminists and Moderates: Religious Diversity and the Latter-Day Saints Church." *Sociology of Religion* 62, no. 1 (2001): 65–86.

Bednarowski, Mary. *The Religious Imagination of American Women*. Bloomington: Indiana University Press, 1990.

Beecher, Maureen Ursenbach, and Lavina Fielding Anderson, eds. *Sisters in Spirit: Mormon Women in Historical and Cultural Perspective*. Chicago: University of Illinois Press, 1987.

Benson, Ezra T. "To the Mothers in Zion." Fireside address, February 22, 1987. https:// www.churchofjesuschrist.org/study/manual/eternal-marriage-student-manual/ womens-divine-roles-and-responsibilities/to-the-mothers-in-zion?lang=eng.

Black, Susan Easton. "Mary, His Mother." *Ensign*, January 1991.

Borresen, Kari. "Mary in Catholic Theology." In *Mary in the Churches*, edited by Hans Kung and Jurgen Moltmann, 48–56. New York: Seabury, 1983.

Bowler, Kate. *Blessed: A History of the American Prosperity Gospel*. New York: Oxford University Press, 2013.

Bowman, Matthew. *The Mormon People: The Making of an American Faith*. New York: Random House, 2012.

Bradley, Martha Sonntag. *Pedestals and Podiums: Utah Women, Religious Authority and Equal Rights*. Salt Lake City: Signature, 2005.

Brekus, Catherine. "Mormon Women and the Problem of Historical Agency." *Journal of Mormon History* 37, no. 2 (2011): 59–87.

———. *Strangers and Pilgrims: Female Preaching in America, 1740–1845*. Chapel Hill: University of North Carolina Press, 1998.

Bringhurst, Newell. *Saints, Slaves, and Blacks: The Changing Place of Black People Within Mormonism*. Westport, CT: Greenwood, 1981.

Brooks, Abigail. "Feminist Standpoint Epistemology: Building Knowledge and Empowerment Through Women's Lived Experience." In *Feminist Research Practice: A Primer*, edited by Sharlene Nagy Hesse-Biber and Patricia Lina Leavy, 53–82. Thousand Oaks, CA: Sage, 2006.

Brooks, Joanna. "Mormonism as Colonialism, Mormonism as Anti-Colonialism, Mormonism as Minor Transnationalism: Historical and Contemporary Perspectives." In *Decolonizing Mormonism: Approaching a Postcolonial Zion*, edited by Gina Colvin and Joanna Brooks, 163–185. Salt Lake City: University of Utah Press, 2018.

Brooks, Joanna, Rachel Hunt Steenblik, and Hannah Wheelwright, eds. *Mormon Feminism: Essential Writings*. New York: Oxford University Press, 2015.

Brooks, Melvin R. *LDS Reference Encyclopedia*. Salt Lake City: Bookcraft, 1960.

Brueggemann, Walter. "The Liturgy of Abundance, the Myth of Scarcity." *Christian Century* 116, no. 10 (1999): 342–347.

Brusco, Elizabeth. *The Reformation of Machismo: Evangelical Conversion and Gender in Colombia*. Austin: University of Texas Press, 1995.

Buerger, John David. *The Mysteries of Godliness: A History of Mormon Temple Worship*. San Francisco: Smith Research Associates, 1994.

Bulbeck, Chilla. *Re-Orienting Western Feminisms: Women's Diversity in a Postcolonial World*. Cambridge: Cambridge University Press, 1998.

Burke, Daniel, and M. J. Lee. "Rob Porter, and Mormonism's #MeToo Moment." *CNN Politics*, February 11, 2018. https://www.cnn.com/2018/02/09/politics/rob-porter-mormonism-metoo/index.html.

Bush Jr., Lester. "Mormonism's Negro Doctrine: An Historical Overview." *Dialogue* 8, no. 1 (Spring 1973): 11–68.

Bushman, Claudia L. *Contemporary Mormonism: Latter-day Saints in Modern America*. Lanham, MD: Rowman & Littlefield, 2008.

———, ed. *Mormon Sisters: Women in Early Utah*. Logan: Utah State University Press, 1997.

Bushman, Claudia, and Caroline Kline, eds. *Mormon Women Have Their Say: Essays from the Claremont Oral History Collection*. Salt Lake City: Greg Kofford Books, 2013.

Bushman, Richard Lyman. *Rough Stone Rolling: A Cultural Biography of Mormonism's Founder*. New York: Knopf, 2005.

Cannon, Katie. *Katie's Canon: Womanism and the Soul of the Black Community*. New York: Continuum, 1995.

Christ, Carol, and Judith Plaskow, eds. *Womanspirit Rising*. New York: Harper & Row, 1979.

Church of Jesus Christ of Latter-day Saints. "Church Provides Updated Guidelines for Preventing and Responding to Abuse." *Church News*, March 26, 2018. https://www.churchofjesuschrist.org/church/news/church-provides-updated-guidelines-for-preventing-and-responding-to-abuse?lang=eng.

———. "Church Releases Statement Condemning White Supremist Attitudes." *Church News*, August 15, 2017. https://www.churchofjesuschrist.org/church/news/church-releases-statement-condemning-white-supremacist-attitudes?lang=eng&_r=1.

———. "Facts and Statistics." Newsroom. Accessed September 22, 2021.https://newsroom.churchofjesuschrist.org/facts-and-statistics/country/botswana.

———. "Facts and Statistics." Newsroom. Accessed September 22, 2021. https://newsroom.churchofjesuschrist.org/facts-and-statistics/country/mexico.

———. "Race and the Priesthood." Accessed January 3, 2020. https://www.churchofjesuschrist.org/study/manual/gospel-topics-essays/race-and-the-priesthood?lang=eng.

———. "Unwed Pregnancy." Acccessed January 3, 2020. https://www.churchofjesuschrist.org/study/manual/gospel-topics/unwed-pregnancy?lang=eng.

Collins, Patricia Hill. *Black Feminist Thought: Knowledge, Consciousness, and the Politics of Empowerment*. Boston: Unwin Hyman, 1990.

———. "Learning from the Outsider Within: The Sociological Significance of Black Feminist Thought." In *Beyond Methodology: Feminist Scholarship as Lived Research*, edited by Mary Margaret Fonow and Judith A. Cook, 35–57. Bloomington: Indiana University Press, 1991.

Colvin, Gina. "#110: Mormonism, Liberation Theology and Womanism: A Conversation with Fatimah Salleh and Janan Graham." *A Thoughtful Faith*, August 24, 2015. Podcast. http://www.athoughtfulfaith.org/mormonism-liberation-theology-and-womanism-a-conversation-with-fatimah-salleh-and-janan-graham/.

———. "The Future of Global Mormonism: Decolonization and Inclusivity." *Exponent II* 34, nos. 2/3 (Fall 2014/Winter 2015): 39–42.

———. "I'll Be at the Ordain Women Event, But . . ." *KiwiMormon* (blog), April 2, 2014. http://www.patheos.com/blogs/kiwimormon/2014/04/ill-be-at-the-ordain-women-event-but/.

———. "There's No Such Thing as a Gospel Culture." *Dialogue* 50, no. 4 (2017): 57–69.

Colvin, Gina, and Joanna Brooks. "Introduction: Approaching a Postcolonial Zion." In *Decolonizing Mormonism: Approaching a Postcolonial Zion*, edited by Gina Colvin and Joanna Brooks, 1–23. Salt Lake City: University of Utah Press, 2018.

Compton, Todd. *In Sacred Loneliness: The Plural Wives of Joseph Smith*. Salt Lake City: Signature, 1997.

Cooke, Miriam. "Saving Brown Women." *Signs* 28, no. 1 (2002): 468–470.

Cornwall, Andrea. "Introduction: Perspectives on Gender in Africa." In *Readings in Gender in Africa*, edited by Andrea Cornwall, 1–19. Oxford: James Currey, 2005.

Cornwall, Marie. "The Institutional Role of Mormon Women." In *Contemporary Mormonism: Social Science Perspectives*, edited by Marie Cornwall, Tim B. Heaton, and Lawrence A. Young, 239–264. Chicago: University of Illinois Press, 1994.

Covey, Stephen R. *The 7 Habits of Highly Effective People: Restoring the Character Ethic*. New York: Fireside, 1990.

Craig, Wesley, Jr. "The Church in Latin America: Progress and Challenge." *Dialogue: A Journal of Mormon Thought* 5, no. 3 (1968): 66–74.

Crenshaw, Kimberlé. "Demarginalizing the Intersection of Race and Sex: A Black Feminist Critique of Antidiscrimination Doctrine, Feminist Theory and Antiracist Politics." *University of Chicago Legal Forum* 1 (1989): 139–167.

———. "Mapping the Margins: Intersectionality, Identity Politics, and Violence Against Women of Color." *Stanford Law Review* 43, no. 6 (1991): 1241–1299.

Daly, Mary. "Be-friending: The Lust to Share Happiness." In *For Lesbians Only: A Separatist Anthology*, edited by S. Hoagland and J. Penelope, 200–211. London: Onlywomen Press, 1988.

———. *Beyond God the Father: Toward a Philosophy of Women's Liberation*. Boston: Beacon, 1973.

———. *The Church and the Second Sex*. Boston: Beacon Press, 1968.

DeMunck, Victor C., and Elisa J. Sobo, eds. *Using Methods in the Field: A Practical Introduction and Casebook*. Walnut Creek, CA: Altamira, 1998.

Derr, Jill Mulvay. "The Significance of 'O My Father' in the Personal Journey of Eliza R. Snow." *BYU Studies Quarterly* 36, no. 1 (1996): 85–126.

Derr, Jill Mulvay, Janath Russell Cannon, and Maureen Ursenbach Beecher. *Women of Covenant: The Story of Relief Society*. Salt Lake City: Deseret Books, 1992.

Devault, Marjorie L. *Liberating Method: Feminism and Social Research*. Philadelphia: Temple University Press, 1999.

Dew, Sheri. "Are We Not All Mothers?" *Ensign*, November 2001. https://www.church ofjesuschrist.org/study/ensign/2001/11/are-we-not-all-mothers?lang=eng

Dube, Musa W. "Postcoloniality, Feminist Spaces, and Religion." In *Postcolonialism, Feminism, and Religious Discourse*, edited by Laura E. Donaldson and Kwok Pui-lan, 100–120. New York: Routledge, 2002.

Du Bois, W. E. B. *Black Reconstruction in America: An Essay Toward a History of the Part Which Black Folk Played in the Attempt to Reconstruct Democracy in America, 1860–1880*. New York: Free Press, 1965.

Dunch, Ryan. "Beyond Cultural Imperialism: Cultural Theory, Christian Missions, and Global Modernity." *History and Theory* 41, no. 3 (2002): 301–325.

Dworkin, Andrea. *Right-Wing Women*. New York: Putnam, 1983.

Ellece, Sibonile Edith. "'Be a Fool Like Me': Gender Construction in the Marriage Advice Ceremony in Botswana—A Critical Discourse Analysis." *Agenda* 25, no. 1 (2011): 43–52.

Espin, Olivia. "Cultural and Historical Influences on Sexuality in Hispanic/Latin Women." In *Race, Class, and Gender*, edited by Margaret L. Anderson and Patricia Hill Collins. Belmont, CA: Wadsworth, 1992.

"The Family: A Proclamation to the World." *Ensign*, November 1995.

Farnsworth, Sonja. "Mormonism's Odd Couple: The Motherhood-Priesthood Connection." In *Women and Authority: Re-emerging Mormon Feminism*, edited by Maxine Hanks, 299–314. Salt Lake City: Signature, 1992.

Finlayson-Fife, Jennifer. "Female Sexual Agency in Patriarchal Culture: The Case of Mormon Women." PhD diss., Boston College, 2007.

Fiorenza, Elizabeth Schüssler. *In Memory of Her: A Feminist Theological Reconstruction of Christian Origins*. New York: Crossroad, 1983.

Ford, Stacilee. "Sister Acts: Relief Society and Flexible Citizenship in Hong Kong." In *Decolonizing Mormonism: Approaching a Postcolonial Zion*, edited by Gina Colvin and Joanna Brooks, 202–228. Salt Lake City: University of Utah Press, 2018.

"Former President of Mormon Church, Gordon B. Hinckley, Gives First Ever Interview." *World Religion News*. Accessed June 22, 2017. http://www.worldreligion news.com/religion-news/former-president-of-mormon-church-gordon-b -hinckley-gives-first-ever-interview.

Gilligan, Carol. *In a Different Voice: Psychological Theory and Women's Development*. Cambridge, MA: Harvard University Press, 1982.

Givens, Terryl. "Christ, Atonement and Human Possibilities in Mormon Thought." In *The Oxford Handbook of Mormonism*, edited by Terryl Givens and Philip Barlow, 260–275. New York: Oxford University Press, 2015.

———. *People of Paradox: A History of Mormon Culture*. New York: Oxford University Press, 2007.

———. *Wrestling the Angel: The Foundations of Mormon Thought: Cosmos, God, Humanity*. New York: Oxford University Press, 2015.

Gjelton, Tom. "With His Choice of Inauguration Prayer Leaders, Trump Shows His Values." *National Public Radio*. January 13, 2017. http://www.npr.org/2017/01/13/509558608/with-his-choice-of-inauguration-prayer-leaders-trump-shows-his-values.

Gluck, Sherna Berger, and Daphne Patai. "Introduction." In *Women's Words: The Feminist Practice of Oral History*, edited by Sherna Berger Gluck and Daphne Patai, 1–6. New York: Routledge, 1991.

Gooren, Henri. "Latter-day Saints Under Siege: The Unique Experiences of Nicaraguan Mormons." *Dialogue* 40, no. 3 (2007): 134–155.

———. "The Mormons of the World: The Meaning of LDS Membership in Central America." In *Revisiting Thomas O'Dea's* The Mormons: *Contemporary Perspectives*, edited by Cardell K. Jacobson, John P. Hoffman, and Tim B. Heaton, 362–388. Salt Lake City: University of Utah Press, 2008.

Graham-Russell, Janan. "On Black Bodies in White Spaces: Conversations of Women's Ordination and Women of African Descent in the Church of Jesus Christ of Latter-day Saints." In *Mormon Feminism: Essential Writings*, edited by Joanna Brooks, Rachel Hunt Steenblik, and Hannah Wheelwright, 268–270. New York: Oxford University Press, 2015.

Griffith, R. Marie. *God's Daughters: Evangelical Women and the Power of Submission*. Berkeley: University of California Press, 1997.

Gross, Rita, and Nancy Falk, eds. *Unspoken Worlds: Women's Religious Lives*. New York: Harper & Row, 1980.

Gulbrandsen, Ornulf. *The State and the Social: State Formation in Botswana and Its Precolonial and Colonial Genealogies*. New York: Berghahn, 2012.

Gutmann, Matthew. *The Meanings of Macho: Being a Man in Mexico City*, 10th anniv. ed. Berkeley: University of California Press, 2007.

Hafen, Bruce C. "Crossing Thresholds and Becoming Equal Partners." *Ensign*, August 2007. https://www.churchofjesuschrist.org/study/ensign/2007/08/crossing-thresholds-and-becoming-equal-partners?lang=eng.

Hall, Dave. "A Crossroads for Mormon Women: Amy Brown Lyman, J. Reuben Clark, and the Decline of Organized Women's Activism in the Relief Society." *Journal of Mormon History* 36, no. 2 (2010): 205–249.

Hanciles, Jehu J. "'Would That All God's People Were Prophets': Mormonism and the New Shape of Global Christianity." *Journal of Mormon History* 41, no. 2 (April 2015): 35–68.

Hanks, Maxine, ed. "Historic Mormon Feminist Discourse—Excerpts." In *Women and Authority: Re-emerging Mormon Feminism*, edited by Maxine Hanks, 69–147. Salt Lake City: Signature, 1992.

Harding, Sandra. "Introduction: Is There a Feminist Method?" In *Feminism and Methodology: Social Science Issues*, edited by Sandra Harding, 1–14. Bloomington: Indiana University Press, 1988.

Hardy, B. Carmon. "Lords of Creation: Polygamy, the Abrahamic Household, and Mormon Patriarchy." *Journal of Mormon History* 20 (Spring 1994): 119–152.

Hardy, Grant. "The Book of Mormon and Social Justice." *Meridian*, March 20, 2011. https://ldsmag.com/article-1-7677/.

Heaton, Tim B., Kristen L. Goodman, and Thomas B. Holman. "In Search of a Peculiar People: Are Mormon Families Really Different?" In *Contemporary Mormonism: Social Science Perspectives*, edited by Marie Cornwall, Tim B. Heaton, and Lawrence A. Young, 87–117. Chicago: University of Illinois Press, 1994.

Hesse-Biber, Sharlene Nagy, Patricia Leavy, and Michelle L. Yaiser. "Feminist Approaches to Research as a Process: Reconceptualizing Epistemology, Methodology, and Method." In *Feminist Perspectives on Social Research*, edited by Sharlene Nagy Hesse-Biber, Patricia Leavy, and Michelle L. Yaiser, 3–26. Oxford: Oxford University Press, 2004.

Hinckley, Gordon B. "Reverence and Morality." *Ensign*, May 1987, 46–47.

———. "Women of the Church." *Ensign*, November 1996. https://www.churchof jesuschrist.org/study/ensign/1996/11/women-of-the-church?lang=eng.

Hinga, Teresa M. "Jesus Christ and the Liberation of Women in Africa." In *The Will to Arise: Women, Tradition, and the Church in Africa*, edited by Mercy Amba Oduyoye and Musimbi R. A. Kanyoro, 183–194. Maryknoll, NY: Orbis, 1992.

Hoagland, Sarah. *Lesbian Ethics: Toward New Values*. Palo Alto, CA: Institute of Lesbian Studies, 1989.

Hodgson, Dorothy L. *The Church of Women: Gendered Encounters Between Maasai and Missionaries*. Bloomington: Indiana University Press, 2005.

hooks, bell. *Feminist Theory: From Margin to Center*. New York: Routledge, 2015.

Howe, Daniel Walker. "Emergent Mormonism in Context." In *The Oxford Handbook of Mormonism*, edited by Terryl Givens and Philip Barlow, 24–37. New York: Oxford University Press, 2015.

Hoyt, Amy. "Agency, Subjectivity and Essentialism with Traditional Religious Cultures: An Ethnographic Study of an American Latter-day Saint Community." PhD diss., Claremont Graduate University, 2007.

———. "Beyond the Victim/Empowerment Paradigm: The Gendered Cosmology of Mormon Women." *Feminist Theology* 16, no. 1 (2007): 89–100.

———. "Reconceptualizing Agency." *Element* 5, no. 2 (Fall 2009): 69–85.

Hurtado, Aida, and Mrinal Sinha. *Beyond Machismo: Intersectional Latino Masculinities*. Austin: University of Texas Press, 2016.

Iannaccone, Laurence R., and Carrie A. Miles. "Dealing with Social Change: The Mormon Church's Response to Change in Women's Roles." *Social Forces* 68, no. 4 (1990): 1231–1250.

Ingoldsby, Bron B. "The Latin American Family: Familialism Vs. Machismo." *Journal of Comparative Family Studies* 22, no. 1 (1991): 57–62.

Ingram, Aleah. "Church Leaders Speak About Dowry in Africa." *LDS Daily*, January 25, 2016. http://www.ldsdaily.com/church-lds/church-leaders-speak-about -dowry-in-african-culture/.

Inouye, Melissa Wei-Tsing. "Culture and Agency in Mormon Women's Lives." In *Women and Mormonism: Historical and Contemporary Perspectives*, edited by Kate Holbrook and Matthew Bowman, 230–246. Salt Lake City: University of Utah Press, 2016.

———. "The Oak and the Banyan: The 'Glocalization' of Mormon Studies." *Mormon Studies Review* 1, no. 1 (2014): 70–79.

Isasi-Díaz, Ada Maria. *En la Lucha: Elaborating a Mujerista Theology*. Minneapolis: Fortress, 2004.

———. *Mujerista Theology: A Theology for the Twenty-First Century*. Maryknoll, NY: Orbis, 1996.

Izzard, Wendy. "The Impact of Migration on the Roles of Women in Botswana: Patterns, Causes, and Consequences." *Final Report: National Migration Study* 3 (1982): 654–707.

Jacobson, Cardell K., John P. Hoffman, and Tim B. Heaton, eds. *Revisiting Thomas O'Dea's* The Mormons: *Contemporary Perspectives*. Salt Lake City: University of Utah Press, 2008.

Jagger, Alison. "Feminist Politics and Epistemology: The Standpoint of Women." In *The Feminist Standpoint Theory Reader: Intellectual and Political Controversies*, edited by Sandra Harding, 55–66. New York: Routledge, 2004.

Jenkins, Philip. "Letting Go: Understanding Mormon Growth in Africa." *Journal of Mormon History* 35 (Spring 2009): 1–25.

Jensen, Kipton E. "The Politics of Faith-Based HIV Prevention Policies and Programs in Botswana." In *The Faith Sector and HIV/AIDS in Botswana: Responses and Challenges*, edited by Lovemore Togarasei, Sana K. Mmolai, and Fidelis Nkomazana, 44–69. Cambridge: Cambridge Scholars Publishing, 2011.

"John and Mary, Beginning Life Together." *New Era*, June 1975, 7–8.

Johnson, Allen G. *Privilege, Power, and Difference*. New York: McGraw Hill, 2018.

Juschka, Darlene M. "General Introduction." In *Feminism in the Study of Religion: A Reader*, edited by Darlene M. Juschka, 8–18. New York: Continuum, 2001.

Kachipande, Sitinga. "Botswanan or Batswana? It's Complicated." *Voices of Africa* (blog). April 17, 2015. https://tinyurl.com/y2lwkpyj.

Kaufman, Debra. *Rachel's Daughters: Newly Orthodox Jewish Women*. New Brunswick: Rutgers University Press, 1991.

Keeney, Allison, and Susan Woster. "Motherhood." In *Mormon Women Have Their Say: Essays from the Claremont Oral History Collection*, edited by Claudia Bushman and Caroline Kline, 73–86. Salt Lake City: Greg Kofford Books, 2013.

Kim, Grace ji-Sun, and Susan M. Shaw. *Intersectional Theology: An Introductory Guide*. Minneapolis: Fortress, 2018.

Kimball, Edward L., and Andrew E. Kimball Jr. *Spencer W. Kimball: Twelfth President of The Church of Jesus Christ of Latter-day Saints*. Salt Lake City: Bookcraft, 1977.

Kimball, Spencer W. *The Teachings of Spencer W. Kimball*. Salt Lake City: Deseret Books, 1982.

Kincheloe, Joe. *Critical Pedagogy Primer*. New York: Peter Lang International, 2008.

Kiskilili. "Renaming the 'Priesthood Ban.'" *Zelophehad's Daughters* (blog), June 8, 2008. http://zelophehadsdaughters.com/2008/06/08/renaming-the-priesthood-ban/.

Kline, Caroline. "The Mormon Conception of Women's Nature and Role: A Feminist Analysis." *Feminist Theology* 22, no. 2 (2014): 186–202.

———. "Saying Goodbye to the Final Say: The Softening and Reimagining of Mormon Male Headship Ideologies." In *Out of Obscurity: Mormonism Since 1945*, edited by Patrick Mason and John Turner, 214–233. New York: Oxford University Press, 2016.

Knowlton, David. "Thoughts on Mormonism in Latin America." *Dialogue* 25, no. 2 (1992): 41–53.

Larson, Mary A. "Research Design and Strategies." In *Handbook of Oral History*, edited by Thomas L. Charlton, Lois E. Myers, and Rebecca Sharpless, 105–134. Lanham, MD: Altamira, 2006.

Lazreg, Marnia. "Decolonizing Feminism." In *African Gender Studies: A Reader*, edited by Oyeronke Oyewumi, 67–80. New York: Palgrave Macmillan, 2005.

LDS Family Services. "Adoption and the Unwed Mother." *Ensign*, February 2002. https://www.churchofjesuschrist.org/study/ensign/2002/02/adoption-and-the-unwed-mother?lang=eng.

LeBaron, E. Dale. "Botswana." In *Encyclopedia of Latter-day Saint History*, edited by Arnold K. Garr, Donald Q. Cannon, and Richard O. Cowan, 124–125. Salt Lake City: Deseret, 2000.

Lindholm, Philip. *Latter-Day Dissent: At the Crossroads of Intellectual Inquiry and Ecclesiastical Authority*. Salt Lake City: Greg Kofford, 2010.

Mahmood, Saba. *Politics of Piety: The Islamic Revival and the Feminist Subject*. Princeton: Princeton University Press, 2005.

Makgala, Christian John. "A Survey of Race Relations in Botswana, 1800–1966." *Botswana Notes and Records* 36 (2004): 11–26.

Mangena, Fainos. "The Search for an African Feminist Ethic: A Zimbabwean Perspective." *Journal of International Women's Studies* 11, no. 2 (September 2009): 18–30.

Matope, Nogget, Nyevero Marunzani, Efirtha Chauraya, and Beatrice Bondai. "Lobola and Gender Based Violence: Perceptions of Married Adults in Gweru Urban, Zimbabwe." *Journal of Education Research and Behavioral Sciences* 2, no. 11 (November 2013): 192–200.

Mauss, Armand. *All Abraham's Children: Changing Mormon Conceptions of Race and Lineage*. Chicago: University of Illinois Press, 2003.

Mbiti, John. *African Religions and Philosophies*. Oxford: Heinemann, 1969.

McConkie, Bruce R. *Mormon Doctrine, 2nd ed*. Salt Lake City: Bookcraft, 1966.

McDannell, Colleen. *Sister Saints: Mormon Women Since the End of Polygamy.* New York: Oxford University Press, 2019.

McIntosh, Marjorie Keniston. *Yoruba Women, Work, and Social Change.* Bloomington: Indiana University Press, 2009.

McIntosh, Peggy. "White Privilege: Unpacking the Invisible Knapsack." In *Race, Class and Gender: An Anthology*, 9th ed., edited by Margaret Andersen and Patricia Hill Collins, 74–78. Boston: Wadsworth, 2015.

McLeod, John. *Beginning Postcolonialism.* Manchester, UK: Manchester University Press, 2000.

Meagher, Michelle. "Patriarchy." In *The Concise Encyclopedia of Sociology*, edited by George Ritzer and J. Michael Ryan, 441–442. Oxford: Wiley-Blackwell, 2011.

Meekers, Dominique, and Ghyasuddin Ahmed. "Adolescent Sexuality in Southern Africa: Cultural Norms and Contemporary Behavior." Paper presented at the International Union for the Scientific Study of Population General Conference, Beijing, China, October 1997. https://www.psi.org/wp-content/uploads/1997/10/WP02.pdf.

Menkiti, Ifeanyi A. "Person and Community in African Traditional Thought." In *African Philosophy: An Introduction*, edited by Richard Wright, 171–182. Lanham, MD: University Press of America, 1984.

Meyers, Donald. "New Mormon Missionary Training Center Building Plan Upsets Residents." *Salt Lake Tribune*, May 16, 2012. http://archive.sltrib.com/story.php?ref=/sltrib/news/54118360–78/building-church-residents-heaton.html.csp.

Miles, Carrie. "LDS Family Ideals Versus the Equality of Women: Navigating the Changes since 1957." In *Revisiting Thomas F. O'Dea's* The Mormons: *Contemporary Perspectives*, edited by Cardell K. Jacobson, John P. Hoffman, and Tim B. Heaton, 101–134. Salt Lake City: University of Utah Press, 2008.

Mitchem, Stephanie Y. *Introducing Womanist Theology.* Maryknoll, NY: Orbis, 2002.

Mohanty, Chandra Talpade. *Feminism Without Borders: Decolonizing Theory, Practicing Solidarity.* Durham, NC: Duke University Press, 2004.

———. "Under Western Eyes: Feminist Scholarship and Colonial Discourse." In *Third World Women and the Politics of Feminism*, edited by Chandra Talpade Mohanty, Ann Russo, and Lourdes Torres, 51–80. Bloomington: Indiana University Press, 1991.

Mookodi, Godisang. "Male Violence Against Women in Botswana: A Discussion of Gendered Uncertainties in a Rapidly Changing Environment." *African Sociological Review* 8, no. 1 (2004): 118–138.

Morell, Robert, and Lahoucine Ouzgane. "African Masculinities: An Introduction." In *African Masculinities: Men in Africa from the Late Nineteenth Century to the Present*, edited by Lahoucine Ouzgane and Robert Morell, 1–20. New York: Palgrave Macmillan, 2005.

Morgenegg, Ryan. "LDS Family Services No Longer Operating as Adoption Agency." *Church News*, July 1, 2014. https://www.churchofjesuschrist.org/church/news/lds-family-services-no-longer-operating-as-adoption-agency?lang=eng.

Morin, Karin M., and Jeanne Kay Guelke, eds. *Women, Religion and Space: Global Perspectives on Gender and Faith.* Syracuse: Syracuse University Press, 2007.

Morton, Nelle. *The Journey Is Home.* Boston: Beacon, 1985.

Mueller, Max Perry. *Race and the Making of the Mormon People.* Chapel Hill: University of North Carolina Press, 2017.

Murove, Munyaradzi Felix, ed. *African Ethics: An Anthology of Comparative and Applied Ethics.* Scottsville, South Africa: University of KwaZulu-Natal Press, 2009.

Navarro, Marysa. "Against *Marianismo.*" In *Gender's Place: Feminist Anthropologies of Latin America,* edited by Rosario Montoya, Lessie Jo Frazier, and Janise Hurtig, 257-272. New York: Palgrave MacMillan, 2002.

Nelson, Russell M. "The Correct Name of the Church." Address given at the Semiannual General Conference of the Church of Jesus Christ of Latter-day Saints, October 2018. https://www.churchofjesuschrist.org/study/general-conference/2018/10/the-correct-name-of-the-church?lang=eng.

———. "Let God Prevail." Address given at the Semiannual General Conference of the Church of Jesus Christ of Latter-day Saints, October 4, 2020. https://www.churchofjesuschrist.org/study/general-conference/2020/10/46nelson?lang=eng

Newell, Linda King. "The Historical Relationship of Mormon Women and Priesthood." In *Women and Authority: Re-emerging Mormon Feminism*, edited by Maxine Hanks, 23–48. Salt Lake City: Signature, 1992.

Newell, Linda King, and Valeen Tippets Avery. *Mormon Enigma: Emma Hale Smith.* Chicago: University of Illinois Press, 1994.

Nkomazana, Fidelis. "The Botswana Religious Landscape." In *The Faith Sector and HIV/AIDS in Botswana: Responses and Challenges*, edited by Lovemore Togarasei, Sana K. Mmolai, and Fidelis Nkomazana, 2–21. Cambridge: Cambridge Scholars Publishing, 2011.

Oaks, Dallin H. "The Gospel Culture." *Ensign*, March 2012. https://www.churchofjesuschrist.org/study/ensign/2012/03/the-gospel-culture?lang=eng.

———. "Priesthood Authority in the Family and the Church." Address given at the Church of Jesus Christ of Latter-day Saints Semiannual General Conference. Salt Lake City, UT, October, 2005.

Oduyoye, Mercy Amba. *African Women's Theology.* Cleveland, OH: Pilgrim, 2001.

Okazaki, Chieko. *Aloha.* Salt Lake City: Deseret Books, 1995.

———. "Baskets and Bottles." Address given at the Church of Jesus Christ of Latter-day Saints Annual General Conference, Salt Lake City, UT, April 1996. https://www.churchofjesuschrist.org/study/general-conference/1996/04/baskets-and-bottles?lang=eng.

———. *Being Enough.* Salt Lake City: Bookcraft, 2002.

Orsi, Robert A. "Abundant History: Marian Apparitions as Alternative Modernity." *Historically Speaking* 9, no. 7 (September/October 2008): 12–16.

———. *Thank You, St. Jude: Women's Devotion to the Patron Saint of Lost Causes.* New Haven: Yale University Press, 1998.

Packer, Boyd K. "Follow the Rule." BYU Devotional. January 14, 1977. https://speeches
.byu.edu/talks/boyd-k-packer_follow-rule/.

———. "For Time and All Eternity." *Ensign*, November 1993. https://www.churchof
jesuschrist.org/study/ensign/1993/11/for-time-and-all-eternity?lang=eng.

Pala, Achola. "Definitions of Women and Development: An African Perspective."
Signs 3, no. 1 (1977): 9–13.

Parker, Lyn, ed. *The Agency of Women in Asia*. Singapore: Marshall Cavendish Academic, 2005.

Parry, Benita. "Problems in Current Theories of Colonial Discourse." *Oxford Literary
Review* 9, no. 1 (1987): 27–58.

Parsons, Robert. "Hagoth and the Polynesians." In *The Book of Mormon: Alma, the Testimony of the World*, edited by Monte S. Nyman and Charles D. Tate Jr., 249–262.
Provo, UT: Religious Studies Center, Brigham Young University, 1992.

Paulsen, David L., and Martin Pulido. "'A Mother There': A Survey of Historical
Teachings About Mother in Heaven." *BYU Studies Quarterly* 50, no. 1 (2011): 71–97.

Payne, Paulette. "Hallelujah and Amen: The African-American Religious Aesthetic
and Black Women in the Church of Jesus Christ of Latter-day Saints in Southwest
Atlanta, Georgia." Master's thesis, Clark Atlanta University, 2009.

———. Panel, Black, White and Mormon Conference in Salt Lake City, October 9,
2015. http://thc.utah.edu/lectures-programs/bwm-conference/raceandmormon
women.php.

Pearson, Carol Lynn. *Daughters of Light*. Salt Lake City: Bookcraft, 1982.

Pena, Manuel. "Class, Gender and Machismo: The 'Treacherous-Woman' Folklore of
Mexican Male Workers." *Gender and Society* 5, no. 1 (1991): 30–46.

Petroff, Elizabeth Alvilda. "Introduction: The Visionary Tradition in Women's Writing; Dialogue and Autobiography." In *Medieval Women's Visionary Literature*,
edited by Elizabeth Alvilda Petroff, 3–59. New York: Oxford University Press, 1986.

Phillips, Layli. "Womanism: On Its Own." In *The Womanist Reader*, edited by Layli
Phillips, xix–lv. New York: Routledge, 2006.

Piper, John. "A Vision of Biblical Complementarity: Manhood and Womanhood
Defined According to the Bible." In *Recovering Biblical Manhood and Womanhood:
A Response to Evangelical Feminism*, edited by John Piper and Wayne Grudem,
31–59. Wheaton, IL: Crossway, 2012.

Plaskow, Judith. *Standing Again at Sinai: Judaism from a Feminist Perspective*. San
Francisco: HarperSanFrancisco, 1990.

———. "We Are Also Your Sisters: The Development of Women's Studies in Religion."
Women's Studies Quarterly 21, nos. 1/2 (1993): 9–21.

Pui-lan, Kwok. *Introducing Asian Women's Theology*. Sheffield, UK: Sheffield Academic Press, 2000.

Quinn, D. Michael. *Early Mormonism and the Magic Worldview*. Salt Lake City:
Signature, 1998.

———. *Mormon Hierarchy: Origins of Power*. Salt Lake City: Signature, 1994.

Ram, Kalpana. "Too 'Traditional' Once Again: Some Poststructuralists on the Aspirations of the Immigrant/Third World Female Subject." *Australian Feminist Studies* 8, no.17 (1993): 5–28.

Reader, Jennifer, and Kate Holbrook, eds. *At the Pulpit: 185 Years of Discourses by Latter-day Saint Women*. Salt Lake City: Church Historian's Press, 2017.

Reeve, W. Paul. *Religion of a Different Color: Race and the Mormon Struggle for Whiteness*. New York: Oxford University Press, 2015.

Riess, Jana. *The Next Mormons: How Millennials Are Changing the LDS Church*. New York: Oxford University Press, 2019.

Ritchie, Donald. *Doing Oral History*. Oxford: Oxford University Press, 2003.

RJH. "Common-law Marriages." *By Common Consent* (blog). January 17, 2006. https://bycommonconsent.com/2006/01/17/common-law-marriage/.

Robbins, Lynn G. "Agency and Love in Marriage." *Ensign,* October 2000. https://www .churchofjesuschrist.org/study/ensign/2000/10/agency-and-love-in-marriage? lang=eng.

Rockwood, Jolene Edmunds. "The Redemption of Eve." In *Sisters in Spirit: Mormon Women in Historical and Cultural Perspective*, edited by Maureen Ursenbach Beecher and Lavina Fielding Anderson, 3–36. Chicago: University of Illinois Press, 1987.

Roediger, David. *The Wages of Whiteness: Race and the Making of the American Working Class*. New York: Verso, 1999.

Ruether, Rosemary Radford. *Sexism and God-Talk: Toward a Feminist Theology*. Boston: Beacon, 1983.

Rutherford, Taunalyn. "Conceptualizing Global Religions: An Investigation of Mormonism in India." PhD diss., Claremont Graduate University, 2018.

Salleh, Fatimah. "God of the Gentiles, Theology from the Margins." Paper presented at Sunstone's Theology from the Margins Conference, Salt Lake City, UT, March 2015. https://www.sunstonemagazine.com/2015-theology-from-the-margins -conference-keynote-speech-by-fatimah-salleh/.

Salo, Elaine. "Social Construction of Masculinity on the Racial and Gendered Margins of Cape Town." In *From Boys to Men: Social Constructions of Masculinity in Contemporary Society*, edited by T. Shefer, K. Ratele, N. Shabalala, and R. Buikema, 160–180. Cape Town: University of Cape Town Press, 2007.

Schensul, Steven L., Jean J. Schensul, and Margaret D. LeCompte. *Essential Ethnographic Methods: Observations, Interviews, and Questionnaires*. Walnut Creek, CA: Altamira, 1999.

Scott, Richard G. "How to Obtain Revelation and Inspiration for Your Personal Life." *Ensign*, May 2012. https://www.churchofjesuschrist.org/study/ensign/2012/05/ saturday-afternoon-session/how-to-obtain-revelation-and-inspiration-for-your -personal-life.html?lang=eng#title1.

———. "To Heal the Shattering Consequences of Abuse." *Ensign*, May 2008, 40–43.

Segura, Denise A., and Jennifer L. Pierce. "Chicana/o Family Structure and Gender Personality: Chodorow, Familism, and Psychoanalytic Sociology Revisited." *Signs* 19, no. 1 (1993): 62–91.

Sharpe, Jenny. *Ghosts of Slavery: A Literary Archaeology of Black Women's Lives*. Minneapolis: University of Minnesota Press, 2003.

Shipps, Jan. *Mormonism: The Story of a New Religious Tradition*. Chicago: University of Illinois Press, 1985.

Shirts, Kathryn H. "The Role of Susa Young Gates and Leah Dunford Widtsoe in the Historical Development of the Priesthood/Motherhood Model." *Journal of Mormon History* 44, no. 2 (April 2018): 104–139.

Silberschmidt, Margarethe. "Poverty, Male Disempowerment, and Male Sexuality: Rethinking Men and Masculinities in Rural and Urban East Africa." In *African Masculinities*, edited by Lahoucine Ouzgane and Robert Morrell, 189–204. New York: Palgrave Macmillan, 2005.

Smith, Dorothy. *The Conceptual Practices of Power: A Feminist Sociology of Knowledge*. Boston: Northeastern University Press, 1990.

Smith, Joseph Fielding. *The Way to Perfection*. Salt Lake City: Deseret News Press, 1931.

Smith, Linda Tuhiwai. *Decolonizing Methodologies: Research and Indigenous Peoples, 2nd ed*. London: Zed, 2012.

Soothill, Jane E. *Gender, Social Change and Spiritual Power: Charismatic Christianity in Ghana*. Boston: Brill Academic, 2007.

"South Africa—Family Life in Colored Families." *Marriage and Family Encyclopedia*. Accessed May 1, 2018. http://family.jrank.org/pages/1615/South-Africa-Family -Life-in-Colored-Families.html.

Spelman, Elizabeth V. *Inessential Woman: Problems of Exclusion in Feminist Thought*. Boston: Beacon, 1988.

Spivak, Gayatri. "Can the Subaltern Speak?" In *Marxism and the Interpretation of Culture*, edited by Cary Nelson and Lawrence Grossberg, 271–314. London: Macmillan, 1988.

Sprague, Joey, and Mark Zimmerman. "Overcoming Dualism: A Feminist Agenda for Sociological Methodology." In *Theory on Gender/Feminism on Theory*, edited by Paula England, 255–280. New York: Aldine DeGruyter, 1993.

Stack, Peggy Fletcher. "Black Lives Matter, LDS Leader Dallin Oaks Tells BYU Audience, and Is a Cause All Should Support." *Salt Lake Tribune*, October 27, 2020. https://www.sltrib.com/religion/2020/10/27/black-lives-matter-lds/.

———. "Error in Printed LDS Church Manual Could Revive Racial Criticisms." *Salt Lake Tribune*, January 18, 2020. https://www.sltrib.com/religion/2020/01/18/error -printed-lds-church/.

———. "Feeling Excluded, Black Mormon Women Ask: 'Do They See Me?'" *Salt Lake Tribune*, October 9, 2015. http://www.sltrib.com/home/3048039–155/feeling -excluded-black-mormon-women-ask.

———. "For Many Black Mormons, Racism Is a Bigger Issue Than Sexism." *Salt Lake Tribune*, September 4, 2014. http://archive.sltrib.com/story.php?ref=/sltrib/ news/58361569–78/women-says-black-church.html.cspT.

———. "Landmark 'Mormon Doctrine' Goes out of Print." *Salt Lake Tribune*, May 21, 2010. http://archive.sltrib.com/story.php?ref=/ci_15137409.

———. "LDS Closing School in New Zealand." *Salt Lake Tribune*, July 17, 2006. https://archive.sltrib.com/story.php?ref=/utah/ci_4060944.

———. "A Mormon Mystery Returns: Who Is Heavenly Mother?" *Salt Lake Tribune*, May 16, 2013. http://archive.sltrib.com/story.php?ref=/sltrib/news/56282764-78/eternal-female-god-heaven.html.csp.

Stack, Peggy Fletcher, and David Noyce. "LDS Church Changes Temple Ceremony; Faithful Feminists Will See Revisions and Additions as a 'Leap Forward.'" *Salt Lake Tribune*, January 2, 2019. https://www.sltrib.com/religion/2019/01/02/lds-church-releases/.

Stapley, Jonathan. *The Power of Godliness: Mormon Liturgy and Cosmology*. New York: Oxford University Press, 2018.

Sterzer, Rachel. "BYU Professor Teaches How to Take the Fear out of Dating." *Deseret News*, September 10, 2015. http://www.deseretnews.com/article/865636457/Taking-the-fear-out-of-dating.html?pg=all.

Stevens, Elizabeth. "Marianismo: The Other Face of Machismo in Latin America." In *Female and Male in Latin America*, edited by A. Pescatello, 89–101. Pittsburg: University of Pittsburg Press, 1973.

Stewart, David G., Jr. "Growth, Retention, and Internationalization." In *Revisiting Thomas O'Dea's* The Mormons: *Contemporary Perspectives*, edited by Cardell K. Jacobson, John P. Hoffmann, and Tim B. Heaton, 328–361. Salt Lake City: University of Utah Press, 2008.

Stoll, David. *Is Latin America Turning Protestant? The Politics of Evangelical Growth*. Berkeley: University of California Press, 1990.

Sue, Christina A. *Land of the Cosmic Race: Race Mixture, Racism, and Blackness in Mexico*. New York: Oxford University Press, 2013.

Suggs, David N. *A Bagful of Locusts and the Baboon Woman: Constructions of Gender, Change, and Continuity in Botswana*. Fort Worth, TX: Harcourt, 2002.

Taylor, Sheila. "The Problem of Female Salvation in LDS Theology." *Element* 5, no. 2 (2009): 1–14.

Toscano, Margaret. "Is There a Place for Heavenly Mother in Mormon Theology? An Investigation into Discourses of Power." *Sunstone* 133 (2004): 14–22.

Toscano, Margaret, and Paul Toscano. "The Divine Mother." In *Strangers in Paradox: Explorations in Mormon Theology*, 47–59. Salt Lake City: Signature, 1990.

Tullis, F. LaMond. *Mormons in Mexico: The Dynamics of Faith and Culture*. Logan: Utah State University Press, 1987.

———. "Three Myths About Mormons in Latin America." *Dialogue* 7, no. 1 (1981): 79–87.

Ulrich, Laurel Thatcher. "Stirring up LDS History." Lecture, Sunstone and Friends of the Marriott Library, University of Utah, Salt Lake City, December 11, 2011. https://stream.lib.utah.edu/index.php?c=details&id=8263.

Upton, Rebecca. "'Women Have No Tribe': Connecting Carework, Gender, and Migration in an Era of HIV/AIDS in Botswana." In *Global Dimensions of Gender and Carework*, edited by Mary K. Zimmerman, Jacquelyn S. Litt, and Christine E. Bose, 360–369. Stanford, CA: Stanford Social Sciences, 2006.

Van Allen, Judith. "Radical Citizenship: Powerful Mothers and Equal Rights." In *Power, Gender, and Social Change in Africa*, edited by Muna Ndulo and Margaret Grieco, 59–76. Cambridge: Cambridge Scholars Publishing, 2009.

Van Beek, Walter E. A. "Church Unity and the Challenge of Cultural Diversity: A View from Across the Sahara." In *Directions for Mormon Studies in the Twenty-First Century*, edited by Patrick Q. Mason, 72–98. Salt Lake City: University of Utah Press, 2016.

Vance, Laura. "Evolution of Ideals for Women in Mormon Periodicals, 1897–1999." *Sociology of Religion* 63, no. 1 (2002): 91–112.

Walch, Tad. "Essays on Mormon History, Doctrine Find New Visibility in Official App, Sunday School." *Deseret News*, December 26, 2016. https://www.deseretnews.com/article/865669945/Essays-on-Mormon-history-doctrine-find-new-visibility-in-official-app-Sunday-School.html.

Walker, Alice. *In Search of Our Mothers' Gardens.* San Diego: Harcourt Brace Jovanovich, 1983.

Weaver, Mary Jo. *New Catholic Women: A Contemporary Challenge to Traditional Religious Authority.* Bloomington: Indiana University Press, 1995.

White, Caroline. "'Close to Home' in Johannesburg: Gender Oppression in Township Households." *Women's Studies International Forum* 16, no. 2 (1993): 149–163.

Widtsoe, John A. *Priesthood and Church Government*, rev. ed. Salt Lake City: Deseret Books, 1954.

Wilcox, Linda P. "The Mormon Concept of a Mother in Heaven." In *Sisters in Spirit: Mormon Women in Historical and Cultural Perspective*, edited by Maureen Ursenbach Beecher and Lavina Fielding Anderson, 64–77. Urbana: University of Illinois Press, 1992.

Wilcox, W. Bradford. *Soft Patriarchs, New Men: How Christianity Shapes Fathers and Husbands.* Chicago: University of Chicago Press, 2004.

Williams, Delores S. *Sisters in the Wilderness: The Challenge of Womanist God-Talk.* Maryknoll, NY: Orbis, 1993.

———. "Womanist Theology: Black Women's Voices." *Christianity and Crisis* 47, no. 3 (March 2, 1987): 66–70.

Williamson, Robert. *Latin America: Cultures in Conflict.* New York: Palgrave MacMillan, 2006.

World Atlas. "The Major Ethnic Groups of Botswana." Accessed July 19, 2018. https://www.worldatlas.com/articles/the-major-ethnic-groups-of-botswana.html.

World Council of Churches. "Together Towards Life: Mission and Evangelism in Changing Landscapes." March 9, 2012. http://archived.oikoumene.org/en/resources/documents/wcc-commissions/mission-and-evangelism/together-towards-life-mission-and-evangelism-in-changing-landscapes.html.

Wright-Rios, Edward. *Searching for Madre Matiana: Prophecy and Popular Culture in Modern Mexico*. Santa Fe: University of New Mexico Press, 2014.

Young, Brigham. "The Persecutions of the Saints—Their Loyalty to the Constitution—The Mormon Battalion—The Laws of God Relative to the African Race." *Journal of Discourses* 10 (1863): 104–111. http://contentdm.lib.byu.edu/cdm/ref/collection/JournalOfDiscourses3/id/4266.

Young, Lani Wendt. "Rejoice in the Diversity of Our Sisterhood: A Samoan Mormon Feminist Voice on Ordain Women (2014)." In *Mormon Feminism: Essential Writings*, edited by Joanna Brooks, Rachel Hunt Steenblik, and Hannah Wheelwright, 273–278. New York: Oxford University Press, 2016.

Zinn, Maxine Baca, Pierrette Hondagneu-Sotelo, and Michael A. Messner. "Introduction: Sex and Gender Through the Prism of Difference." In *Gender Through the Prism of Difference*, edited by Maxine Baca Zinn, Pierrette Hondagneu-Sotelo, and Michael A. Messner, 1–12. New York: Oxford University Press, 2011.

Index

Abrahamsen, Rita, 73
abstinence, 61–62, 70, 87. *See also* chastity
abundance: and church restructuring, 162–
    63; internal, 142–46; Mary and, 154–58;
    mentality, 140; metaphysical bounty,
    23, 134–38, 142, 145–46, 158; parable of
    loaves and fishes, 135–37; paradigm,
    168; and plenty, 142–45, 152; rejection of
    scarcity, 135–42, 218n23; and revelation,
    146–50; womanist theology of, 4, 23,
    129, 131–35, 150–54, 158–60
abundant events, 134–35
abuse: Mormon women's opposition to, 10,
    22, 27; sexual, 59, 111, 124, 164. *See also*
    alcohol, alcoholism; domestic abuse
Addiction Recovery Program, 165
adoption, 22, 59, 71–75, 82
agency, 2, 3, 7–9, 17–18, 21, 32–36, 38,
    162, 201n18; and female subordination,
    38–39; and growth, 35–36, 38 43; and
    revelation, 11, 23, 93
alcohol, 86–87; alcoholism, 26, 27, 29, 139;
    Word of Wisdom, 30, 48, 65, 139
alienation: and oppression, 3, 122, 126;
    rejection of, 10, 22, 27, 52, 112, 162
Allred, Janice, 14, 132
ambivalence, 63, 102, 106, 124–26, 129
Anderson, Lavina Fielding, 13
androcentrism, 5, 8, 19, 131
angels, 100, 147–48, 152, 156
apartheid, 103, 121, 144
Aquino, Maria Pilar, 31

autonomy: LDS women's, 13, 22, 95, 139–
    41, 143; western notions of, 6–7, 10, 32,
    68. *See also* independence

baptism, 18, 43, 48, 70–71, 87, 109, 123, 166
Baptist denomination, 122–23
Batswana Traditional Religion, 54
Beaman, Lori, 15
Bednarowski, Mary, 125–26
Beecher, Maureen Ursenbach, 13
Benemérito de las Américas, 51–52, 165–66
Benson, Ezra Taft, 63
Bible, 12, 31–32, 44, 118, 158
biraciality, 118–19
Black people, 4; in Botswana, 16–17, 145–
    46 (*see also chapter 2*); God as Black, 94;
    and LDS leaders, 79, 118–19; in South
    Africa, 79, 103–5, 120–21, 142–44, 168; in
    the United States, 99–101, 103–13, 121–
    24, 135–36, 142. *See also* racial restriction
    in LDS church; womanist
Book of Mormon: and conversion, 44, 60,
    87; origins, 10, 13; and prosperity theol-
    ogy, 134; and race, 12, 56, 101, 139
Botswana: historical background, 22–23;
    women on abundance, 146–50. *See also*
    chapter 2
Bradley, Martha, 13
Brekus, Catherine, 7–8, 32, 38
bridewealth, 22, 59, 66, 77–84. *See also*
    lobola
Brooks, Abigail, 113, 117

Brooks, Joanna, 12, 51–52, 56
Brusco, Elizabeth, 29, 48
Buddhism, 132, 151
Bushman, Claudia, 13

Cannon, Katie, 110
Cape Coloured people, 103–5, 144, 155
Cape Verde, 113–14
care ethics, 9–10
Caribbean, 109
Carlson, April, 18, 27
Carlson, Silvia, 18, 25
chastity, 22, 65–71, 87, 104
Christ, Carol, 5
class: and machismo, 29; Mormonism's values, 31, 44, 50, 64; oppression, 6; privilege, 23, 102, 112–17, 167; and rural Batswana, 18; as structure, 4–5, 8, 16, 21; white middle, 3, 13, 21, 50, 132–33, 193n17. *See also* intersectionality
Collins, Patricia Hill, 102
colonialism: British, 16–17, 53–54, 200n1; decolonization, 17, 19, 162–63; gender and, 6, 29, 92; Mary and, 154–56; Mormonism and, 56–57, 83, 95, 167, 199n88; neocolonialism, 50, 56; and oppression, 10; Portuguese, 113, 144; postcolonialism, 56–57, 73, 80, 105; and religion, 21, 84
Colvin, Gina, 51, 83–84,121
complementarianism. *See* gender
Congregational denomination, 77
conversion: to Christianity, 54; to Mormonism, 26, 30, 35, 44, 48, 56, 65, 87, 109, 161
correlation, LDS, 11, 51
Covey, Stephen, 140
Craig, Jr., Wesley, 44
Crenshaw, Kimberlé, 4

Daly, Mary, 5
decision-making authority, 15, 39, 42, 52, 96, 138, 142, 165, 189n49
decolonization. *See* colonialism
Derr, Jill, 13
Dew, Sheri, 62
divorce, 1, 37–38, 115, 117; church encouragement not to, 164; difficulty of obtaining, 71
domestic abuse, 26, 36–43, 50, 52, 90, 103, 108–9; anti-abuse training, 40–41, 164–65; as future emphasis for LDS Church, 164–65; lobola and, 80

dreams, 78, 109, 146–50, 158–59, 165, 167
Dube, Musa, 56
Du Bois, W.E.B., 112
Dunch, Ryan, 84
Dutch Reformed Church, 59

Ellece, Sibonile Edith, 85
equality. *See* gender, equality
English, in LDS global churches, 55, 94–95, 201n10
evangelicalism, 7, 39, 48, 105, 133
Eve, 14, 62, 142, 154, 159, 188n46

Fall, the, 142, 154
feminist/feminism: author positionality, 2–3; intersectional, 4, 25, 27, 50, 102, 105, 159; Mormon women of color, 10, 15, 52, 83, 99–100, 111–12, 121–22, 128, 164; non-feminist, 2–3; scriptural interpretation, 132; theology, 31, 155–56, 159; white, 3–5, 19, 24, 99, 112–13, 163, 207n100. *See also* standpoint theory; womanist; women's studies in religion
feminist scholarship, 5–10, 68, 74, 79–80, 102; critiques of religion, 21–22; research methodologies, 5–10, 20, 56–57
Finlayson-Fife, Jennifer, 66
Fiorenza, Elizabeth Schüssler, 5–6, 186n10
Ford, Stacilee, 41

gender: and colonialism 6, 29, 92; complementarianism, 2–3, 14–15, 23, 27, 41, 108, 155, 162, 168; equality, 1–5, 8–10, 19, 22, 42, 52, 102–3, 111–12, 161–63, 168; and freedom from oppression, 103–11; and globalization, 3, 92, 94–95; masculinities, 37, 42, 52, 92, 165; and Mormonism, 13–16; Western norms, 17, 23. *See also* marriage, equal partnership
General Conference, 50, 55, 86, 110, 119, 132, 166, 222n7
Gilligan, Carol, 9–10
Givens, Terryl, 11, 120
globalization/global: and gender norms, 3, 92, 94–95; growth, 2, 11, 55, 83; and Latter-day Saints, 12, 24, 51, 58, 133, 151–52, 160, 162–69; South, 1–2, 15, 17, 52, 55–59, 80, 84, 97, 102
God: blessings from, 62, 152; children of, 160; the Father: 81–82, 109, 126, 131; Joseph Smith's vision of, 10; in Mormon women's spirituality, 31–36, 58, 65,

76–82, 109, 145, 149; the Mother (*see* Heavenly Mother); personal, 23, 27, 35, 50. *See also* prayer
Gooren, Henri, 30, 92
"gospel culture," 83
Gospel Topics essays, 119–20
Graham-Russell, Janan, 100, 121
grandchildren, 60–62
Griffith, Marie, 7, 39, 186n22
Gross, Rita, 5

Hall, Dave, 13
Hanciles, Jehu, 83
Hardy, B. Carmon, 14
hatred, 28–29, 33
Heavenly Mother, 14, 33, 126–27, 131–32, 148–50, 160; sacred silence, 148
hermeneutics, cultural, 85
Hesse-Biber, Sharlene Nagy, 20
Hinckley, Gordon B., 148
HIV (Human immunodeficiency virus), 59–60, 65, 95, 146
Hoagland, Sarah, 39, 141
Hoyt, Amy, 3, 6–9, 15, 74–75, 82
Huntington, Prescindia, 147–48

Iannaccone, Laurence, 63
immigrants, 18, 115–16
independence: personal, 6, 22, 89–90, 120; political, 16, 54
Indigenous peoples: and Mormonism, 10, 12, 16, 19–20, 52, 55–56, 101, 139; values, 52, 97
infidelity, 22, 25–27, 30, 48
Ingoldsby, Bron, 29
Inouye, Melissa Wei-Tsing, 166
interdependence, 8–9
intersectionality: centrality in study's methodology, 16–17, 21–22, 25, 27, 50, 57, 80, 102, 105, 163, 169; definition, 4–5; and Mormon feminism, 99, 128, 159. *See also* womanist
Inuit, 139
Isasi-Díaz, Ada Maria, 6, 116
Izzard, Wendy, 61, 64

Jenkins, Philip, 83
Jesus Christ: and abundance, 135–37, 149, 153, 157–58; Eve as Christ figure, 154; Joseph Smith's vision of, 10; in LDS scripture, 87; and Mary (*see* Mary of Nazareth); as model of growth for LDS

leadership, 219n24; testimony of, 48, 109–10, 123; whiteness of Mormon, 100
Job (figure), 31, 154
Johnson, Allen, 113
justice, 9–10, 22, 35, 133; and abundance, 135, 138–39, 157–58; injustice, 95, 102, 128; *See also* social justice

Kimball, Spencer W., 63, 86
kinship theology, 167
Knight, Gladys, 122
Knight, Lydia, 147–48

Lamanites, 101, 139
Lazreg, Marnia, 80
LGBTQ+, 124, 126, 168; gay men, 108; lesbian community ethics, 141
Liahona (magazine), 50
lobola: definition, 66, 77; navigating as a Latter-day Saint, 78–84, 96

machismo, 29–30, 34, 36, 48, 192n7, 192n8
Mahmood, Saba, 3, 6–7, 32
Mangena, Fainos, 68
marriage: common-law, 70–71, 205n65, 205n66; companionate, 22, 59, 84–92; equal partnership, 14–15, 42, 85–88, 90–92, 111; interracial, 118–20, 214n72, 214n74; and money, 42, 44–46, 66, 77, 87–91; stability in, 69, 105, 107, 109; unity in, 84–92, 96. *See also* divorce; domestic abuse; lobola; polygamy; temple, and female submission; temple, and sealing; unwed pregnancies
Mary of Nazareth, 23, 134, 154–59
masculinities, 37, 42, 52, 92, 165, 197n61. *See also* patriarchy
Mbiti, John, 68
McConkie, Bruce R., 118, 120
McDannell, Colleen, 15, 58, 81, 94–95
McIntosh, Peggy, 112
Methodist denomination, 109
methodology (for study), 16–21
Mexico: background, 22; women on abundance, 142–46. *See also chapter 1*
Miles, Carrie, 63
mission presidents, 16, 71
Mohanty, Chandra Talpade, 56–57
Mookodi, Godisang, 79, 90
Mormon/Mormonism: adoption and adaptation to, 2, 17, 23, 44, 55, 57, 59, 73, 80–84, 93, 162; Americentrism, 52, 162;

empowering for women, 47, 49, 75, 77,
    95, 101, 139; feminists, 2, 15, 99, 111, 128,
    164; founding, 10–12; growth of, 2, 11,
    55, 83; hierarchy, 11, 16, 33, 43, 52, 55, 84,
    93, 100, 110, 123–24, 131–32, 138, 140, 150,
    152, 159; and Indigenous peoples, 10, 12,
    16, 19–20, 52, 56, 97, 101; masculinities,
    37, 42, 52, 92, 165; as liberation, 3, 8–9,
    14, 22, 159; as liberation for Batswana
    LDS women, 95, 104–7, 126–29; as lib-
    eration for Mexican LDS women, 27–31,
    35, 41–43, 49–52, 58; racial restriction
    (*see* racial restriction in LDS church);
    and social mobility (*see* social mobility)
motherhood: of God (*see* Heavenly
    Mother); as LDS women's nurturing
    role, 14–15, 45–46, 62–64, 107, 213n63;
    single, 1, 59–64, 67, 71; stay-at-home or
    employed, 13, 46, 90, 62–64, 114–17, 146,
    198n75, 202n31; unwed, 72–73, 104, 155,
    204n52. *See also* Mary of Nazareth
mujerista theology, 35, 116

Native Americans. *See* Indigenous peoples
negotiation: of Batswana and LDS identity,
    57–58, 69, 74–75, 82–84, 93, 96, 168;
    skill, 39
Nelson, Russell M., 13
Newell, Linda King, 13
New Thought Movement, 133–34
non-oppressive connectedness: abundance
    (*see* womanist, theology of abundance);
    and Batswana relationships, 23, 56, 58,
    71–72, 75, 96–97, 167; definition, 3–5;
    and elimination of oppression, 23, 102,
    106, 109–12, 117; and liberation, 22,
    27–28, 34–35, 43, 49, 52; and lobola, 81;
    moral paradigm, 4, 8, 22, 52, 97, 103, 122,
    139, 145, 161–63, 166, 169

Oaks, Dallin, 78–79
obedience: to God, 49, 65, 81, 134, 155; to
    husbands, 37–38, 40, 80, 86, 92; to LDS
    Church leaders, 32; to parents, 36. *See
    also* temple, and female submission
Oduyoye, Mercy Amba, 6, 85
Okazaki, Chieko, 23, 132, 159; *Being
    Enough*, 152–53; theologian, 151
oral histories, methodology, 17–20, 26–27,
    163
Orsi, Robert, 7, 33, 134

Pasifika people, 12, 99, 164
passivity, 38, 42, 155
patriarchy: and American women of color,
    108, 124, 127; authoritarian, 15, 39; and
    Batswana LDS women, 56–58, 66–69,
    77, 85, 89, 92–93, 96; definition, 14–16;
    in the LDS Church, 14–17, 21–22, 26–28,
    144, 162; and Mexican LDS women, 33–
    35, 39–42, 47, 52; and religion, 2–3, 5–8,
    21, 32; soft or benevolent, 14, 92, 189n47
Payne, Paulette, 111
Pentecostal denomination, 54, 60, 109, 134,
    193n17
Petroff, Elizabeth Alvilda, 149–50
Plaskow, Judith, 5–6
plural consciousness, 75, 82, 116–17
plural marriage. *See* polygamy
polygamy, 10–12, 14, 16, 38, 86, 122–23,
    195n44
positionality, 2–5, 20–21, 26, 105, 132–33
poverty: escape from, 44, 46, 52; and pros-
    perity theology, 133; systemic, 104–5,
    120, 144, 154–55
prayer: to Heavenly Mother, 148; with LDS
    leaders, 35; in marriage relationships,
    36–38; in personal relationships, 64,
    81–82, 88, 109; and personal revelation,
    73, 93, 122, 125, 144
priesthood: all-male, 14, 76; ban (*see* ra-
    cial restriction in LDS church); -led
    structure, 77, 96; priesthood ordination,
    137–38; white male leaders (*see* white/
    whiteness, of male leadership); women
    and, 13, 168, 209n144; women's reflec-
    tions on authority, 34–35, 92–94, 107–10
Primary organization, 30, 68, 153
Proclamation on the Family, 62, 85, 106,
    214n63
prosperity theology, 133–34, 137
Pui-lan, Kwok, 6

race: artwork, 94; biraciality, 118–19; Indig-
    enous (*see* Indigenous peoples); interra-
    cial marriage (*see* marriage, interracial);
    mestizo, 16; mixed race, 16, 101, 103, 113,
    119, 144; racial restriction (*see* racial
    restriction in LDS church). *See also*
    intersectionality, Black people; white/
    whiteness
racial restriction in LDS church, 12, 56,
    100–101, 119, 122–23, 168, 210n3

racism, 12, 53, 56, 99, 104, 111, 112, 119–20, 142, 215n76
refugees, 141
Relief Society, 28, 68; and correlation, 11, 13; early, 13, 152; hybridity of Batswana women in, 72–75; presidents, 45, 60, 69–70, 76, 164; and social mobility, 26, 44–47, 69, 95, 167, 198n70. *See also* Okazaki, Chieko
Reorganized Church of Jesus Christ of Latter Day Saints, 10
revelation: and agency, 11, 23, 93; and Mexican visionary culture, 146–50; Okazaki and, 152; personal, 11, 23, 93–94, 102, 122–24, 128; revelators, 100, 123
Robbins, Lynn G., 86
Roman Catholicism: conversion to Mormonism, 30–31, 59, 77, 113; Mariology, 134, 155; Mexican visionary culture, 147; women, 7, 33, 128
rural locations, 18, 59, 61, 94–95
Ruether, Rosemary Radford, 5, 156
Rutherford, Taunalyn, 92

sadness, 33, 51, 165
Salleh, Fatimah, 136–37, 158
Samoan, 107, 164
sangoma, 168
scarcity, 133, 135–42, 145, 153, 158, 218n23. *See also* abundance
Scientology, 86
self-development, 22, 27, 42, 48–49, 52
self-sacrifice, 141
Setswana culture, 55, 58, 63, 67, 72, 75, 78, 81–82, 85, 92, 94
Seventh-Day Adventists, 109
sexual abuse. *See* abuse, sexual
single women, 1, 30, 36, 59–61, 67, 71–73, 104–5, 117, 168
Smith, Emma Hale, 12, 38
Smith, Joseph, 109, 122; teachings, 11–13, 75, 147, 152; and Black people, 100, 118
Smith, Joseph, III, 10
Smith, Linda Tuhiwai, 19–20
Snow, Eliza R., 131
social justice, 111, 139, 213n52, 218n6
social mobility: LDS Church as social vehicle, 26–27, 30, 43–47, 49–52, 139; practical skills, 45; and skill building, 26, 28, 44–47; upward mobility, 44, 134. *See also* marriage, and money

South Africa: LDS church members from, 103–4, 120–21, 144, 155, 168; history, 17, 54, 61; lobola, 79
Spelman, Elizabeth, 21
spirits, 125, 134, 147–48
Spivak, Gayatri, 57, 80
Stack, Peggy Fletcher, 111
stake president, 35–37, 40–41, 47, 87, 107
standpoint theory, 113, 116–17
Stapley, Jonathan, 167
Stevens, Evelyn, 29
Stokes, Cathy, 111
subaltern, 57
submission, female, 7, 29, 32, 35, 39, 50, 93, 187n31, 209n145
Suggs, David, 60–61, 64

Taylor, Sheila, 15
temple: and ambiguity, 124–25; and community, 69; covenants, 58, 64, 88; and dreams, 146, 148; and female submission, 14, 42, 85–86, 96, 125, 188n46; and the LDS racial restriction, 12, 56, 100–101, 119, 122–23, 168; and lobola, 82; recommend interview, 34; and sealing, 12, 64–65, 74–78, 81–83, 86, 146; and women blessing, 127
theology. *See* abundance; feminist, theology; kinship theology; mujerista theology; prosperity theology; womanist
Third Convention, 16
Toscano, Margaret, 14, 131–32
traditional religious women, 2n1, 2–3, 7–8, 22, 161–62
transformation: self, 7, 41–43, 49; structural, 6, 31–32, 63, 126, 157
Trump, Donald, 134

Ubuntu, 68
Ulrich, Laurel Thatcher, 95
United States: background, 23; women on abundance, 135–42. *See also chapter 3*

Van Allen, Judith, 63
van Beek, Walter E. A., 55, 79, 83
visions: and dreams, 26, 78, 147–51, 158–59, 163, 166–69; Joseph Smith's, 10–11

Walker, Alice, 4, 110
Weaver, Mary Jo, 155–56
Western ideas and norms: business attire,

55; feminism, 5–6, 50, 52, 56–57, 163; gender norms, 17, 23; individualism, 68; and lobola, 79–80; liberalism, 2, 3, 5–7, 24, 63; and marriage, 84–93; and Mormonism, 56, 58, 63–64, 69, 73–76, 83–84, 94–97; notions of agency, 32; white middle-class women, 21, 50

White, Caroline, 79, 207n100

white/whiteness: "and delightsome," 56; feminism, 3–5, 19, 24, 163, 207n100; interracial marriage (*see* marriage, interracial); middle class, 3, 13, 21, 50; of Mormon feminism, 99–103, 111–12, 132–33; of Mormon leadership, 2, 12, 16–17, 22, 51, 55, 73, 78–82, 94, 104, 110, 120–21, 167, 187n37; privilege, 9, 23, 97, 116–17, 131, 160; race relations in Botswana, 53–54; study subjects, 2, 15

Williams, Delores, 6, 35, 153–54

womanism/womanist: definition, 110, 218n7, 220n50; frameworks, 4–5, 21–22, 35, 110; theology of abundance, 4, 23, 129, 131–35, 150–54, 158–60

Woman's Exponent, 131

women's studies in religion, 3, 5–7, 20–24

work, women outside the home, 42–46, 58, 61, 90, 115–17, 121, 145

World Council of Churches, 169

worship services (LDS), 27–28, 30, 55, 149

Young, Brigham, 10, 100, 118

Young, Lani Wendt, 164–65

Young Women's Organization, 68–70, 144, 153

Zion, 63, 101, 129, 131

Zion Christian Church, 76

CAROLINE KLINE is the assistant director
of the Center for Global Mormon Studies
at Claremont Graduate University.

The University of Illinois Press
is a founding member of the
Association of University Presses.

———————————————————

University of Illinois Press
1325 South Oak Street
Champaign, IL 61820-6903
www.press.uillinois.edu